D1193122

HOMELESS IN AMERICA

HOW COULD IT HAPPEN HERE?

ISSN 1536-5204

HOMELESS IN AMERICA

HOW COULD IT HAPPEN HERE?

Susan M. Turner

INFORMATION PLUS® REFERENCE SERIES
Formerly published by Information Plus, Wylie, Texas

GALE®

361.1
Tur
2003

THOMSON

™

GALE

Detroit • New York • San Diego • San Francisco • Cleveland • New Haven, Conn. • Waterville, Maine • London • Munich

Homeless in America: How Could It Happen Here?
Susan M. Turner

Project Editor
Ellice Engdahl

Editorial
Andrew Claps, Paula Cutcher-Jackson,
Kathleen J. Edgar, Dana Ferguson, Debra
Kirby, Prindle LaBarge, Elizabeth Manar,
Sharon McGilvray, Charles B. Montney,
Heather Price

Permissions
Mari Masalin-Cooper

Product Design
Cynthia Baldwin

Composition and Electronic Prepress
Evi Seoud

Manufacturing
Keith Helmling

© 2004 by Gale. Gale is an imprint of the Gale
Group, Inc., a division of Thomson Learning,
Inc.

Gale and Design™ and Thomson Learning™
are trademarks used herein under license.

For more information, contact
The Gale Group, Inc.
27500 Drake Rd.
Farmington Hills, MI 48331-3535
Or you can visit our Internet site at
http://www.gale.com

ALL RIGHTS RESERVED
No part of this work covered by the copyright
hereon may be reproduced or used in any
form or by any means—graphic, electronic, or
mechanical, including photocopying, record-
ing, taping, Web distribution, or information
storage retrieval systems—without the written
permission of the publisher.

For permission to use material from this product, submit your request via Web at
http://www.gale-edit.com/permissions, or you
may download our Permissions Request form
and submit your request by fax or mail to:

Permissions Department
The Gale Group, Inc.
27500 Drake Rd.
Farmington Hills, MI 48331-3535
Permissions Hotline: 248-699-8006 or
800-877-4253, ext. 8006
Fax: 248-699-8074 or 800-762-4058

Cover photograph reproduced by permission
of PhotoDisc.

Since this page cannot legibly accommodate
all copyright notices, the acknowledgments
constitute an extension of the copyright
notice.

While every effort has been made to ensure
the reliability of the information presented in
this publication, The Gale Group, Inc. does not
guarantee the accuracy of the data contained
herein. The Gale Group, Inc. accepts no payment for listing; and inclusion in the publication of any organization, agency, institution,
publication, service, or individual does not
imply endorsement of the editors or publisher.
Errors brought to the attention of the publisher and verified to the satisfaction of the
publisher will be corrected in future editions.

LIBRARY OF CONGRESS CATALOGING-IN-PUBLICATION DATA

ISBN 0-7876-5103-6 (set)
ISBN 0-7876-7340-4
ISSN 1536-5204

Printed in the United States of America
10 9 8 7 6 5 4 3 2 1

TABLE OF CONTENTS

are described. Diminishing options related to welfare reform are discussed.

PREFACE

Homeless in America: How Could It Happen Here? is one of the latest volumes in the Information Plus Reference Series. The purpose of each volume of the series is to present the latest facts on a topic of pressing concern in modern American life. These topics include today's most controversial and most studied social issues: abortion, capital punishment, care for the elderly, crime, health care, the environment, immigration, minorities, social welfare, women, youth, and many more. Although written especially for the high school and undergraduate student, this series is an excellent resource for anyone in need of factual information on current affairs.

By presenting the facts, it is Gale's intention to provide its readers with everything they need to reach an informed opinion on current issues. To that end, there is a particular emphasis in this series on the presentation of scientific studies, surveys, and statistics. These data are generally presented in the form of tables, charts, and other graphics placed within the text of each book. Every graphic is directly referred to and carefully explained in the text. The source of each graphic is presented within the graphic itself. The data used in these graphics are drawn from the most reputable and reliable sources, in particular from the various branches of the U.S. government and from major independent polling organizations. Every effort has been made to secure the most recent information available. The reader should bear in mind that many major studies take years to conduct, and that additional years often pass before the data from these studies are made available to the public. Therefore, in many cases the most recent information available in 2003 dated from 2000 or 2001. Older statistics are sometimes presented as well if they are of particular interest and no more recent information exists.

Although statistics are a major focus of the Information Plus Reference Series, they are by no means its only content. Each book also presents the widely held positions and important ideas that shape how the book's subject is discussed in the United States. These positions are explained in detail and, where possible, in the words of their proponents. Some of the other material to be found in these books includes: historical background; descriptions of major events related to the subject; relevant laws and court cases; and examples of how these issues play out in American life. Some books also feature primary documents or have pro and con debate sections giving the words and opinions of prominent Americans on both sides of a controversial topic. All material is presented in an even-handed and unbiased manner; the reader will never be encouraged to accept one view of an issue over another.

HOW TO USE THIS BOOK

It is a sad but undeniable fact that in the midst of the tremendous wealth of the United States, there are still many people who cannot afford a place to live. For some, this is a temporary condition, lasting months or years, but many who become homeless find it extremely difficult to earn enough money to afford housing again. Many organizations, both public and private, work to assist the homeless and the potentially homeless, but all studies agree that there are far more in need of help than ever receive it. This book explores these and other issues, presenting the statistics and facts that illuminate the overall state of the homeless in the United States and the state of those programs that aid them.

Homeless in America: How Could It Happen Here? consists of seven chapters and three appendices. Each of the chapters is devoted to a particular aspect of homelessness in the United States. For a summary of the information covered in each chapter, please see the synopses provided in the Table of Contents at the front of the book. Chapters generally begin with an overview of the basic facts and background information on the chapter's topic, then proceed to examine subtopics of particular interest. For example, Chapter 2: The Demographics of Homelessness, begins by discussing the estimated number of homeless people in the United States and trends in the overall homeless population over time. The next section describes the characteristics of the homeless population. Covered, for instance, is the level of education of homeless people, whether they are alone or part of a homeless family, and the genders, races, and ethnicities of this population. While demonstrating that the homeless are highly diverse, special attention is given to segments that are over-represented among the homeless, e.g., single men. The chapter than examines the typical duration of a spell of homelessness and how likely it is that a formerly homeless person will become homeless again. The chapter concludes with a look at the rural homeless population. Readers can find their way through a chapter by looking for the section and sub-section headings, which are clearly set off from the text. They can also refer to the book's extensive index if they already know what they are looking for.

Statistical Information

The tables and figures featured throughout *Homeless in America: How Could It Happen Here?* will be of particular use to the reader in learning about this issue. These tables and figures represent an extensive collection of the most recent and important statistics on homelessness, housing, and related issues—for example, graphics in the book cover the percentage of the homeless who are children; how much money families of different sizes need to earn in order to stay out of poverty; the availability of low-rent housing units by region; a survey of where homeless people sleep during a typical week; and federal tax expenditures on housing. Gale believes that making this information available to the reader is the most important way in which we fulfill the goal of this book: to help readers to understand the issues and controversies surrounding homelessness in the United States and to reach their own conclusions.

Each table or figure has a unique identifier appearing above it for ease of identification and reference. Titles for the tables and figures explain their purpose. At the end of each table or figure, the original source of the data is provided.

In order to help readers understand these often complicated statistics, all tables and figures are explained in the text. References in the text direct the reader to the relevant statistics. Furthermore, the contents of all tables and figures are fully indexed. Please see the opening section of the index at the back of this volume for a description of how to find tables and figures within it.

Appendices

In addition to the main body text and images, *Homeless in America: How Could It Happen Here?* has three appendices. The first is the Important Names and Addresses directory. Here the reader will find contact information for a number of government and private organizations that can provide further information on homelessness. The second appendix is the Resources section, which can also assist the reader in conducting his or her own research. In this section, the author and editors of *Homeless in America: How Could It Happen Here?* describe some of the sources that were most useful during the compilation of this book. The final appendix is the detailed Index, which facilitates reader access to specific topics in this book.

ADVISORY BOARD CONTRIBUTIONS

The staff of Information Plus would like to extend their heartfelt appreciation to the Information Plus Advisory Board. This dedicated group of media professionals provides feedback on the series on an ongoing basis. Their comments allow the editorial staff who work on the project to make the series better and more user-friendly. Our top priorities are to produce the highest-quality and most useful books possible, and the Advisory Board's contributions to this process are invaluable.

The members of the Information Plus Advisory Board are:

- Kathleen R. Bonn, Librarian, Newbury Park High School, Newbury Park, California

- Madelyn Garner, Librarian, San Jacinto College— North Campus, Houston, Texas

- Anne Oxenrider, Media Specialist, Dundee High School, Dundee, Michigan

- Charles R. Rodgers, Director of Libraries, Pasco-Hernando Community College, Dade City, Florida

- James N. Zitzelsberger, Library Media Department Chairman, Oshkosh West High School, Oshkosh, Wisconsin

COMMENTS AND SUGGESTIONS

The editors of the Information Plus Reference Series welcome your feedback on *Homeless in America: How Could It Happen Here?* Please direct all correspondence to:

Editors

Information Plus Reference Series

27500 Drake Rd.

Farmington Hills, MI 48331-3535

ACKNOWLEDGMENTS

The editors wish to thank the copyright holders of material included in this volume and the permissions managers of many book and magazine publishing companies for assisting us in securing reproduction rights. We are also grateful to the staffs of the Detroit Public Library, the Library of Congress, the University of Detroit Mercy Library, Wayne State University Purdy/ Kresge Library Complex, and the University of Michigan Libraries for making their resources available to us.

Following is a list of the copyright holders who have granted us permission to reproduce material in Information Plus: Homeless in America. *Every effort has been made to trace copyright, but if omissions have been made, please let us know.*

For more detailed source citations, please see the sources listed under each individual table and figure.

Applied Survey Research and **Monterey County Department of Social Services (California):** Figure 2.4, Table 2.8, Figure 4.1

Association of Gospel Rescue Missions: Figure 1.1, Table 1.3

Centers for Disease Control & Prevention, National Center for HIV, STD, and TB Prevention: Table 7.2

International Union of Gospel Missions: Table 2.6

Louisiana Department of Social Services: Figure 2.5, Figure 2.6

National Coalition for the Homeless: Table 6.1

National Coalition for the Homeless, Los Angeles Coalition to End Hunger & Homelessness, and National Welfare Monitoring and Advocacy Partnership: Figure 4.3

National League of Cities: Figure 2.2, Figure 2.3, Table 2.4, Table 4.2

Urban Institute: Table 1.4, Figure 1.1, Figure 1.2, Table 2.1, Table 3.7, Figure 3.13, Figure 7.3, Figure 7.5, Figure 7.6

Urban Institute and U.S. Department of Health and Human Services: Table 1.6, Table 1.7, Figure 1.3, Table 1.8

U.S. Census Bureau: Figure 2.1, Table 2.2, Figure 3.1, Figure 3.2, Figure 3.3, Figure 3.4, Figure 3.5, Figure 3.6, Table 3.4, Figure 3.7, Figure 3.8, Figure 3.9, Table 3.1, Table 3.2, Table 3.6, Table 4.1, Figure 5.1, Table 5.3, Figure 7.2

U.S. Conference of Mayors: Table 1.1, Table 1.5, Table 2.3, Table 2.5

U.S. Department of Commerce, Bureau of Economic Analysis: Figure 3.10, Figure 3.11

U.S. Department of Education: Figure 4.2, Table 4.3

U.S. Department of Education, Office of Elementary and Secondary Education: Table 2.7

U.S. Department of Health and Human Services, Agency for Healthcare Research and Quality: Figure 7.1

U.S. Department of Health and Human Services, Health Resources and Services Administration, Bureau of Primary Health Care: Table 7.3

U.S. Department of Housing and Urban Development: Figure 2.1, Figure 5.2, Table 5.2, Table 5.5, Table 5.6, Table 5.7

U.S. Department of Housing and Urban Development and U.S. Department of Health and Human Services: Table 1.2

U.S. Department of Justice, U.S. Courts: Figure 3.11

U.S. Department of Labor, Bureau of Labor Statistics: Figure 3.8, Figure 3.12, Table 3.5

U.S. General Accounting Office: Table 5.1, Table 5.4, Table 5.8, Figure 7.4

Women's and Children's Health Policy Center, Johns Hopkins Bloomberg School of Public Health: Table 7.1

CHAPTER 1

THE NATURE OF HOMELESSNESS

From ancient Mesopotamia to the 21st-century United States, the homeless have been with us. They are society's castoffs who must sleep on the streets. In order to understand a culture that is defined by a lack of something—in this case, a permanent place to live—one must also explore the lives of the people who have what others lack. Social researchers—educators, sociologists, economists, political scientists—have studied homelessness in the past and present and determined that homelessness is a complex social phenomenon caused by a combination of poverty, misfortune, illness, and behavior.

HISTORICAL ATTITUDES TOWARD THE HOMELESS

Views of homelessness have changed over time. The condition today is viewed by most people as a result of poverty or structural flaws in society. In earlier times, the homeless have been blamed for their own misfortune, their conditions assigned to laziness, drunkenness, and crime; that view persists to this day, with drug addiction added to the causes of homelessness. Distinctions, however, have always been made. The English Poor Laws of 1601, for example, distinguished between the "worthy" and "unworthy" poor. The so-called worthy poor—widows, the elderly, the disabled, and children—were not held responsible for poverty and homelessness and sometimes received aid when aid was available, but others were viewed as idlers, derelicts, vagrants, and criminals.

English colonists bound for North America brought their beliefs with them. Some thought that the community should intervene to reduce homelessness but still believed that for most people homelessness was the consequence of weakness or flawed character. The colonists established poorhouses where the homeless and those unable to care for themselves could be sent; those ending in the poorhouse—or the workhouse, as it was sometimes called—were put to work doing hard or unpleasant tasks,

the hope being that such labor would reform the shiftless and they would then get steady employment. The modern view of homelessness—as a systemic condition for which society is responsible—would not take hold for some time yet to come.

Poorhouses failed to reduce homelessness and went out of fashion by the early 1900s. By that time the United States was becoming more and more urban and industrial. Factory work paid low wages for long hours. Homelessness became an urban phenomenon.

Attitudes toward the homeless began to change early in the 20th century. Social science began studying the problem systematically and investigators interviewed homeless people for the first time. They discovered that most of the homeless wanted to work to earn enough to pay for housing and their upkeep, but had problems finding work that paid enough to cover housing.

Attitudes changed further during the Great Depression (1929–34). After the market crash of 1929, Americans faced a decade of hard times worse than anything they had known before. Millions of people lost their jobs, many lost their homes, and most of those who still had work struggled to make ends meet. A severe drought struck the central United States in the 1930s destroying the livelihoods of millions of farmers; they streamed out of the so-called Dust Bowl that the Plains States had become. Widespread hardship felt by nearly everyone produced sympathy for the homeless and led to demands that government come to their aid. President Hoover, who advocated minimal federal involvement in solving such problems, came under severe criticism, and it is commonly held that his stance was at least in part a cause of his defeat in the 1932 elections.

The subsequent Franklin D. Roosevelt administration, as part of its New Deal program, passed a number of laws intended to reduce homelessness and poverty. The Social

TABLE 1.1

Main causes of homelessness reported by big city mayors, 2002

The following causes of homelessness were identified by the majors of the cities listed in response to an open ended question on the main or primary causes of homelessness in their respective cities. Twenty five mayors participated in the survey.

Number of positive survey responses	Causes of homelessness	Cities replying in the affirmative that the listed cause of homelessness was one of the main or primary causes in their city
21	Lack of affordable housing	Boston, Burlington, Charleston, Cleveland, Denver, Kansas City, Los Angeles, Louisville, Miami, Nashville, New Orleans, Philadelphia, Phoenix, Portland, Providence, Salt Lake City, San Antonio, Seattle, St. Louis, St. Paul, and Washington, D.C.
20	Mental illness and the lack of needed services	Boston, Burlington, Charleston, Charlotte, Chicago, Cleveland, Denver, Los Angeles, Louisville, Miami, Nashville, New Orleans, Norfolk, Phoenix, Portland, Salt Lake City, San Antonio, Seattle, St. Louis, and Trenton
19	Substance abuse and the lack of needed services	Boston, Burlington, Charleston, Charlotte, Chicago, Denver, Kansas City, Los Angeles, Louisville, Miami, Nashville, New Orleans, Norfolk, Phoenix, Portland, Salt Lake City, Seattle, St. Louis, and Trenton
17	Low-paying jobs	Boston, Burlington, Charleston, Charlotte, Chicago, Cleveland, Denver, Louisville, Miami, Nashville, Philadelphia, Phoenix, Portland, Salt Lake City, St. Louis, and Washington, D.C.
11	Domestic violence	Burlington, Charlotte, Chicago, Denver, Nashville, New Orleans, Phoenix, Portland, San Antonio, Seattle, and St. Louis
7	Unemployment	Chicago, Denver, New Orleans, Norfolk, San Antonio, St. Louis, and Washington, D.C.
6	Poverty	Charlotte, Los Angeles, San Antonio, Seattle, St. Louis, and Washington, D.C.
6	Prison release	Cleveland, Denver, New Orleans, Phoenix, Seattle, and Washington, D.C.
5	Downturn in the economy	Charleston, Kansas City, Norfolk, Salt Lake City, and Trenton
5	Limited life skills	Burlington, Charleston, Kansas City, Nashville, and San Antonio
3	Changes and cuts in public assistance programs	Chicago, Portland, and St. Louis

Cities whose mayors participated in the survey with their respective state abbreviations:

Boston, MA	Kansas City, KS	Norfolk, VA	San Antonio, TX
Burlington, VT	Los Angeles, CA	Philadelphia, PA	Seattle, WA
Charleston, NC	Louisville, KY	Phoenix, AZ	St. Louis, MO
Charlotte, SC	Miami, FL	Portland, OR	St. Paul, MN
Chicago, IL	Nashville, TN	Providence, RI	Trenton, NJ
Cleveland, OH	New Orleans, LA	Salt Lake City, UT	Washington, DC
Denver, CO			

SOURCE: Created by Information Plus from data in Eugene T. Lowe et al., *A Status Report on Hunger and Homelessness in America's Cities 2002,* The United States Conference of Mayors, Washington, DC, December 2002

Security Act of 1935 was important because it established programs that channeled funds directly to the elderly and to children of single mothers—two groups that had always suffered most from poverty and homelessness. The United States Housing Act of 1937 established housing and home loan programs for low-income people.

The New Deal laws marked a turning point in attitudes toward the homeless. More resources were added in the 1960s by further legislation, especially the formation of the Department of Housing and Urban Development in 1965. With new laws and bureaucracies in place, American society acknowledged that people could become poor and homeless because of circumstances beyond their control, and that the government should help such people. This basic idea has continued to guide federal policy since, although the shape and implementation of programs has continuously changed. Other political priorities drew attention away from the plight of the poor and homeless during the 1970s and early 1980s. Funding for many programs was cut or frozen. The late 1980s and early 1990s saw renewed interest in the problem, and new ideas surfaced on how best to help those in need. Over the past decade or so, policy has focused on getting people out of poverty as rapidly as possible. Amendments to legislation in the 1990s were designed to accelerate the process whereby those on welfare were employed as rapidly as possible.

DEFINING HOMELESSNESS

A Legislative Definition

During a period of growing concern about homelessness in the mid-1980s, the first major piece of federal legislation aimed specifically at helping the homeless was adopted: the Stewart B. McKinney Homeless Assistance Act of 1987 (PL 100-77), today known as the McKinney-Vento Homeless Assistance Act. Part of the act laid out the official government definition of a homeless person:

> An individual who lacks a fixed, regular, and adequate nighttime residence [or]
>
> An individual who has a primary nighttime residence that is:
>
> A. A supervised or publicly operated shelter designed for temporary living accommodations (including welfare hotels, congregate shelters, and transitional housing for the mentally ill);
>
> B. An institution that provides a temporary residence for individuals intended to be institutionalized; or
>
> C. A public or private place not designed for, or ordinarily used as, a regular sleeping accommodation for human beings.

A Problem Definition

There are those who disagree with the government's definition of a homeless person. Homeless advocates feel that the definition should be broadened to include groups of people who, while they may have somewhere to live, do not really have a home in the conventional sense. Considerable debate has resulted over expanding the classification to include people in situations such as the following:

TABLE 1.2

Common methods for collecting planning information

Method	Usual places to find people for study	Usual period of data collection and of estimate	Probable complexity of data collected
Full counts and other non-probability methods			
Analysis of agency records	Specific agency	Varies; usually not done to develop a population estimate	Whatever the agency routinely records in its case documents
Simple count, involving significant amounts of data by observation or from minimal agency records (e.g., Boston, Nashville, Minnesota quarterly shelter survey)	Shelters, streets	1 night; point-in-time estimate	Enumeration, + very simple population characteristics (gender, adult/child, race)
Simple count with brief interview (e.g., Pasadena, Colorado)	Shelters, meal programs, streets	1 night; point-in-time estimate	Enumeration + basic information as reported by respondent
Screener, counts and brief interviews for anyone screened in, plus unduplication using unique identifiers (Kentucky)	Service agencies of all types	Several weeks or months; point-in-time and period prevalence estimate	Enumeration + basic information as reported by respondent
Complete enumeration through multiple agency search and referral (Ohio, First et al.), followed by extensive interview (also unduplication)	Service agencies and key informants	Several weeks or months; point-in-time and period prevalence estimate	Usually extensive
Probability-based methods			
Block probability with substantial interview (e.g., Rossi, Vernez et al., DC*MADS)	Streets	Several weeks or months; point-in-time estimate	Usually extensive
Other probability approaches	Abandoned buildings, conventional housing in poor neighborhoods	Several days or weeks; point-in-time estimate	Enumeration + basic information as reported by respondent
Service-based random sampling (e.g., Rossi; UI 1987; DC*MADS; NSHAPC)	Usually homeless assistance programs	Several weeks, months, or years; point-in-time estimate	Usually extensive
Shelter and other service tracking systems that allow unduplication across all services in a jurisdiction over time	Service agencies	Ongoing; point-in-time or period prevalence for periods of any length	Whatever the system collects, but usually simple data for administrative purposes
Other interesting methods			
Surveys of the housed population (e.g., Link)	At home	Multi-year; produces period prevalence for periods asked about	Basic information as reported by respondent
Longitudinal studies (e.g., in Los Angeles, Oakland, Minneapolis, New York City)	Shelters, soup kitchens, streets	Multi-year; does not produce a population estimate	Extensive information, collected from the same person at several points in time

SOURCE: Martha R. Burt, "Table 3. Demographics and Geography: Estimating Needs," in *Practical Lessons: The 1998 National Symposium on Homelessness Research*, edited by Linda B. Fosburg and Deborah L. Dennis, U.S. Department of Housing and Urban Development and the U.S. Department of Health and Human Services, Washington, DC, August 1999

- People engaging in prostitution who spend each night in a different hotel room, paid for by clients.

- Children in foster or relative care.

- A family or single person living with their parents, with no clear expectation of when the arrangement will end, because the family/individual cannot afford a home.

- People living in stable but inadequate housing (having no plumbing or heating, for example).

- People doubled up in conventional dwellings for the short term.

- People in hotels paid for by vouchers to the needy.

- Elderly people living with family members because they cannot afford to live elsewhere.

Official definitions are important because total counts of the homeless influence levels of funding authorized by Congress for homeless programs. With the availability of federal funds since the passage of the McKinney Act, institutional constituencies have formed advocating for additional funding, an effort in which more expansive definitions are helpful.

CAUSES OF HOMELESSNESS

In a 2002 survey of mayors of big cities, most mayors named the lack of affordable housing as a cause of homelessness; 21 of 25 mayors surveyed identified this problem as a cause. (See Table 1.1.) The next three causes identified by mayors, in rank order, were mental illness and lack of services to treat it (20 of 25), substance abuse and lack of treatment services (19 of 25), and low-paying jobs (17 of 25). The lowest ranking cause cited by three mayors was changes and cuts in public assistance programs (3 of 25). Other causes cited are variations on the same basic themes:

TABLE 1.3

Survey of the homeless served by selected rescue missions, 1998-99

(In percent)

	1999	1998
Gender		
Male	77%	78%
Female	23%	22%
Age Groups		
Under 18	11%	12%
18-25	10%	10%
26-35	21%	23%
36-45	29%	30%
46-65	24%	21%
65+	5%	5%
Race/Ethnic Groups		
Caucasian	42%	40%
Afro-American	39%	42%
Hispanic	14%	12%
Asian	1%	2%
Native American	4%	5%
Families Served		
Couples	12%	12%
Women with children	67%	66%
Men with children	5%	7%
Intact families	16%	16%
Other Information		
Veterans - Male	30%	32%
Veterans - Female	3%	4%
Served in Korea	16%	8%
Served in Vietnam	38%	42%
Served in Persian Gulf War	8%	8%
Homeless less than 1 year	69%	61%
Never before homeless	33%	N/A
Homeless once before	29%	N/A
Homeless twice before	17%	N/A
Homeless 3 or more times before	20%	N/A
More than 6 month resident of city	76%	72%
Unemployed in last 6 months	54%	52%
Lost government benefits last 12 months	17%	22%
Prefer programs with spiritual emphasis	81%	79%
In long-term rehab - Male	30%	32%
In long-term rehab - Female	19%	25%

SOURCE: "1999 Snap Shot Survey of the Homeless," Association of Gospel Rescue Missions, Kansas City, MO, November 1999 [Online] http://www.agrm.org/statistics/99-snap.html [accessed September 12, 2003]

TABLE 1.4

Basic demographic characteristics of NSHAPC cases, by homeless status, 1996

Characteristics	Currently homeless clients (N = 2938)	Formerly homeless clients (N = 677)	U.S. adult population
Sex			
Male	68(%)	54(%)	48(%)
Female	32	46	52
Race/Ethnicity			
White non-Hispanic	41	46	76
Black non-Hispanic	40	41	11
Hispanic	11	9	9
Native American	8	2	1
Other	1	2	3
Age			
17	1	0	NA
18–21	6	2	7
22–24	5	2	5
25–34	25	17	21
35–44	38	36	22
45–54	17	26	17
55–64	6	11	11
65 and older	2	6	17
Education/Highest Level of Completed Schooling			
Less than high school	38	42	18
High school graduate/G.E.D.	34	34	34
More than high school	28	24	48
Marital Status			
Never married	48	45	23
Married	9	9	60
Separated	15	14	a
Divorced	24	25	10
Widowed	3	6	7
Living Situation			
Client ages 17 to 24			
Clients in families			
Men	*	*	NA
Women	3	1	NA
Single clients			
Men	5	2	NA
Women	4	1	NA
Client ages 25 and older			
Clients in families			
Men	2	3	NA
Women	9	13	NA
Single clients			
Men	62	50	NA
Women	16	30	NA
Veteran Status	**23**	**22**	**13**

Note: Numbers do not sum to 100 percent due to rounding.
NA Not available.
* Denotes values that are less than 0.5 but greater than 0 percent.
a Included in "married."
NSHAPC stands for National Survey of Homeless Assistance Providers and Clients.

SOURCE: Adapted from Martha R. Burt et al., "Table 3.1: Basic demographic characteristics, by homeless status," in *Homelessness: Programs and the People They Serve: Findings of the National Survey of Homeless Assistance Providers and Clients*, Urban Institute, Washington, DC, December 1999

domestic violence, unemployment, poverty, prison release, downturn of the economy, and limited life skills.

Based on this survey of knowledgeable individuals whose job includes managing the problem, homelessness emerges as a complex social problem arising from three fundamental and interacting causes: lack of means, medical conditions, and behavioral problems.

COUNTING THE HOMELESS

Methodology

An accurate count of the U.S. homeless population has proved to be a problem for statisticians. The most formidable obstacle is the nature of homelessness itself. Typically, researchers contact people in their homes using in-person or telephone surveys to obtain information regarding income, education levels, household size, ethnicity, and other demographic data. Since homeless people cannot be counted "at home," researchers have been forced to develop new methods for collecting data on these transient groups. Martha Burt, Ph.D., a lead researcher with the U.S. Department of Housing and Urban Development (HUD) and the U.S. Department of Health and Human

FIGURE 1.1

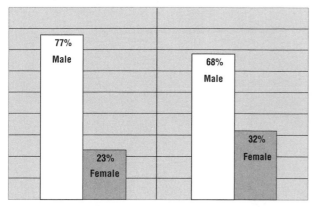

Gender breakdown of the homeless population as reported in two different studies, 1996 and 1999

1999 Survey by the Association of Gospel Rescue Missions

1996 Survey by the Urban Institute

77% Male

23% Female

68% Male

32% Female

SOURCE: Created by Information Plus from data in Martha R. Burt et al., "Table 3.1: Basic demographic characteristics, by homeless status" in *Homelessness: Programs and the People They Serve: Findings of the National Survey of Homeless Assistance Providers and Clients*, Urban Institute, Washington, DC, 1999 and "1999 Snap Shot Survey of the Homeless," Association of Gospel Rescue Missions, Kansas City, MO, November 1999 [Online] http://www.agrm.org/statistics/99-snap.html [accessed September 12, 2003]

Services (DHHS) has explored this issue and published a table of the most common methods of data collection for homeless people. (See Table 1.2.)

An actual count of people without homes would, of course, be the ideal method of establishing their number and, failing that, estimates based on record searches at homeless service provider locations. Alternatively, sampling combined with projections, so-called probabilistic methods, can be used. Point-in-time counts, called "snapshots," enumerate the number of homeless at a particular point in time and at a particular place. Longitudinal studies are used to follow individuals over a period of time to determine if they become homeless.

COMPARING METHODS AND RESULTS. As Table 1.2 reveals, methods vary in scope and design. Different designs will produce different results even if the intention is the same—namely to enumerate the homeless population. Table 1.3 shows results of surveys conducted by the Association of Gospel Rescue Missions (AGRM) in 1998 and 1999. Table 1.4 shows results from an Urban Institute study conducted in 1996. Data in Table 1.3 are based on the "snapshot" method—counts of a population at a point in time. AGRM counted all people receiving homeless services during one specific night in each year. Data in Table 1.4 are based on a sample of 76 geographical areas selected by the Urban Institute as being representative of all service

providers in the United States. The Urban Institute then compared its results by demographic characteristics to the total population as enumerated by the U.S. census. The male/female ratios in the AGRM study are quite different from the Urban Institute's study, with AGRM finding, both in 1998 and 1999, that males were more than three-quarters of the homeless (77 percent in 1999), whereas the Urban Institute's study showed that males were just over two-thirds of the homeless population (68 percent). (See Figure 1.1.) Both studies showed that males were more numerous among the homeless than females, but the proportions were different. Census data show that women outnumber men in the U.S. population by a small margin—50.9 percent of the population was female and 49.1 percent male in the 2000 census of the population.

The Official Count: The U.S. Census Survey

The official U.S. Census, which takes place at 10-year intervals, is intended to count everyone in the United States. The results of the census are critical for determining how much federal money goes into different programs and to various regions of the country. Representation of the population in Congress is also based on the census. Since the U.S. Census Bureau counts people in their homes, counting the homeless presents special challenges.

A PROBLEM OF METHODOLOGY. In 1990 census officials, on what was known as Shelter and Street Night, or S-Night, counted homeless persons in the following locations:

- Emergency shelters for the homeless
- Pre-identified street locations
- Youth shelters
- Shelters for abused women

The results of this count were released the following year, categorized under the heading, "Count of Persons in Selected Locations Where Homeless Persons Are Found." Homeless advocates criticized the methods and results as inadequate and charged that they provided a low estimate of homeless people in the United States. In response, a spokesman for the Bureau of the Census, in a 1991 press release, emphasized that "S-Night was not intended to, and did not, produce a count of the 'homeless' population of the country." S-Night results were not a reflection of the prevalence of homelessness over a given year, but rather a count of homeless persons identified during a single night, a "snapshot," like the census itself.

CENSUS ACCUSED OF UNCONSTITUTIONALITY. The National Law Center on Homelessness and Poverty alleged that the methodology of the S-Night count was unconstitutional. In 1992 the Law Center, the U.S. Conference of Mayors, the cities of Baltimore and San Francisco,

TABLE 1.5

City data on homelessness, 2002

City	Percent increase in requests for emergency shelter	Percent increase in requests by families for emergency shelter	Shelter beds	Transitional housing units	Family break-up for shelter?	Family leave during day	Percentage need unmet	Turn away families?	Turn others away?
Boston	3.0	5.6	decreased	same	yes	no	2	yes	yes
Burlington	11.0	NA	increased	increased	no	no	28	yes	no
Charleston	15.0	15.0	same	same	no	no	0	yes	no
Charlotte	10.0	10.0	same	increased	yes	no	50	yes	yes
Chicago	NA	NA	increased	same	yes	no	0	no	no
Cleveland	15.0	10.0	same	increased	no	no	0	no	no
Denver	15.0	5.0	same	same	no	yes	15	yes	yes
Kansas City	25.0	20.0	decreased	decreased	no	no	56	no	no
Los Angeles	10.0	16.0	increased	increased	yes	no	21	yes	yes
Louisville	9.0	6.0	same	same	no	no	65	no	no
Miami	23.0	8.0	increased	same	no	no	10	no	no
Nashville	15.0	15.0	decreased	same	yes	no	0	no	no
New Orleans	20.0	20.0	increased	increased	yes	yes	20	yes	yes
Norfolk	30.0	30.0	same	same	yes	yes	15	yes	yes
Philadelphia	NA	NA	same	increased	no	no	0	no	no
Phoenix	NA	17.0	decreased	decreased	yes	yes	60	yes	yes
Portland, OR	23.0	35.0	same	decreased	yes	yes	25	yes	yes
Providence	22.0	16.0	NA	NA	no	no	0	yes	yes
Salt Lake City	0.0	58.0	same	increased	no	no	0	yes	yes
San Antonio	8.0	19.0	increased	same	yes	no	9	yes	yes
Seattle	0.0	0.0	same	increased	no	no	0	no	no
St. Louis	64.0	61.0	same	same	yes	yes	58	yes	yes
St. Paul	NA	-2.0	same	increased	no	no	49	no	no
Trenton	15.0	5.0	same	increased	no	yes	15	yes	yes
Washington, DC	18.0	15.0	increased	decreased	no	no	15	no	no

NA = not available

SOURCE: Eugene T. Lowe et al., "City Data on Homelessness," in *A Status Report on Hunger and Homelessness in America's Cities, 2002: A 25-City Survey*, The United States Conference of Mayors, Washington, DC, December 2002

15 local homeless organizations, and 7 homeless people (the plaintiffs) filed suit in the federal district court in Washington, D.C. They charged the Census Bureau with excluding segments of the homeless population in the 1990 population count by not counting those in hidden areas and by not allocating adequate funds for S-Night.

In its suit, the Law Center cited an internal Census Bureau memorandum that stated, in part, "We know we will miss people by counting the 'open' rather than 'concealed' (two studies showed that about two-thirds of the street population sleep concealed)." Studies funded by the Census Bureau indicated that up to 70 percent of the homeless street population in Los Angeles were missed, as were 32 percent in New Orleans, 47 percent in New York City, and 69 percent in Phoenix. Advocates were greatly concerned that this underrepresentation would negatively affect the funding of homeless initiatives.

In 1994 the district court dismissed the case, ruling that the plaintiffs' case was without merit. The court ruled that failure to count all the homeless was not a failure to perform a constitutional duty; the Constitution does not give individuals a right to be counted or a right to a perfectly accurate census. The court stated that the "methods used by the bureau on S-Night were reasonably designed to count as nearly as practicable all those persons residing in the United States and, therefore, easily pass constitutional muster."

CENSUS 2000 LIMITS INFORMATION. The Bureau of the Census undertook a special operation, called Service-Based Enumeration (SBE), for the 2000 census. From March 27–29, 2000, census workers focused solely on counting the homeless population at the locations where they were most likely to be found. For the SBE, the Bureau released the following schedule:

- Monday, March 27, 2000—Emergency and transitional shelters, hotels, motels, or other facilities. Enumerators will leave blank questionnaires for residents who usually stay at the shelter, but who are away at the time of the enumeration.

- Tuesday, March 28, 2000—Soup kitchens, regularly scheduled mobile food vans.

- Wednesday, March 29, 2000, from 4 A.M. to 7 A.M. only—Outdoor locations. Census workers will complete the census forms for each person at an outdoor location.

The SBE methods were considered an improvement over the methods used in the 1990 census survey. Homeless citizens and advocates alike expected to see an increase in the number of homeless persons reported by the Census Bureau in the 2000 census as compared with the count reported for the 1990 census. Expectations that the higher population counts would translate into higher funding levels for those providing services to the homeless were also raised.

An Associated Press story dated June 27, 2001, reported that the U.S. Census Bureau would not be releasing a specific homeless count because of the liability issues raised after the 1990 census. The Bureau stated that it would have only one category showing the number of persons tabulated at "emergency and transitional shelters." The people who, in 2000, were counted at domestic-violence shelters, family crisis centers, soup kitchens, mobile food vans, and targeted nonsheltered outdoor locations (i.e. street people, car dwellers, etc.) during the March 2000 SBE night were to be included in the category of "other non-institutional group quarters population." This category is overly inclusive; it includes, for instance, students living in college dormitories. The homeless portion of the category cannot be extracted.

According to Edison Gore, deputy chief of the Census Bureau's decennial management division, rather than release information on homeless people, the bureau planned to publish a special report on people sleeping in shelters. Bureau officials said the homeless people they did find during the exhaustive, three-day SBE count were included in total population figures for states, counties, and municipalities. Researchers voiced concern that the numbers teased from these data sets will be flawed.

People involved in the receipt or delivery of services to the homeless were worried that their programs would suffer from the lack of SBE night information. A detailed homeless count is thought to be essential for city officials and advocacy groups to plan budgets for shelters and other homeless outreach programs. Results from the U.S. Conference of Mayors 2002 study illustrate the negative impact that inadequate information and funding can have on the delivery of human services. (See Table 1.5.) For example, Kansas City has an unmet need of 56 percent due to lack of resources. Homeless program funding for most cities is already strained. Eighty-eight percent of cities surveyed in 2002 showed increased requests for emergency shelter services. The highest increase (64 percent) was reported in St. Louis and the lowest (3 percent) was reported in Boston. Shelter requirements for families with children have increased 88 percent overall, with the highest increase in St. Louis (61 percent) and the lowest in Denver and Trenton, New Jersey (5 percent).

Only Estimates Are Available

The actual number of homeless people is unknown. The Urban Institute estimated that 3.5 million people were homeless at some point of time during the year 1996 (*America's Homeless II—Populations and Services*, The Urban Institute, Washington, D.C., February 1, 2000). The 2000 Census counted 170,706 individuals in emergency and transitional shelters, down from 178,638 individuals in 1990 (*Emergency and Shelter Population: 2000*, U.S. Census Bureau, Washington, D.C., October 2001). The Bureau expressly stated that this number is not a total count of the homeless. In its Fiscal Year 2004 budget summary, the U.S. Department of Housing and Urban Development put the number of those chronically homeless at 150,000 and stated that this population was less than 10 percent of all homeless individuals. If the 150,000 figure was at least 10 percent, the homeless population was around 1.5 million people in 2003. In a 2002 press release, HUD put the number of homeless at 650,000 on any given night ("Martinez Names Mangano Director of Interagency Homeless Council," HUD No. 02-005, January 10, 2002).

PUBLIC INTEREST IN HOMELESSNESS

Since the mid-1990s public interest in the homeless has declined, in part because of the strong economy of the 1990s. Earlier, in the mid- to late 1980s, the country showed more concern about homelessness. Public initiatives to draw attention to the cause were popular. In 1986 the American public demonstrated concern over the plight of the homeless by initiating the Hands Across America fundraising effort. Some 6 million people locked hands across 4,152 miles to form a human chain across the country, bringing an outpouring of national attention and concern to the issue. In 1986 popular comedians Robin Williams, Whoopi Goldberg, and Billy Crystal hosted the HBO comedy special *Comic Relief,* to help raise money for the homeless. The show was a hit and became an annual event. Magazines, art shows, books, and songs turned the nation's attention toward homelessness. Well-funded research studies came out by the dozens. The country was awash in statistical information regarding the homeless.

In 2003 one could only see *Comic Relief* in reruns. The annual fundraiser ran out of steam in 1996 with the exception of one revival show two years later. No new resurgence of interest by the public in the homeless problem has appeared thus far in the 21st century although the problem remains and the demand for services has increased as reported by the U.S. Conference of Mayors in 2002. "The Real Face of Homelessness," in the January 20, 2003, issue of *Time* explores a change in the national mood about homelessness. In New Orleans, for instance, park benches in certain areas have been removed in order to prevent street people from sleeping on them. A campaign was launched in Philadelphia to discourage giving money to panhandlers. In Orlando one can land in jail for sleeping on the sidewalk. In San Francisco Proposition N ("Care not Cash") reduced county housing support payments from $395 to $59 a month, assisting the homeless with food and shelter instead. According to a *Time*/CNN poll also cited in the article, 36 percent of the 1,006 adults polled favored making panhandling illegal and 47 percent thought it should be illegal to sleep in public places.

Research studies, once so plentiful, are now outdated, but some well-funded research centers and organizations continue to study the homeless population. A look at leading organizations follows.

The Urban Institute

The Urban Institute is a nonprofit policy research organization located in Washington, D.C. The Institute conducts research projects, publishes newsletters and books regarding social issues, and evaluates government programs. It is dedicated to examining society's problems and developing methods to solve them. The Institute's work is designed to help improve government decisions and increase citizens' awareness of important social issues. Funding comes from a variety of government, corporate, and private organizations and people.

The Urban Institute study *Homelessness: Programs and the People They Serve*, published in December 1999, was a landmark in homelessness research. The program was designed specifically to update a 1987 Institute study. The survey was based on a statistical sample of 76 metropolitan and nonmetropolitan areas, including small cities and rural areas. It provided relevant information about homeless service providers and examined the characteristics of those who use the services. The analysis presented information about homelessness in national, urban, suburban, and rural areas. It was still one of the most comprehensive research studies available on the subject of homelessness in America as of summer 2003.

The U.S. Conference of Mayors

The U.S. Conference of Mayors is the official organization of the leaders of cities with populations of 30,000 or more. More than 1,000 cities send their chief elected official, the mayor, to the annual conference. Since 1982 the U.S. Conference of Mayors has conducted and published an annual survey to bring attention to the shortage of emergency services—food, shelter, medical care, and income assistance—in the nation's largest cities. The survey tracks the increases or reductions in the demand for emergency services from year to year, including services for the homeless. This study has become one of the leading sources of homelessness research today.

The National Coalition for the Homeless

The National Coalition for the Homeless (NCH) is an advocacy group of homeless persons, activists, service providers, and people dedicated to ending homelessness. NCH serves as a national clearinghouse for information and works as a referral resource to enhance the public's understanding of homelessness. NCH believes that homelessness can be eliminated through public education, legislative advocacy, and grassroots movements.

Other Organizations

Homes for the Homeless (HFH) is a New York City-based program designed to find long-term solutions for homeless people in New York. HFH designed an innovative and successful program, the American Family Inn, used as a model for permanent solutions to homelessness. HFH is affiliated with the Institute for Children and Poverty, and together they conduct research studies to uncover strategies for fighting poverty and homelessness.

The National Alliance to End Homelessness (NAEH) is a nationwide federation of public, private, and nonprofit organizations operating on the assumption that homelessness can be ended. Alliance members work to advance the implementation of practical, community-based solutions to homelessness.

The National Law Center on Homelessness and Poverty states that its mission is "to alleviate, ameliorate and end homelessness by serving as the legal arm of the nationwide movement to end homelessness," and works to protect the rights of homeless people and to end homelessness in America. It uses three main strategies to achieve this goal: impact litigation, policy advocacy, and public education. The Law Center conducts research studies and distributes the results by publishing fact sheets and a monthly newsletter.

HOMELESS SERVICES

A substantial number of organizations provide services to the homeless across the country. Faith-based organizations have been providing assistance to the needy throughout history, including programs for the homeless. More recently, secular non-profits have also begun providing such assistance. Since 1987, with the passage of the McKinney Act, federal funding targeted to the homeless has been available. It reached a peak of $1.5 billion in 1995, up from $350 million in 1987. HUD's FY (fiscal year) 2004 budget allocated $1.3 million for homeless programs; additional funds were spent by 50 other government agencies, including the Department of Health and Human Services and the Veterans Administration.

The most recent comprehensive study of assistance programs dates to 1996. In that year, according to the Urban Institute, about half of all assistance programs were located in central cities, 19 percent in suburban fringe communities, the rest in rural areas. (See Table 1.6.) All told, 39,664 programs operated nationwide, with the

TABLE 1.6

Homeless assistance programs by sponsorship, type, and area designation, 1996

Areas and program types	Total number of programs	Percentage by sponsor type			
		Faith-based non-profit	Secular non-profit	Govern-ment	For-profit
All program types	39,664	31.8	47.3	13.4	0.6
Central cities					
All	19,388	36.8	45.9	9.9	0.7
Housing	7,894	28.7	53.8	9.6	0.8
Food	6,018	63.4	28.3	2.6	0.2
Health	1,379	7.5	56.8	29.1	0.7
Other	4,097	23.5	53.0	14.6	1.2
Suburbs					
All	7,694	35.1	48.0	7.4	1.1
Housing	3,230	24.2	53.6	8.7	1.8
Food	3,020	53.0	40.0	2.6	0.4
Health	251	2.9	51.0	32.0	2.6
Other	1,192	26.2	52.9	11.0	0.4
Rural areas					
All	12,583	21.9	48.9	22.6	0.2
Housing	4,754	15.5	56.6	18.6	NA
Food	3,965	37.6	49.1	10.3	0.7
Health	1,110	1.8	11.1	68.4	NA
Other	2,754	18.3	50.7	28.6	NA

NA Not available.

Rows may not added to 100 percent because programs that did not identify their source of sponsorship in the survey are not listed.

SOURCE: Adapted from Laudan Y. Aron and Patrick T. Sharkey, "Table 1a: NSHAPC Programs by Urban/Rural Status," in *The 1996 National Survey of Homeless Assistance Providers and Clients: A Comparison of Faith-Based and Secular Non-Profit Programs,* The Urban Institute and the U.S. Department of Health and Human Services, Washington, DC, March 2002 [Online] http://aspe.hhs.gov/hsp/homelessness/NSHAPC02/ [accessed July 2, 2003]

TABLE 1.7

Homeless assistance programs by sponsorship, type, and region, 1996

Regions and program types	Number of programs	Percentage by sponsor type			
		Faith-based non-profit	Secular non-profit	Govern-ment	For-profit
All programs	39,664	31.8	47.3	13.4	0.6
Northeast					
All programs	7,097	28.6	53.6	10.1	0.6
Housing	2,870	16.4	61.3	12.9	0.6
Food	2,401	53.1	37.2	3.6	0.5
Health	306	6.6	69.1	14.1	0.7
Other	1,521	17.4	62.1	14.5	0.7
South					
All programs	11,101	39.0	40.7	13.6	0.5
Housing	4,309	30.0	50.3	10.3	1.1
Food	4,113	58.1	32.2	6.1	NA
Health	863	4.7	26.9	57.0	0.1
Other	1,817	33.5	43.5	17.9	0.1
Midwest					
All programs	11,853	31.6	43.7	16.2	0.5
Housing	4,678	24.5	47.6	16.9	0.4
Food	3,945	54.6	34.3	6.7	0.8
Health	736	2.8	39.7	35.5	NA
Other	2,494	16.8	52.6	24.0	0.4
West					
All programs	9,333	25.8	54.6	12.4	1.0
Housing	3,892	21.2	62.9	8.0	1.0
Food	2,478	42.4	51.0	1.7	0.2
Health	816	6.0	34.7	53.8	1.7
Other	2,147	22.3	51.3	17.2	1.6

NA Not available.

Rows may not added to 100 percent because programs that did not identify their source of sponsorship in the survey are not listed.

SOURCE: Adapted from Laudan Y. Aron and Patrick T. Sharkey, "Table 1b: NSHAPC Programs by Region of the Country," in *The 1996 National Survey of Homeless Assistance Providers and Clients: A Comparison of Faith-Based and Secular Non-Profit Programs,* The Urban Institute and the U.S. Department of Health and Human Services, Washington, DC, March 2002 [Online] http://aspe.hhs.gov/hsp/homelessness/NSHAPC02/ [accessed July 2, 2003]

largest number in the South and Midwest and the lowest in the Northeast (see Table 1.7). Some of these programs were aimed directly at homeless people, such as those supporting shelters. Others were programs open to a wider group of needy people that included most or all of the homeless (e.g., free clinics for the poor).

Homeless services provide assistance in three major areas: housing, food, and health. In 1996, 40 percent of the programs consisted of housing assistance such as shelters, permanent housing, and housing vouchers. Provision of food through such outlets as soup kitchens, food pantries, and mobile food distribution accounted for 33 percent of services. Seven percent of the assistance programs were related to health care, which included not only physical and mental health care but also assistance to those with drug and alcohol addictions as well as care for sufferers of HIV/AIDS. Nationwide there were 15,878 housing programs, 13,003 food programs, and 2,740 health programs. An additional 8,043 programs provided assistance on an outreach basis, through drop-in centers and through programs offering financial help for housing.

The Urban Institute also studied the utilization rates of homeless services. Figure 1.2 illustrates the scope of food programs, with 26 percent of the surveyed providers expecting between 101 and 299 requests daily, and 11 percent expecting more than 300 contacts a day. For walk-in services (labeled "other programs" on the graph) and health programs, about half this percentage expected the same volume of clients. For example, 5 percent of walk-in programs expected more than 300 people a day, as did 4 percent of health programs. Housing programs served the lowest number of people per day: on average, only 2 percent of the programs expected 300 contacts a day. Food, health, and walk-in services (such as job counseling) are, by nature, geared toward multiple returns and have high traffic. Housing programs, by contrast, provide single-client service delivery over a longer period of time. Housing programs are

FIGURE 1.2

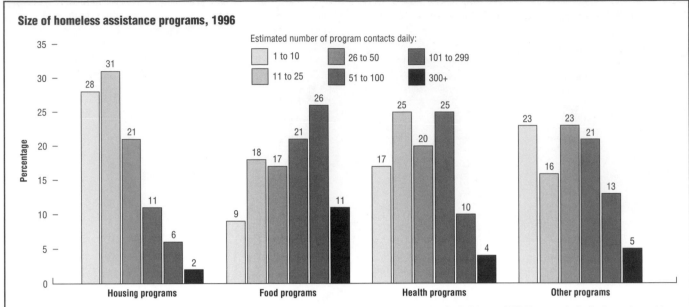

Size of homeless assistance programs, 1996

Note: These are program staff estimates of how many program contacts their own program expected on an average day in February 1996. They contain duplication and cannot be added together to get the total number of people served on an average day. Housing programs include emergency, transitional, permanent housing, and voucher programs; food programs include pantries, soup kitchens, and mobile food programs; health programs include general health, mental health, alcohol/drug, and HIV/AIDS programs; other programs include outreach, drop-in centers, financial/housing assistance, and other.

SOURCE: "Figure 4.3: Size of Homeless Assistance Programs," in *Homelessness: Programs and the People They Serve: Findings of the National Survey of Homeless Assistance Providers and Clients,* Urban Institute, Washington, DC, December 1999

FIGURE 1.3

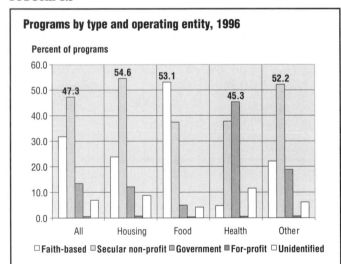

Programs by type and operating entity, 1996

Note: The "Other" category includes outreach, drop-in centers, financial/housing assistance, and miscellaneous aid programs.

SOURCE: Created by Information Plus from Laudan Y. Aron and Patrick T. Sharkey, "Table A1: Number of NSHAPC Programs by Type of Agency Operating Programs," in *The 1996 National Survey of Homeless Assistance Providers and Clients: A Comparison of Faith-Based and Secular Non-Profit Programs,* The Urban Institute and the U.S. Department of Health and Human Services, Washington, DC, March 2002 [Online] http://aspe.hhs.gov/ homelessness/NSHAPC02/ [accessed July 2, 2003]

Secular non-profit organizations provided nearly half (47.3 percent) of all homeless services in 1996. (See Figure 1.3.) Secular organizations were also most prominent in providing housing (54.6 percent of all housing programs) and "other" services (52.2 percent); other services included outreach, drop-in centers, and financial/housing assistance. Faith-based organizations were most active in providing food services (53.1 percent of all such programs); these include food pantries, soup kitchens, and mobile food distribution. Government agencies led in the provision of health services (45.3 percent of all such services).

Special Population Services

Many homeless assistance programs are open to anyone who wants to use them, but other programs are designed to serve only specific groups of people. The population served may be defined in several different ways: men by themselves, women by themselves, households with children, youth by themselves, battered women, or veterans, for example. The Urban Institute study revealed that less than one-third of all homeless service programs named a specific population group as a focus.

After meeting the basic needs of food, shelter, and health care, homeless programs provide for other special needs. According to the Urban Institute, 40.6 percent of emergency shelters do not target their assistance to a particular group of people and 30.3 percent focus their assistance on those suffering domestic violence. (See Table

also geared specifically toward helping the homeless while many food, health, and walk-in programs are open to a wider group of people.

TABLE 1.8

Homeless assistance programs by type, sponsorship, and focus, 1996

Program type and focus	Programs by all sponsors		Faith-based non-profit		Secular non-profit		Government	
	Number	Percent	Number	Percent	Number	Percent	Number	Percent
Emergency shelter with	5,320	100%	1,520	100%	3,480	100%	320	100%
No specialization		40.6		63.2		30.4		44.6
Mental health (MH) focus		3.7		2.5		4.1		5.2
Chemical dependency (CD) focus		8.6		15.5		5.3		12.6
MH/CD focus		1.4		2.7		0.9		1.0
HIV/AIDS focus		1.4		1.8		1.3		0.3
Domestic violence focus		30.3		5.2		42.1		20.1
Youth focus		8.3		1.7		11.3		6.8
Family focus		5.6		7.4		4.5		9.3
Transitional shelter with	4,149	100%	1,181	100%	2,535	100%	433	100%
No specialization		43.4		54.8		35.6		57.6
Mental health focus		8.3		3.5		9.6		14.2
Chemical dependency focus		14.4		16.6		15.2		4.2
MH/CD focus		5.2		2.9		6.3		5.2
HIV/AIDS focus		3.1		1.2		4.2		1.7
Domestic violence focus		14.0		7.7		18.2		6.6
Youth focus		4.4		5.6		4.6		0.2
Family focus		7.1		7.6		6.3		10.2
Permanent housing with	1,719	100%	205	100%	980	100%	534	100%
No specialization		63.6		61.6		52.8		84.2
Mental health focus		15.7		8.8		22.1		6.6
Chemical dependency focus		5.2		11.0		5.2		2.9
MH/CD focus		5.8		5.6		7.8		2.2
HIV/AIDS focus		9.8		13.0		12.1		4.2
Soup kitchen with	3,284	100%	2,131	100%	1,057	100%		NA
No specialization		83.2		84.9		79.4		NA
Mental health focus		6.1		4.4		9.8		NA
Chemical dependency focus		6.7		7.6		5.2		NA
Family focus		2.4		2.9		1.6		NA
HIV/AIDS focus		1.5		0.2		4.0		NA

NA Not available

SOURCE: Adapted from Laudan Y. Aron and Patrick T. Sharkey, "Table 6: What Special Focus Do NSHAPC Programs Have?," in *The 1996 National Survey of Homeless Assistance Providers and Clients: A Comparison of Faith-Based and Secular Non-Profit Programs,* The Urban Institute and the U.S. Department of Health and Human Services, Washington, DC, March 2002 [Online] http://aspe.hhs.gov/homelessness/NSHAPC02/ [accessed July 2, 2003]

1.8.) The transitional shelters that report specialized assistance programs divide their focus between domestic violence and chemical dependence, around 14 percent for each. Permanent housing programs that target specific population groups focus heavily on those in need of mental health services (15.7 percent of programs).

CHAPTER 2
THE DEMOGRAPHICS OF HOMELESSNESS

THE AUTHORITATIVE ESTIMATES

Our view of the homeless phenomenon is of necessity hindsight because data sufficient to assess homelessness nationally date to 1996. No census or other governmental program is in place to track the homeless population. The situation is succinctly summarized in a report published by the U.S. Department of Housing and Urban Development, or HUD (*Evaluation of Continuums of Care For Homeless People*, Washington, DC, May 2002), as follows:

> Basically, there are only three sources or original data on which to base estimates of incidence (the number of people homeless on a single day) for the nation as a whole—HUD's 1984 effort (HUD, 1984), the Urban Institute's 1987 study (Burt and Cohen, 1989), and the 1996 National Survey of Homeless Providers and Clients (Burt, Aron, and Lee, 2001). Any national estimates offered by anyone for any years other than 1984, 1987, and 1996 are projections or manipulations of one of these three data sources, and include assumptions of population change or growth that are not grounded in data. HUD's 1984 study was based on a survey of providers, who supplied their best guesses as to the size of the homeless population in their cities. Only the 1987 and 1996 studies are based on statistically reliable samples of homeless people using homeless assistance programs. Using these three data sources, the number of people homeless at any one time appears to have grown substantially from the mid-1980s until the mid-1990s—from 250,000–350,000 in 1984 (HUD's "most reliable range") to 500,000–600,000 in 1987, to 640,000–840,000 in 1996. Best guesses or projections of the number of people homeless during the course of a year come from various different sources (Burt, Aron, and Lee, 2001; Culhane et al., 1994; Link et al., 1994, 1995) (there are no truly reliable national data). These estimates, using very different approaches, nevertheless converge on figures that between 2.5 and 3.5 million people (including children) experience at least one night of homelessness within a given year.

Even these data, considered by the government to be reliable, are based on very small samples. The 1996 data, the most recent and most widely used (including in this presentation), were based on interviews with 6,300 homeless program representatives, held in February 1996, and interviews with 4,200 users of homeless programs conducted in October 1996. The total number of people homeless at some point in the year 1996 was derived by projection from this sample. While such methods of estimating are common in statistical analysis, they also show that current knowledge about the phenomenon is, at best, partial.

HOW NUMBERS ARE USED

The ordinary citizen, hearing of the homeless, envisions people, including children, who live on the street permanently and sleep in cardboard boxes under bridges or in cars. There are, of course, people in this category, but they are the minority among the homeless. HUD has labeled such people the chronically homeless and estimates their number at around 150,000, close to the number of people counted by the Census Bureau as inhabiting emergency and transitional shelters in the 2000 census count (170,706 individuals). Most of the homeless are not chronically but temporarily homeless. After some period of homelessness, they find permanent shelter or move in with relatives; the last condition is also counted as homelessness by some and those who are "doubled up" are also included in the homeless category by certain programs, as will be shown below.

A clearer picture of the homeless population envisions a group of people who are, on any day, without proper shelter. When agencies or the media cite numbers in the 600,000–800,000 range, they mean the size of the homeless population at any one point in time. Individuals are continuously joining this population while others are continuously leaving it. If all those who pass through this status in a given year are counted, the total number reaches somewhere between 2.5 and 3.5 million individuals.

TABLE 2.1

Number likely to be homeless at least once in a given year

	New homeless spells begun in last week	Average week estimate	Annual projection
	A	B	C
February 1996	52,000	842,000	3.5 million
October 1996	36,900	444,000	2.3 million

Note: The projection is developed by taking column A times 51 weeks and adding the result to column B. Column B represents the estimated constant population of homeless in any one week. The assumption is that a population of the size shown in column A is continuously passing into and also out of homeless status throughout the year. Data for February were based on the estimates of homeless program employees, data for October on interviews with the homeless.

SOURCE: Adapted from "Number Likely to Be Homeless at Least Once in a Given Year," in *America's Homeless II: Populations and Services*, Urban Institute, Washington, DC, February 2000

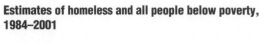

FIGURE 2.1

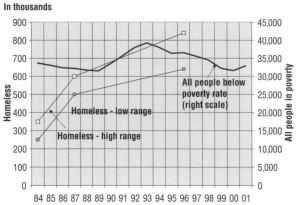

Estimates of homeless and all people below poverty, 1984–2001

SOURCE: Created by Information Plus from data in *Evaluation of Continuous Care for Homeless People*, U.S. Department of Housing and Urban Development, Washington, DC, May 2002 and "Table 2. Poverty Status of People by Family Relationship, Race, and Hispanic Origin: 1959 to 2001," in *Historical Poverty Tables*, U.S. Census Bureau, Washington, DC [Online] http://www.census.gov/hhes/poverty/histpov/hstpov2.html [accessed September 5, 2003]

The manner in which the annual projections for 1996 were derived is shown in Table 2.1 for two different months of 1996 using two sets of data. The data for October, projected from counts of homeless services seekers, show that an estimated 36,900 individuals began spells of homelessness during the week surveyed, while the total number of people in the homeless population in any one week was estimated to be 444,000. The annual projection assumes that every week 36,900 become homeless and an equal number pass out of the homeless status. Multiplying 36,900 51 times, for the weeks remaining in the year, and adding that total to the average homeless population, produces the 2.3 million count of those who were homeless at least once in 1996. The number does not mean that there were 2.3 million homeless during the entire span of 1996.

Counting Children

Sometimes stories in the media or on Web sites cite 600,000 homeless and 1 million homeless children (see for instance "Are Shelters the Answer to Family Homelessness," *USA Today,* January 1, 2003). Such statements double-count the homeless by using two different sources of incompatible data. These confusing numbers come about because, under the McKinney-Vento Homeless Assistance Act, the U.S. Department of Education (USDE) is required to file a report on homeless children served by the act. USDE obtains the data from school districts; school districts use different methods of estimation. In its 2000 report to Congress (*Education for Homeless Children and Youth Program*, Washington, D.C.), USDE reported an estimated 930,032 children as being homeless. More on this subject is presented below; the point is that these data were drawn on records for a full year, whereas homeless counts have been point-in-time snapshots.

GROWTH PATTERNS

The data from three surveys mentioned in the HUD report above are plotted in Figure 2.1 together with Census Bureau data on the population living below the poverty level. People living below the poverty threshold decreased between 1984 and 1989 from 33.7 to 31.5 million. This population then increased from 1989 to 1993 to 39.3 million, declining after that year to 31.6 million people in 2000 during the boom of the 1990s, with a new uptick shown from 2000 to 2001 of 1.3 million people, ending in that year with 32.9 million people living below the poverty line. Between 1984 and 1996, years for which comparable estimates for the homeless are available, the total number of people living in poverty increased 8.4 percent.

The number of homeless, using the high range of the estimates, was 350,000 in 1984 and increased to 840,000 people by 1996, an increase of 140 percent. Using the low range estimate, numbers increased from 250,000 in 1984 to 640,000 in 1996, a 156 percent increase.

Comparing these two sets of data suggests that homelessness is not strongly correlated to the population living below the poverty line—or that the number of the homeless were underestimated in the early years of the period shown—or that the homeless were an increasingly larger proportion of the poor. There is, however, a very definite relationship between poverty and homelessness, suggesting that the other two explanations are probably more on target; the most likely reason for the difference in homeless and poverty trends is an undercount of the homeless.

TABLE 2.2

Population in emergency and transitional shelters, 1990 and 2000

| Area | Population in shelters | | | | Total 2000 U.S. population |
| | 1990 | | 2000 | | |
	Number	Percent	Number	Percent	Percent
United States	178,638	100.0	170,706	100.0	100.0
Region					
Northeast	60,077	33.6	52,369	30.7	19.0
Midwest	27,245	15.3	28,438	16.7	22.9
South	42,407	23.7	42,471	24.9	35.6
West	48,909	27.4	47,428	27.8	22.5

SOURCE: Adapted from Annetta C. Smith and Denise I. Smith, "Table 1. Population in Emergency and Transitional Shelters for the United States, Regions, States, and Puerto Rico: 1990 and 2000," in *Emergency and Transitional Shelter Population: 2000*, U.S. Census Bureau, Washington, DC, October 2001

Homeless counts have been based on surveys centered around facilities that provide services to the homeless (such as shelters and soup kitchens). These are permanent sites where some contact with the homeless is possible. The number of such facilities has increased substantially since the passage of the McKinney Act of 1987. Shelter/housing for the homeless increased from an estimated 275,000 in 1988 to 607,000 beds in 1996; big city food service programs increased from 97,000 to 380,100 between 1987 and 1996 (*America's Homeless II: Populations and Services*, The Urban Institute, Washington, D.C., February 2000). With an ever larger base of support facilities, the ability of researchers to reach more and more precise estimates of populations served has improved.

What is clear at present is that trend data on the growth or decline of homelessness, comparable in precision to data collected by the Census Bureau on poverty levels, are still not available. Other but more limited data are on hand supporting the relationship between poverty and homelessness. Data collected by the U.S. Census Bureau for the population in emergency and transitional shelters show a decline in that population from 178,638 in the 1990 census to a total of 170,706 in the 2000 census. In that period the economy was exhibiting strong growth. Table 2.2 shows these data together with regional breakdowns. In 2000, 30.7 percent of the sheltered population was found in the Northeast, a region with 19 percent of the total U.S. population. The West had 27.8 percent of the sheltered and 22.5 percent of the total population. The Midwest and the South had smaller shares of the sheltered than of the total population, suggesting that in the last two census years, homelessness was at higher levels on the two coasts than in the center of the country.

In 2000 New York state had 31,856 persons in emergency and transitional shelters according to the Census Bureau. Data extending from January 2002 to January 2003 for New York City alone, from the Coalition for the Homeless, show a month-by-month pattern during a period of worsening economic conditions. Homeless in shelters numbered 31,064 in January 2002 and had risen to 38,463 a year later. Numbers increased every month except between May and June 2002, when there was a small decline.

Needs Profiled by Mayors

In *A Status Report on Hunger and Homelessness in America's Cities, 2002: A 25-City Survey*, the United States Conference of Mayors presented 16 years of survey data profiling needs in urban areas. (See Table 2.3.)

In 2002 requests for emergency shelter increased in the cities surveyed by an average of 19 percent, with 88 percent of the cities reporting some increase and 12 percent reporting no increase or a decline. Demand for shelter by entire homeless families increased by slightly more than overall demand (20 percent), although this figure does not appear in the table. The annual survey has not always tracked homeless families separately from homeless individuals.

An average of 30 percent of the requests for emergency shelter by all homeless people went unmet in 2002, a decrease from 2001 but higher than in most years since 1987. Fifty-six percent reported the possibility of having to turn away single homeless people.

Officials in all cities surveyed expected that requests for emergency shelter would increase in 2003, including requests by homeless families. People remained homeless an average of six months in the survey cities. Eighty-two percent of the city mayors said that the length of time people stayed homeless increased during 2002. Officials further reported that the increase in funding from HUD had been successful in helping homeless families and individuals into transitional and permanent housing. The troubled economic situation and ever tightening state budgets caused a great deal of pessimism among mayors in 2002 regarding how they would deal with issues of homelessness in the future.

In the Conference of Mayors' survey, lack of affordable housing was the most often mentioned cause of homelessness in 21 of 25 cities. This lack of housing is of key importance in the study of homelessness. Insufficient housing options for low-income people are a root cause. In the surveyed cities, the average wait for public housing was 19 months. The city officials also estimate that low-income households spend an average of 51 percent of their income on housing. Disproportionate housing costs are another precipitating factor that bears scrutiny.

Philip Mangano, Executive Director of the Interagency Council on Homelessness, in a keynote address on May 20, 2003, at the Policy Academy in Chicago, blamed the lack of affordable housing on what he called "affluenza."

TABLE 2.3

Hunger and homelessness in large urban areas, 1987–2002

(Data are the cumulative and summary results of an annual 25 city survey. The cities surveyed change from year to year.)

Indicator	1987	1988	1989	1990	1991	1992	1993	1994	1995	1996	1997	1998	1999	2000	2001	2002
Hunger																
Increase in demand for emergency food	18%	19%	19%	22%	26%	18%	13%	12%	9%	11%	16%	14%	18%	17%	23%	19%
Cities in which demand for food increased	92%	88%	96%	90%	93%	96%	83%	83%	72%	83%	86%	78%	85%	83%	93%	100%
Increase in demand by families for food assistance	18%	17%	14%	20%	26%	14%	13%	14%	10%	10%	13%	14%	15%	16%	19%	17%
Portion of those requesting food assistance who are families with children	67%	62%	61%	75%	68%	68%	67%	64%	63%	62%	58%	61%	58%	62%	54%	48%
Demand for emergency food unmet	18%	15%	17%	14%	17%	21%	16%	15%	18%	18%	19%	21%	21%	13%	14%	16%
Cities in which food assistance facilities must turn people away	67%	62%	73%	86%	79%	68%	68%	73%	59%	50%	71%	47%	54%	46%	33%	32%
Cities which expect demand for emergency food to increase next year	84%	85%	89%	100%	100%	89%	100%	81%	96%	96%	92%	96%	84%	71%	100%	100%
Homelessness																
Increase in demand for emergency shelter	21%	13%	25%	24%	13%	14%	10%	13%	11%	5%	3%	11%	12%	15%	13%	19%
Cities in which demand increased	96%	93%	89%	80%	89%	88%	81%	80%	63%	71%	59%	72%	69%	76%	81%	88%
Demand for emergency shelter unmet	23%	19%	22%	19%	15%	23%	25%	21%	19%	20%	27%	26%	25%	23%	37%	30%
Cities in which shelters must turn people away	65%	67%	59%	70%	74%	75%	77%	72%	82%	81%	88%	67%	73%	56%	44%	56%
Cities which expect demand for shelter to increase next year	92%	89%	93%	97%	100%	93%	88%	71%	100%	100%	100%	93%	92%	72%	100%	100%
Composition of homeless population																
Single men	49%	49%	46%	51%	50%	55%	43%	48%	46%	45%	47%	45%	43%	44%	40%	41%
Families with children	33%	34%	36%	34%	35%	32%	34%	39%	36%	38%	36%	38%	36%	36%	40%	41%
Single women	14%	13%	14%	12%	12%	11%	11%	11%	14%	14%	14%	14%	13%	13%	14%	13%
Unaccompanied youth	4%	5%	4%	3%	3%	2%	4%	3%	4%	3%	4%	3%	7%	7%	4%	5%
Children	NA	25%	25%	23%	24%	22%	30%	26%	25%	27%	25%	25%	19%	22%	NA	NA
Severely mentally ill	23%	25%	25%	28%	29%	28%	27%	26%	23%	24%	27%	24%	31%	37%	22%	23%
Substance abusers	35%	34%	44%	38%	40%	41%	48%	43%	46%	43%	43%	38%	21%	26%	34%	32%
Employed	22%	23%	24%	24%	18%	17%	18%	19%	20%	18%	17%	22%	14%	15%	20%	22%
Veterans	NA	26%	26%	26%	23%	18%	21%	23%	23%	19%	22%	22%			11%	10%

SOURCE: "Hunger and Homelessness in America's Cities: A Sixteen-Year Comparison of Data," in *A Status Report on Hunger and Homelessness in America's Cities, 2002: A 25-City Survey*, The United States Conference of Mayors, Washington, DC, December 2002

Homeless in America: How Could It Happen Here?

FIGURE 2.2

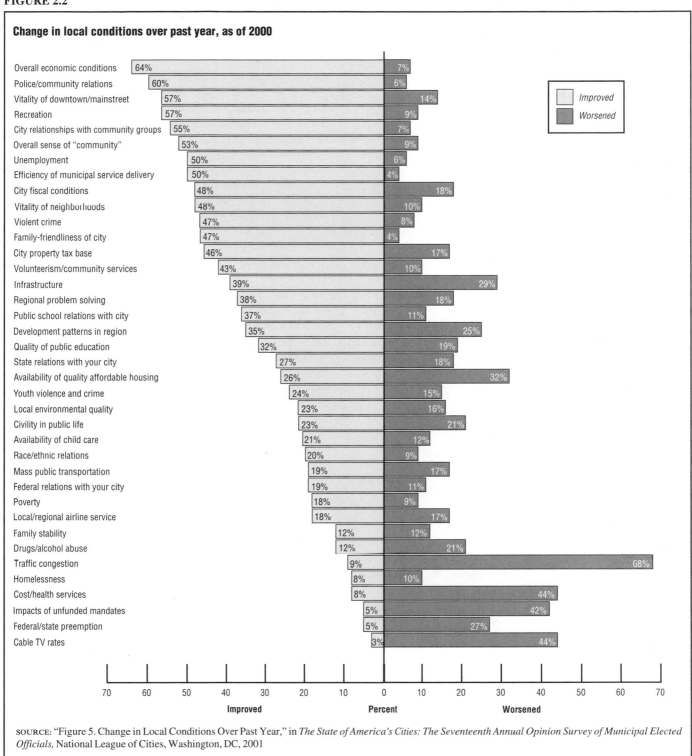

Change in local conditions over past year, as of 2000

Condition	Improved	Worsened
Overall economic conditions	64%	7%
Police/community relations	60%	6%
Vitality of downtown/mainstreet	57%	14%
Recreation	57%	9%
City relationships with community groups	55%	7%
Overall sense of "community"	53%	9%
Unemployment	50%	6%
Efficiency of municipal service delivery	50%	4%
City fiscal conditions	48%	18%
Vitality of neighborhoods	48%	10%
Violent crime	47%	8%
Family-friendliness of city	47%	4%
City property tax base	46%	17%
Volunteerism/community services	43%	10%
Infrastructure	39%	29%
Regional problem solving	38%	18%
Public school relations with city	37%	11%
Development patterns in region	35%	25%
Quality of public education	32%	19%
State relations with your city	27%	18%
Availability of quality affordable housing	26%	32%
Youth violence and crime	24%	15%
Local environmental quality	23%	16%
Civility in public life	23%	21%
Availability of child care	21%	12%
Race/ethnic relations	20%	9%
Mass public transportation	19%	17%
Federal relations with your city	19%	11%
Poverty	18%	9%
Local/regional airline service	18%	17%
Family stability	12%	12%
Drugs/alcohol abuse	12%	21%
Traffic congestion	9%	68%
Homelessness	8%	10%
Cost/health services	8%	44%
Impacts of unfunded mandates	5%	42%
Federal/state preemption	5%	27%
Cable TV rates	3%	44%

70 60 50 40 30 20 10 0 10 20 30 40 50 60 70

Improved   Percent   Worsened

SOURCE: "Figure 5. Change in Local Conditions Over Past Year," in *The State of America's Cities: The Seventeenth Annual Opinion Survey of Municipal Elected Officials,* National League of Cities, Washington, DC, 2001

He suggested that the affluenza of the mid-1980s and 1990s caused the destruction of old affordable housing and its replacement with "artificial housing and neighborhoods implanted like pacemakers."

The National League of Cities

In 2000 the National League of Cities surveyed a random sample of the nation's municipal elected officials regarding issues and problems they face in governing American cities (*The State of America's Cities: The Seventeenth Annual Opinion Survey of Municipal Elected Officials,* National League of Cities, Washington, D.C., 2001). When asked to indicate whether various conditions had improved or worsened in their cities in the previous year, 10 percent of the officials reported that homelessness had worsened in their cities, while 8 percent said homelessness had improved. (See Figure 2.2.) When city officials were

TABLE 2.4

Most deteriorated city conditions, 1996–2000[1]

Traffic congestion	49%
Availability of housing	19%
Infrastructure	16%
Cost and availability of health services	15%
Impacts of unfunded mandates	14%
Development patterns in the region	12%
Quality of education	11%
Unemployment	10%
City fiscal conditions	10%
Cable TV rates	9%
Drug/alcohol abuse	7%

[1] Percent of city officials listing item as one of the three most deteriorated city conditions during the past five years.

SOURCE: "Table 3. Most Deteriorated City Conditions," in *The State of America's Cities: The Seventeenth Annual Opinion Survey of Municipal Elected Officials*, National League of Cities, Washington, DC, January 2001

FIGURE 2.3

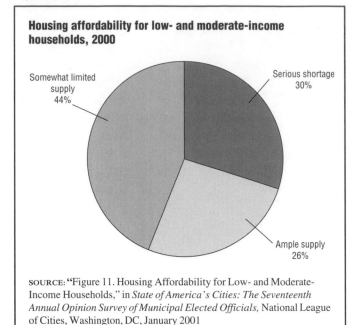

Housing affordability for low- and moderate-income households, 2000

SOURCE: "Figure 11. Housing Affordability for Low- and Moderate-Income Households," in *State of America's Cities: The Seventeenth Annual Opinion Survey of Municipal Elected Officials*, National League of Cities, Washington, DC, January 2001

asked to list the top three "most deteriorated" conditions in their cities, homelessness was not even in the top ten, as it had been in previous years, but "availability of housing" ranked second at 19 percent. (See Table 2.4.) The 2000 *State of America's Cities* survey asked respondents to characterize the situation in their cities with respect to housing affordability for low- and moderate-income households. The response: nearly three-quarters (74 percent) said there is either a "somewhat limited supply" (44 percent) or a "serious shortage" (30 percent) of affordable housing. (See Figure 2.3.) Only one in four (26 percent) responded that affordable housing was in "ample supply."

PROFILES OF THE HOMELESS
Gender and Race

Studies of the homeless and surveys of officials knowledgeable about homeless clients conducted in the 1990s and later show similar patterns of gender and racial data for the homeless, although the percentages vary from study to study.

Data for 2002, collected from 25 cities in the U.S. Conference of Mayors' study cited earlier, show that in most cities surveyed, males outnumber females among the homeless. (See Table 2.5.) Single males were most numerous in Chicago (66 percent of the homeless). Single women were most numerous in Portland, Oregon (20 percent). All the homeless clients in Providence, Rhode Island, were parts of families; the lowest percentage of those in families (among cities reporting on the category) was in Los Angeles (13 percent). Gender breakdowns of family members were not provided.

The racial composition of the homeless varied from city to city in the Mayors' survey. Whites were in the majority in Burlington, Vermont (89 percent), Salt Lake City (69 percent), Portland, Oregon (58 percent), Phoenix (49 percent), Seattle (44 percent), and Denver (37 percent).

Hispanics were the largest group in San Antonio (49 percent). In all other cities surveyed, African Americans were in the majority, the highest percentages encountered in St. Louis (94 percent) and Washington, D.C. (82 percent).

The Association of Gospel Rescue Missions (AGRM), formerly International Union of Gospel Missions (IUGM), has been surveying the homeless at more than 100 missions serving inner cities since 1989 and provides a 13-year view of the demographics of the homeless. (See Table 2.6.) The AGRM surveys are based on large numbers of homeless served. In 1997, for example, 15,000 homeless were surveyed; in AGRM's 2002 survey (not yet available in detail), more than 20,000 persons were queried.

AGRM data show that men were 81 percent of the homeless in 1989 but 77 percent in 2001. Homeless women have been rising as a proportion of the homeless population at a steady rate over more than a decade. In 1989 the racial/ethnic composition of the homeless was 51 percent white, 35 percent black, 11 percent Hispanic, 1 percent Asian, and 2 percent Native American. In 2001 whites were 41, blacks 39, Hispanics 11, Asians 1, and Native Americans 5 percent of the homeless population served by the Gospel Rescue Missions.

In the most recent comprehensive study of the homeless (Urban Institute, 1996), males were 68 and females 32 percent of the homeless. They were 41 percent white, 40 percent black, 11 percent Hispanic, 8 percent Native American, and 1 percent of other races (see Table 1.4 in Chapter 1).

The surveys thus exhibit similar patterns. More of the homeless are male than female, but these proportions have

TABLE 2.5

Composition of the homeless population in 25 major cities, 2002

(Percent)

City	Families	Single Men	Single Women	Youth	African-American	White	Hispanic	Asian	Native American	Mentally ill	Substance abusers	Employed	Veterans	Single parent families	Family members who are children
Boston	35	51	13	0	43	39	16	1	1	30	46	27	0	95	63
Burlington	26	49	16	9	7	89	1	1	2	56	46	30	17	50	55
Charleston	18	55	27	0	52	42	6	0	0	41	55	69	33	87	33
Charlotte	0	0	0	0	0	0	0	0	0	0	0	0	0	83	66
Chicago	16	66	19	5	78	11	10	--	1	16	50	16	0	95	66
Cleveland	25	54	19	2	78	19	2	--	--	25	40	20	10	98	70
Denver	66	24	9	1	26	37	31	1	5	56	56	35	18	43	40
Kansas City	66	33	0	1	0	0	0	0	0	20	28	0	17	81	49
Los Angeles	13	74	13	0	48	21	26	3	2	21	0	5	9	88	71
Louisville	16	61	18	5	49	45	2	1	1	5	8	16	7	0	9
Miami	0	0	0	0	51	20	28	1	0	26	52	25	3	90	52
Nashville	24	56	15	5	60	35	5	0	0	40	75	23	15	65	0
New Orleans	41	38	16	5	70	25	2	1	2	32	20	29	17	87	64
Norfolk	52	30	18	0	59	40	1	0	0	35	42	45	9	75	60
Philadelphia	59	30	11	0	80	13	6	1	0	0	0	0	0	90	72
Phoenix	38	57	0	5	17	49	23	0	13	0	0	0	0	0	0
Portland, OR	40	37	20	4	17	58	16	6	3	26	58	12	11	75	54
Providence	100	0	0	0	38	34	21	0	1	19	28	61	1	81	73
Salt Lake City	22	59	19	0	14	69	13	1	3	25	35	35	22	41	56
San Antonio	52	32	11	5	24	26	49	--	--	29	32	22	4	69	65
Seattle	32	49	18	1	39	44	9	3	5	26	23	0	0	76	17
St. Louis	82	10	7	0	94	6	--	--	--	1	6	7	3	94	68
St. Paul	32	57	11	0	53	32	10	0	4	0	0	28	16	98	64
Trenton	75	12	12	0	80	15	5	0	0	10	62	10	4	75	70
Washington, DC	43	45	11	1	82	5	12	1	0	24	25	31	19	85	65

-- represents a percent that is less than 1 but greater than 0.

SOURCE: "Composition of the Homeless Population," in *A Status Report on Hunger and Homelessness in America's Cities, 2002: A 25-City Survey*, The United States Conference of Mayors, Washington, DC, December 2002

The Demographics of Homelessness

TABLE 2.6

Demographic profile of homeless served by Union of Gospel Missions, 1989–2001

(Percent)

	1989	1990	1991	1992	1993	1994	1995	1996	1997	1998	1999	2000	2001
Males	81	82	81	82	80	82	81	79	79	78	77	76	77
Females	19	18	19	18	20	18	11	21	21	22	23	24	23
Age													
Under 18	8	9	12	9	9	8	12	11	12	12	11	11	12
18-25	17	16	14	13	11	12	28	13	11	10	10	11	10
26-35	25	28	29	29	28	29	28	26	21	23	21	20	20
36-45	23	24	24	25	27	29	17	28	30	30	29	29	29
46-65	21	19	17	19	17	18	17	18	22	21	24	25	26
Over 65	6	4	4	5	4	4	4	4	4	5	5	4	3
Race													
Caucasian	51	53	46	46	41	42	37	45	46	40	42	42	44
African-American	35	35	37	37	44	40	45	38	36	42	39	41	39
Hispanic	11	7	13	12	11	12	13	11	12	12	14	13	11
Asian	1	1	1	2	1	2	2	1	1	2	1	1	1
Native American	2	4	3	3	3	4	3	5	5	5	4	3	5
Families served													
Couples	31	17	18	20	23	20	15	12	11	12	12	12	13
Women with children	46	63	60	49	50	60	62	63	63	66	67	66	62
Men with children	3	4	5	12	5	5	6	5	5	7	5	8	8
Intact families	9	16	17	19	22	15	17	20	21	16	16	14	17
Other issues													
Veterans - male	31	33	33	29	33	28	33	34	32	32	30	29	26
Homeless less than one year	50	43	60	47	38	56	54	58	60	61	69	65	64
More than 6 month resident of city		60	68	67	70	67	71	68	67	72	76	71	69
Unemployed over 6 months			54	61	56	51	51	50	55	52	54	58	51
In drug/alcohol rehab - males			31	28	27	30	31	32	31	32	30	82	78
In drug/alcohol rehab - females						28	23	30	26	25	19	27	24
Prefer spiritual emphasis in programs								66	76	79	81	82	78
Lost government benefits in last 12 months									20	22	17	17	16

Note: Since 1989, the International Union of Gospel Missions has surveyed more than 100 rescue missions that make up part of its U.S. membership on the third Friday of October.

SOURCE: Adapted from "Table of Snapshot Survey Results: 1989–1998," in *The Changing Face of America's Homeless: IUGM Issues Tenth Annual Survey*, International Union of Gospel Missions Press Release, Kansas City, MO, November 23, 1998, updated from subsequent releases issued by IUGM on its Web site [Online] http://www.agrm.org/stats.html [accessed September 8, 2003]

been gradually changing, with more women among the homeless as time has advanced. Blacks appear to have a higher rate of homelessness in proportion to their presence in the U.S. population as a whole (12.9 percent in 2000) than whites (77.1 percent). Hispanic representation is near the Hispanics' share of total population (12.5 percent). Native Americans are among the homeless in greater proportion to their share of total population (1.5 percent); Asian homeless are at a lower proportion to their population (4.2 percent).

Family Structure

In 1996 (Urban Institute), 62 percent of homeless men and 16 percent of homeless women were single. In 2002 (Conference of Mayors), the homeless were 41 percent in families, 41 percent were single men, 13 percent were single women, and 5 percent were unaccompanied youths. The same data from the Conference of Mayors in 1987 showed homeless composition being 33 percent in families, 49 percent single males, 14 percent single females, and 4 percent unaccompanied youths. (See Table 2.3.) Homeless families have, according to the Conference data increased, while single males and single females have decreased.

The AGRM survey data do not present details to make a similar comparison, but AGRM's survey broke out the structure of homeless families as follows for 2001: 62 percent consisted of single women with children while only 8 percent consisted of single men with children. Thirteen percent were couples and 17 percent were intact families with children (see Table 2.6).

Data from the Conference of Mayors (see Table 2.5, last column) show city-by-city estimates of children as a percent of homeless family members. Values range from 9 percent of homeless family members in Louisville, Kentucky, to a high of 73 percent in Providence, Rhode Island.

Age

The Urban Institute, in its comprehensive 1996 study, found that 38 percent of the homeless were between 35 and 44 years of age, 25 percent were 25–34, and 17 percent were 45–54. The AGRM survey for 2001 (see Table 2.6) showed those 36–45 to make up 29 percent, those 26–35 to make up 20 percent, and those 46–55 to make up 26 percent of the homeless. These core populations together were 80 percent of the Urban Institute sample in 1996 and 75 percent of the AGRM survey in 2001. The largest group in both was the 35–45 group, adults in their middle years. AGRM data show an increase of those under 18 from 8 percent to 12 percent of the homeless population between 1989 and 2001.

Education

When the Urban Institute investigated the education of homeless people, it found that 38 percent had less than a high school diploma, 34 percent had completed high school, and 28 percent had some education beyond high school. The homeless were less educated than the population as a whole. In 1996 those with less than a high school education made up 18 percent of the general population, those with high school were (like the homeless) 34 percent, and those with more than a high school education were 48 percent of the population.

Military Background

The Urban Institute study also reported that 23 percent of the homeless were veterans, compared with 13 percent of the total population. Veterans were over-represented among the homeless in 1996 based on Urban Institute data and also earlier among males in the 1990 census of those in emergency and transitional shelters. According to the Veterans Health Administration (VHA), in 1990 veterans were present in shelters at a rate of 149 per 100,000 compared with 126 per 100,000 of other males (*Data on the Socioeconomic Status of Veterans and on VA Program Usage*, Washington, D.C., May 2001).

The National Coalition for Homeless Veterans, citing Department of Veterans Affairs (VA) sources, stated on its Web site in 2003 that 2 percent of homeless veterans are female. Forty-five percent have mental illness and half have or have had problems with drugs. An estimated 275,000 are homeless on any single night; over the course of a year, as many as 500,000 are homeless at least one night. The majority are single. More than two-thirds of homeless veterans served during the Vietnam era.

CHILDREN AND YOUTHS

Homeless children and youths have always received special attention from the public and from welfare agencies. In the terminology of the 19th century, children are perfect representatives of the "worthy" poor in that, if they are homeless, they did nothing to deserve that status. Teenagers who run away from home are included in the category of unaccompanied youth.

Estimates provided by the U.S. Conference of Mayors (see Table 2.3) provide some indication of the prevalence of homelessness for these two categories of persons. In 2002, 41 percent of the homeless population in 25 surveyed cities were in family groups. The Mayors' survey did not provide an estimate of the percentage of the homeless who were children in 2002, but the same survey for 1998 put the proportion of children at 25 percent. In the 1988 through 1998 period, according to the Conference of Mayors, children were never less than 22 percent and were as high as 30 percent in 1993; the average for the 1988–1998 period was 25.2 percent.

The same source shows estimates for "unaccompanied youths," 5 percent of the homeless in 2002. In the 1988–2002 period, the lowest level was 2 percent in 1992 and the highest 7 percent in 1999 and 2000. The average for the period was 4.1 percent. Using the average for children and for unaccompanied youths suggests that children and youth together represent 29 percent of the homeless.

As already mentioned above, the U.S. Department of Education collects estimates of homeless children from selected school district records. The data exclude infants but include some children of preschool age. USDE's tallies show a total of 930,232 children and youths, for 866,899 of whom reported residence status in 2000. (See Table 2.7.) The number of children who lived in shelters (temporary or otherwise), were unsheltered, or had unknown residency was 364,391. All data are for the entire year. These data come close to 1996 estimates on the total population that was homeless during some part of the year. If children represent 29 percent of the homeless based on U.S. Conference of Mayors estimates, the range of total homeless of all ages was somewhere between 1.2 and 3.2 million people in 2000 depending on whether 364,391 or 930,200 children are counted as homeless.

Table 2.7 also shows that of total children estimated by school districts to be homeless, only a portion were enrolled and a smaller number attended school regularly. Among those in elementary school, of 343,340 estimated, 305,920 (89.1 percent) were enrolled and 271,906 (79.2 percent) attended regularly. Those who do attend have less than optimal conditions for educational achievement.

An example of poor results obtained by homeless youths is shown in a 2002 study of unaccompanied homeless youths conducted in Monterey County, California (*Homeless Census and Homeless Youth/Foster Teen Study*, Monterey County, CA, 2002). (See Figure 2.4.) Youth below grade level increased from 21 percent of those aged 16 to 70 percent of those aged 21. The study showed that many of these youth aged 14 to 21 had been in the foster

TABLE 2.7

Homeless children and youths, 2000

	Enrollment and attendance			Shelter status reported		
	Estimated number	Enrolled	Attending		Total	% of total
Not specified	9,999			Sheltered	306,404	35.3
Pre-K	257,076	40,265		Doubled-up	301,195	34.7
Elementary	343,340	305,920	271,906	Unsheltered	38,732	4.5
Junior high	155,964	135,785	119,596	Other[1]	201,313	23.2
High school	163,867	138,794	128,340	Unknown	19,255	2.2
Total	930,232	620,764	519,842	Total	866,899	100.0

[1] Includes other temporary shelter such as motels.

SOURCE: Adapted from "Table 1: Homeless Children and Youth By Grade Level–Estimated Totals, and Numbers Enrolled and Regularly Attending School" and "Table 2: Primary Nighttime Residence of Homeless Children and Youth," in *Education for Homeless Children and Youth Program, Report to Congress, Fiscal Year 2000,* U.S. Department of Education, Office of Elementary and Secondary Education, Washington, DC, 2001

FIGURE 2.4

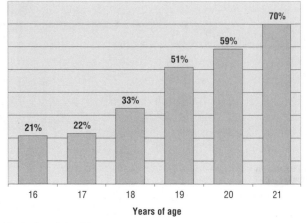

Homeless youth in Monterey County, California who are below grade level, by age, 2002
(Percent)

Standard grade level by age:
8th graders are usually 13–15 years old
9th graders, 14–16 years old
10th graders, 15–17 years old
11th graders, 16–18 years old
12th graders, 17–19 years old

SOURCE: Adapted from "Figure 22 - Percent of homeless youth who are below grade level, by age," in *Homeless Census and Homeless Youth/Foster Teen Study, Monterey County 2002,* Applied Survey Research and Monterey County, Department of Social Services, Monterey, CA, 2002

care system and had become homeless after emancipation. Sixty-four percent of the youths were male and only 13 percent had a high school diploma or GED. The remaining 87 percent were, on average, below their grade level in education.

Although this study was only a countywide survey, it confirmed that those formerly in foster care are represented in higher numbers among the homeless than in the population at large. Ten percent of the unaccompanied homeless youths in the Monterey County study were at one time in the foster care system, while only 3 percent of the general population aged 14 to 21 were ever in foster care.

The Monterey County study also provided information about how the homeless youths surveyed obtained money. Table 2.8 provides a summary of these data, including the fact that 2.9 percent of these homeless youths received unemployment insurance and nearly a third (30.9 percent) received food stamps.

DURATION AND RECURRENCE

For most of the homeless, homelessness is a recurring experience and lasts for months at a time, suggesting that programs that help the homeless do not uniformly help clients solve the fundamental problems that can lead to life on the streets.

The Urban Institute's 1996 study showed that 51 percent of all homeless persons surveyed in that year had been homeless before. AGRM data for 2000 indicate that 67 percent of the homeless surveyed by the organization had been homeless before; the 2001 result was 63 percent. In 2001, 24 percent of AGRM clients had been homeless

once before, 18 percent twice before, and 21 percent three or more times before the current spell.

Thirty-nine percent of homeless studied by the Urban Institute in 1996 had been homeless less than six months. Sixty-four percent of AGRM clients in 2001 had been homeless less than one year.

The state of Louisiana conducted a point-in-time survey of the homeless on November 16 and 17, 1999, to which 2,408 individuals responded. These people were accompanied by 1,012 others; the survey thus represented 3,420 persons. Study results showed that a third of the homeless in the state had been without housing for 3 or fewer months (32.5 percent), and that 10.1 percent had been homeless for between 13 and 24 months. (See Figure 2.5.) The majority of those experiencing homelessness for the first time were aged 30–39; those under 20 made up 13.7 percent of the respondents, while those older than 70 represented 0.4 percent. (See Figure 2.6.)

THE RURAL HOMELESS

Most studies on the homeless have been focused on urban areas, leaving the impression that this problem exists only on city sidewalks. Homelessness is more common in the cities, where the bulk of the population resides, but many areas of rural America also experience the phenomenon. Rural communities have

TABLE 2.8

Means by which homeless youth in Monterey County, California acquire money or money equivalents, 2002

(Percent responding in the affirmative to the listed item)

Are you receiving money from any of the following government sources?

Food stamps	30.9 %
County welfare	25.0
Women, infants and children (WIC)	16.2
General Assistance	13.2
Social Security (SSI/SSA)	10.3
Hotel vouchers	4.4
Disability insurance	2.9
Planned parenthood	2.9
Unemployment insurance	2.9
Temporary assistance for needy families (TANF)	0.0
Other	20.6

Other than income from a job or from government sources, from where does your money for daily living come?

Allowance	0.0 %
Odd jobs	38.1
Family and friends	34.6
Panhandling/begging	23.8
Shoplifting/petty theft	16.5
Drugs	16.2
Receiving no money	15.0
Picking up/recycling cans	11.2
Sex	6.9
Other	4.2

SOURCE: Adapted from "Figure 27 - Are you receiving money from any of the following government sources?," and "Figure 28 - Other than income from a job, where does your money for daily living come from?," in *Homeless Census and Homeless Youth/Foster Teen Study, Monterey County 2002*, Applied Survey Research and Monterey County, Department of Social Services, Monterey, CA, 2002

FIGURE 2.5

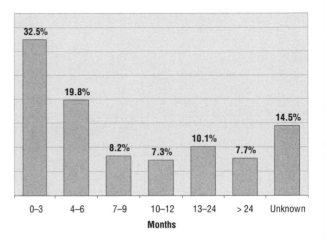

Duration of current homeless period for homeless population in Louisiana, November 16 and 17, 1999

(Percent)

SOURCE: Adapted from "How many months homeless?," in *Louisiana Homeless Demographics and Needs Survey*, Louisiana Department of Social Services, New Orleans, LA [Online] http://www.dss.state.la.us/offocs/assets/applets/Point_in_Time_survey_results.pdf [accessed August 2003]

FIGURE 2.6

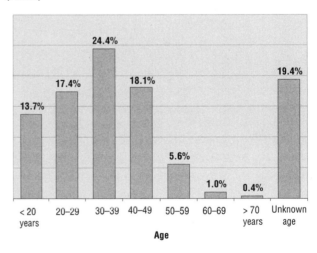

Age first homeless of homeless population in Louisiana, November 16 and 17, 1999

(Percent)

SOURCE: Adapted from "Age First Homeless," in *Louisiana Homeless Demographics and Needs Survey*, Louisiana Department of Social Services, New Orleans, LA [Online] http://www.dss.state.la.us/offocs assets/applets/Point_in_Time_survey_results.pdf [accessed August 2003]

fewer official shelters and fewer public places (heating grates, subways, train stations) where the homeless find temporary shelter. Finding the rural homeless is therefore more difficult for investigators of the problem.

In 1996 the U.S. Department of Agriculture (USDA), in *Rural Homelessness: Focusing on the Needs of the Rural Homeless* (Rural Economic and Community Development, USDA, Washington, D.C., 1996), reported that homeless people in rural areas were more likely to be white, female, married, and currently working than the urban homeless. They were also more likely to be homeless for the first time and generally had experienced homelessness for a shorter period of time than the urban homeless. Findings also included higher rates of domestic violence and lower rates of alcohol and substance abuse.

The National Coalition for the Homeless argues, in *Rural Homelessness* (Fact Sheet #13, March 1999), that the rural homeless are less likely to be found on the street or in the few shelters available in rural areas. When counting the rural homeless, consideration has to be given to those who live in substandard housing, in overcrowded conditions with relatives, and in campers or in cars.

The poverty rate is higher outside metropolitan areas. In 2001, 14.2 percent of the population in rural areas was in poverty compared with 11.1 percent in metropolitan areas (*Current Population Survey*, U.S. Bureau of the Census, Washington, D.C., March 2001 Supplement). The rate for whites was 12.1 percent outside and 9.3 percent inside metro areas; the black rate was 31.4 percent in rural and 21.4 percent in urban areas. The rural homeless population tends to be working, female, married, and white; individuals tend to be homeless for less time than the homeless population generally. Families make up a large percentage of this group.

The 1996 Urban Institute study determined that 21 percent of all homeless people in their study lived in suburban areas, and 9 percent lived in rural communities. This study agrees with the USDA's study on many points. The rural homeless surveyed were more likely to be working, or to have worked recently, than the urban homeless—65 percent of the rural homeless had worked for pay in the last month. Homeless people living in rural areas were also more likely to be experiencing their first spell of homelessness (60 percent). In 55 percent of the cases, the homeless spell lasted three months or less.

The rural homeless are often hidden and thus do not receive the same amount of attention given their urban counterparts. Although housing costs are generally lower in rural areas than in cities, rural incomes are also lower.

The rural homeless may live in shacks rather than shelters or may be taken in by family members. They can be found in cars, abandoned buildings, and even in the woods, when nothing else is available. The rural homeless are also less likely to get social services and benefits than they would in the cities because rural areas generally lack the social support services found in more urban areas.

Several types of rural areas generate higher than average levels of homelessness, including regions that:

- Are primarily agricultural—residents often lose their livelihood because of reduced demand for farm labor or because of a shrinking service sector.

- Depend on declining extractive industries, such as mining or timber.

- Are experiencing economic growth—new or expanding industrial plants often attract more job seekers than can be absorbed.

- Have persistent poverty, such as Appalachia, where the young and able-bodied may have to relocate before they can find work.

CHAPTER 3
EMPLOYMENT AND POVERTY AMONG THE HOMELESS

POVERTY AND HOMELESSNESS

There is an undeniable connection between homelessness and poverty. Those in poverty live from day to day with little or no safety net for times when unforeseen expenses arise. If a family's resources are very small the most elementary needs of food, shelter, and healthcare are often juggled leaving one or more bills unpaid. Decisions about where to spend scant resources are difficult decisions. Should one spend the limited resources on food, a visit to the doctor, buying necessary medicines, or paying the rent? In 2002, a full-time job paying minimum wage provided an income of $10,300 annually, a sum that was below the poverty threshold for a two-person family. Being poor often means being an illness, an accident, or a paycheck away from homelessness.

Housing costs at 2000 fair-market rent for such a family may be out of reach, costing from 50 percent–75 percent of the family income. According to an article titled "Are Shelters the Answer to Family Homelessness?" in *USA Today Magazine* (Ralph da Costa Nunez and Laura M. Caruso, January 1, 2003), low-income and high rent payments often result in sub-standard housing accommodation, doubled-up living, or living on the street or in a public shelter. The necessity of basic sustenance and medical care usually leaves little funding to meet shelter needs. Those in poverty have further difficulties finding housing if they have previously defaulted on their rent payments or perhaps their house payments, with the end result of homelessness. In order to understand homelessness, a study of poverty is useful.

MEASURING POVERTY

Defining poverty and counting the poor is a difficult task. The official poverty measure used in the United States was developed during the 1960s by Mollie Orshansky of the Social Security Administration. Called the poverty index, this measure was based upon the Department of Agriculture's 1955 Household Food Consumption Survey, which had determined that a family of three spent approximately one-third of its income on food. The poverty threshold for a family of three was therefore set at three times the cost of the economy food plan, an amount seen as necessary to cover minimal living expenses. A family whose annual before-tax income was below this poverty threshold was "poor." The government has since revised the poverty threshold regularly to account for inflation and changes in the economy.

The Official Poverty Threshold

In 2002 the U.S. Department of Commerce set the estimated poverty threshold for a family of four at $18,244 (2 adults and 2 related children under 18 years of age). (See Table 3.1.) The annual incomes listed in Table 3.1 establish the poverty threshold for families by size. These amounts include income before taxes but do not include any capital gains or non-cash benefits such as public housing, Medicaid, or food stamps. For example, in 2002 a family of five consisting of a father, mother, two related children under age 18 and an aunt to those children could jointly earn up to $22,007 and still be considered "poor" by the official poverty measure. If, however, all the adults in the family were employed and their annual incomes were as follows: father, $12,000; mother, $8,000; and aunt, $4,000, then the family would have a joint income of $24,000 which is higher than the 2002 poverty threshold figure for a family of five. In 2002 the poverty thresholds ranged from $8,628 for an elderly person living alone to $40,036 for a family of nine or more members with at least one child. (See Table 3.1.)

Concerns about the Accuracy of the Poverty Rate

Social scientists have for years debated about the best and most accurate means of establishing a poverty

TABLE 3.1

Poverty threshold by size of family and number of related children under 18 years of age, 2002

(Dollars)

Size of family	Related children under 18 years of age								
	None	One	Two	Three	Four	Five	Six	Seven	Eight plus
One person (unrelated individual)									
Under 65	9,359								
65 years and over	8,628								
Two Persons									
Householder under 65 years	12,047	12,400							
Householder 65 years and over	10,874	12,353							
Three persons	14,072	14,480	14,494						
Four persons	18,556	18,859	18,244	18,307					
Five persons	22,377	22,703	22,007	21,469	21,141				
Six persons	25,738	25,840	25,307	24,797	24,038	23,588			
Seven persons	29,615	29,799	29,162	28,718	27,890	26,924	25,865		
Eight persons	33,121	22,414	32,812	32,285	31,538	30,589	29,601	29,350	
Nine persons or more	39,843	40,036	39,504	39,057	38,323	37,313	36,399	36,173	34,780

SOURCE: "Poverty Threshold for 2002 by Size of Family and Number of Related Children Under 18 Years," U.S. Census Bureau, Washington, DC, February 2003, [Online] http://www.census.gov/hhes/poverty/threshld/thresh02.html [accessed August 25, 2003]

threshold. The central question that arises in debates about measuring poverty is whether to use an absolute or a relative means of updating the poverty rate on an annual or periodic basis. Once established, an absolute poverty measure is updated to account for price changes (inflation) only. A relative poverty measure is one that is updated based on changes in the median or mean income or compensation of the general population. The relative poverty measure adjusts for changing standards of living. The official poverty measure used by the United States is updated using the absolute means of updating.

In 2001 the "Conveners of the Working Group on Revising the Poverty Measure"—a group of economists, lawyers, professors, and social academics—wrote *An Open Letter on Revising the Official Measure of Poverty* to the Director of the Office of Management and Budget. They wrote to express their concerns over the inadequacy of the official poverty level measurement and to propose a set of guidelines for a revised standard. The letter stated that the current system is one that was established in the 1960s and that it has not been meaningfully adjusted since despite decades of major changes in the social safety net for low-income families.

Three of the items that were specifically listed in the letter as being examples of areas not well accounted for in determining the official poverty rate were:

- Non-cash benefits (food stamps, housing assistance, free school lunch programs) that are not included in the calculation of income

- Out-of-pocket medical expenditures not included in the calculation of costs

- Out-of-pocket child care costs that are not included in the calculation of family costs

The letter criticizes many aspects of the methodology used to determine the official poverty threshold, as did a report published by the National Academy of Sciences in 1995. The debate about how best and most accurately to determine who is and who is not poor has gone on for decades and will likely continue. It is, therefore, worthwhile when reviewing statistics about poverty to keep in mind that they may be skewed by the methods used in calculating them.

WHO ARE THE POOR?

Based on the Official Poverty Rate

An official count of the poor includes all those whose family incomes fall below the poverty threshold figure for that particular size family, as seen in Table 3.1. In 2001, based on those criteria, there were 32.9 million poor in the United States, equivalent to 11.7 percent of the population. (See Table 3.2.) The young, under 18 years old, were poor at a higher rate (16.3 percent) than were adults aged 18 or older, (10.1 percent).

Poor families in 2001 numbered 6.8 million or 9.2 percent of families. (See Table 3.2.) Most of these were white families (4.6 million) although non-Hispanic white families had the lowest rate of poverty (5.7 percent). Poor African American families numbered 1.8 million in 2001 equal to 20.7 percent of all black families. Hispanic families were poor at a rate almost as high as African American families, 19.4 percent.

TABLE 3.2

People and families in poverty by selected characteristics, 2000 and 2001

(Numbers in thousands)

Characteristics	2001 Number	2001 Percent	2000 Number	2000 Percent
Total	**32,907**	**11.7**	**31,581**	**11.3**
Age				
Under 18 years	11,733	16.3	11,587	16.2
18 to 64 years	17,760	10.1	16,671	9.6
65 years and over	3,414	10.1	3,323	9.9
Families				
Total	6,813	9.2	6,400	8.7
White	4,579	7.4	4,333	7.1
Non-Hispanic white	3,051	5.7	2,896	5.4
Black	1,829	20.7	1,686	19.3
Asian, Pacific Islander	234	7.8	233	7.8
Hispanic [1]	1,649	19.4	1,540	19.2
Type of Family				
Married-couple	2,760	4.9	2,637	4.7
White	2,242	4.5	2,181	4.4
Non-Hispanic white	1,477	3.3	1,435	3.2
Black	328	7.8	266	6.3
Asian, Pacific Islander	156	6.6	142	5.9
Hispanic [1]	799	13.8	772	14.2
Female householder, no husband present	3,470	26.4	3,278	25.4
White	1,939	22.4	1,820	21.2
Non-Hispanic white	1,305	19.0	1,226	17.8
Black	1,351	35.2	1,300	34.3
Asian, Pacific Islander	61	14.6	81	22.2
Hispanic [1]	711	37.0	664	36.4
Male householder, no wife present	583	13.1	485	11.3
White	398	11.7	332	10.1
Non-Hispanic white	270	10.3	236	9.2
Black	150	19.4	120	16.3
Asian, Pacific Islander	17	9.1	10	5.4
Hispanic [1]	139	17.0	104	13.6

[1] Hispanics may be of any race.

SOURCE: Adapted from Bernadette D. Proctor and Joseph Dalaker, "Table 1. People and Families in Poverty by Selected Characteristics: 2000 and 2001," in *Poverty in the United States: 2001*, P60-219, U.S. Census Bureau, Washington, DC, September 2002

The highest rates of poverty are seen when one looks at poverty rates by family type. Married couple families had the lowest rates of poverty averaging 4.9 percent in 2001. Male headed single parent families had a rate of poverty of 13.1 percent, less than half that experienced by females whose single parent families had a poverty rate of 26.4 percent. More than a quarter of all female headed single parent families lived below the poverty threshold in 2001. The highest poverty rate listed on Table 3.2 is that experienced by Hispanic females heading up single parent families. Of these families, more than a third (37.0 percent) were poor.

Based on Alternate Poverty Measures

The size of the poverty-stricken segment of the U.S. population varies depending on which method of determining the poverty threshold is used to identify the poor population, the official method or the experimental methods being studied by the U.S. Census Bureau as it grapples with how best to measure poverty. Figure 3.1 presents a comparison of the ways in which the methods used to identify the poverty threshold influence the numbers of people and families categorized as poor.

The experimental methods used by the Census Bureau vary from the official methods in two primary ways. First, they either include medical out-of-pocket expenses in the calculation of the poverty threshold or they deduct these expenses from the calculation of family income, or both. Second, they make adjustments for different housing costs based on geography, by region and/or metropolitan versus rural residences.

Figure 3.1 presents poverty rate data by age group as calculated by the official and the experimental methods used by the Census Bureau. The rate of poverty for children under 18 was higher in 2001 when the official poverty rate results are viewed. When the experimental methods of determining poverty were used they showed a slightly lower rate of poverty for children. Nonetheless, all methods for determining poverty showed a higher rate of poverty for children than for adults aged 18 to 64 years.

Poverty rates for the elderly population showed the most variation when comparing the results of the experimental methods and the official method. (Figure 3.1.) The experimental methods used to study poverty rates make adjustments for medical out-of-pocket expenditures and because the elderly have high out-of-pocket medical expenses, methodologies that adjusted income by reducing medical expenditures resulted in much higher numbers of elderly falling into the ranks of the poor.

Poverty rates varied the most for Hispanics when the experimental poverty methods were applied to the population by race and ethnic group. (See Figure 3.2.) Hispanics and African Americans are more likely to be poor than non-Hispanic whites regardless of the method used to determine the poverty rate.

Trends in the Poverty Rate

For the most part, the poverty rate is linked to the performance of the U.S. economy. When the economy is in recession, the poverty rate increases. Actually, the poverty rate often begins to increase somewhat before a serious economic downturn, and may not begin to decline until some time after a recession ends.

Figure 3.3 demonstrates that during the recession of 1980–82, when many Americans lost their jobs and the economy performed poorly, the poverty rate increased dramatically. In 1979, the year before the recession began, the poverty rate was 11.7 percent; by 1983 it stood at 15.2 percent. After the recession of the early 1980s ended, the poverty rate gradually declined. By 1989 it was down to 12.8 percent, its lowest level since 1979. The United States then endured another recession in 1990–91, and by its end

FIGURE 3.1

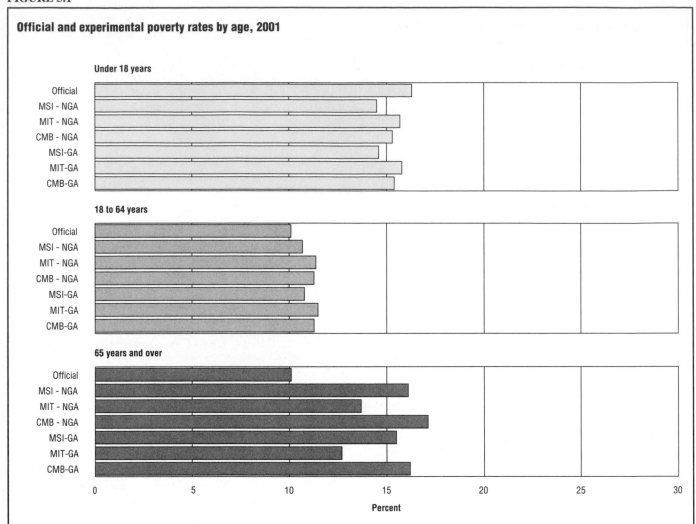

Official and experimental poverty rates by age, 2001

Note: While the experimental measures differ among one another in their computation of medical expenses and geographic variations in costs, they are similar in their scaling of thresholds by family size and their treatment of noncash benefits and child care and work related expenses.

MSI = Medical out-of-pocket expenses (MOOP) subtracted from income.

MIT = MOOP included in the thresholds.

CMB = "Combined" methods.

NGA = No geographic adjustment for housing costs.

GA = Geographic adjustment for housing costs.

SOURCE: Bernadette D. Proctor and Joseph Dalaker, "Figure 7. Experimental Poverty Rates by Age: 2001," in *Poverty in the United States: 2001*, P60-219, U.S. Census Bureau, Washington, DC, September 2002

the poverty level was up to 14.2 percent. With the latest recession that began in March 2001, one can see that both the poverty rate and the number of individuals living in poverty grew between 2000 and 2001. If the pattern normally seen during a recessionary period holds true we can expect these rates to continue to rise until some time after the end of this recessionary period.

Poverty Rates by Category

FAMILIES. The Census Bureau's 2001 report on poverty data included poverty rates by family structure. The recession that started in March 2001 is reflected by rising numbers of people living in poverty across all categories of family structure. The rate of poverty for all families in 2000 was 8.7 percent; by the end of 2001 it had risen to 9.2 percent. (See Table 3.2.) The rate for married couple families in 2000 was 4.7 percent and in 2001 it was 4.9 percent. Single female-headed households had a rate of poverty in 2000 of 25.4 percent; in 2001 that rate rose to 26.4 percent. Single male-headed households saw the largest one-year rise in poverty between 2000 and 2001, from 11.3 percent to 13.1 percent. Single male-headed families, although the smallest group, also saw the greatest increase in overall numbers. In 2000 there were 485,000 single male-headed households in the United States. In 2001 that number had risen to 583,000, an increase of 20.2 percent.

CHILDREN. Taken as a group, the poorest members of U.S. society are children, numbering over 11.7 million in

FIGURE 3.2

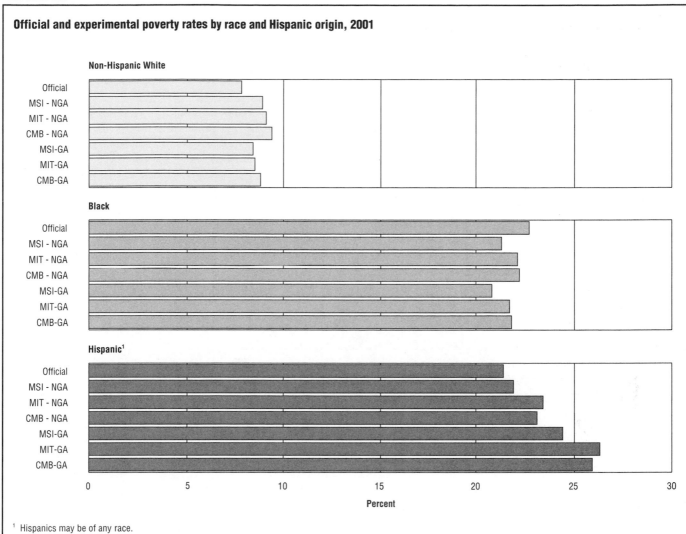

Official and experimental poverty rates by race and Hispanic origin, 2001

[1] Hispanics may be of any race.

Note: While the experimental measures differ among one another in their computation of medical expenses and geographic variations in costs, they are similar in their scaling of thresholds by family size and their treatment of noncash benefits and child care and work related expenses.

MSI – Medical out-of-pocket expenses (MOOP) subtracted from income.

MIT = MOOP included in the thresholds.

CMB = "Combined" methods.

NGA = No geographic adjustment for housing costs.

GA = Geographic adjustment for housing costs.

SOURCE: Bernadette D. Proctor and Joseph Dalaker, "Figure 8. Experimental Poverty Rates by Race and Hispanic Origin: 2001," in *Poverty in the United States: 2001,* P60-219, U.S. Census Bureau, Washington, DC, September 2002

2001. The Census Bureau reported that children had a 6.2 percent higher rate of poverty than those in the population aged 18 or older. According to the Census Bureau's 2001 report nearly half (48.9 percent) of children under 6 years of age and living in a female headed single parent family lived in poverty. These young children were at particularly high risk of poverty compared to their peers who lived in two-parent family households. The poverty rate for children under the age of 6 living in married couple households in 2001 was 9.2 percent. Overall, children under the age of 18 who lived in single-parent households were almost five times more likely (4.8 times) to live in poverty than were children living in a married-couple household, 23.7 percent compared with 4.9 percent.

Over the past few decades the child poverty rate has fallen, from a high of 27.3 percent in 1959 to 16.3 percent in 2001 (see Figure 3.4). The decline in poverty for children was not steady but mirrored, at a higher rate, the fluctuations seen in the poverty rate of adults aged 18 to 64. The age group that has seen the most improvement in poverty rates has been the elderly who started out the period 1959–2001 with the highest rate (35.2 percent) and ended it with a rate equal to that of adults 18 to 64 (10.1 percent).

FIGURE 3.3

Number of poor and poverty rate, 1959–2001
(Numbers in millions, rates in percent)

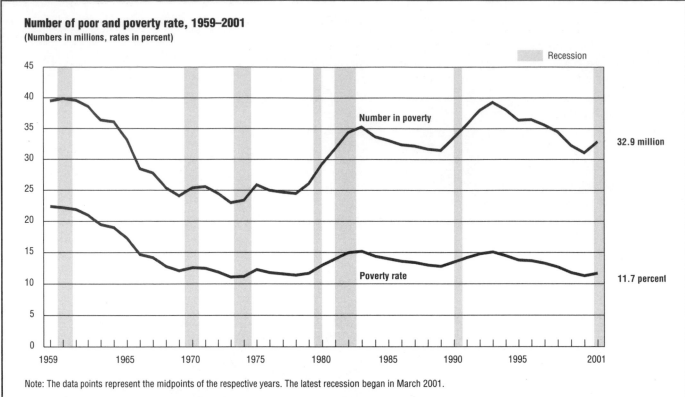

Note: The data points represent the midpoints of the respective years. The latest recession began in March 2001.

SOURCE: Bernadette D. Proctor and Joseph Dalaker, "Figure 1. Number of Poor and Poverty Rate: 1959 to 2001," in *Poverty in the United States: 2001,* P60-219, U.S. Census Bureau, Washington, DC, September 2002

FIGURE 3.4

Poverty rates by age, 1959–2001
(Percent)

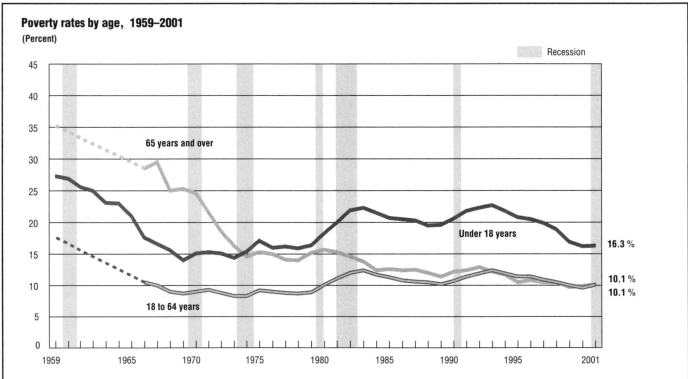

Note: The data points represent the midpoints of the respective years. The latest recession began in March 2001. Data for people 18 to 64 and older are not available from 1960 to 1965.

SOURCE: Bernadette D. Proctor and Joseph Dalaker, "Figure 2. Poverty Rates by Age: 1959 to 2001," in *Poverty in the United States: 2001,* P60-219 U.S. Census Bureau, Washington, DC, September 2002

RACE AND ETHNICITY. Hispanics and African Americans are much more likely to be poor than members of other racial and ethnic groups. Members of these two populations also have higher rates of single-female headed households and lower rates of high school graduation, two indicators of increased likelihood of poverty. (See Figure 3.5.) *Poverty in the United States: 2001* found that the poverty rate for Hispanics (who may be of any race) was 21.4 percent in 2001 and 20.2 percent for Hispanic families. The poverty rate for African Americans was at a record low in 2001 of 22.7 percent, and black families' poverty rate was 21.4 percent. Whites and Asian Americans had the lowest rates of poverty by racial group. Whites had an overall poverty rate of 9.9 percent with the rate for white families at 8.1 percent. Asian Americans and Pacific Islanders were poor at a rate of 10.2 percent in 2001, while their families had a poverty rate equal to that of white families, 8.1 percent.

WORKING STATUS. The poor are often assumed to be the unemployed. Those who are unemployed are more likely to be poor but many people who work are also poor. In 2001 people who worked at any time during the year had a lower poverty rate than those who did not, 5.6 percent versus 20.6 percent. When one looks at family rates of poverty similar results are seen. In families that had at least one worker, the poverty rate was 7.6 percent but rose sharply if the family had no workers to 30.5 percent. (See Figure 3.6.) The same pattern was seen when data on families was divided out by family type. Again, rates of poverty were highest for single female–headed families.

REGION. Poverty rates vary from one part of the United States to another. All regions saw an increase in poverty rates between 2000 and 2001. The South was the region with the highest rate of poverty in 2001, 13.5 percent, up from a rate of 12.8 in 2000. The South was home to 41.1 percent of the nation's poor in 2001 while only 35.7 percent of Americans lived in the South. The poverty rate increases were more modest in other regions between 2000 and 2001. In the Northeast, poverty rates in 2001 were 10.7 percent, compared with 10.3 percent in 2000. In the Midwest, the rates were 9.4 percent in 2001 and 9.3 percent in 2000. The West experienced poverty at a rate of 12.1 percent in 2001, up slightly from 11.8 in 2000.

Poverty rates also vary by residential area. Inner city rates tend to be highest. In 2001 the poverty rate for inside central cities was 16.5 percent. In non-metropolitan areas the rate was 14.2 percent. Suburban poverty rates tend to be the lowest. In 2001 they were 8.2 percent.

EMPLOYMENT AND WAGES

The poverty rate is established by counting the number of families with before-tax income that is lower than the poverty threshold set for a family that size. This means that

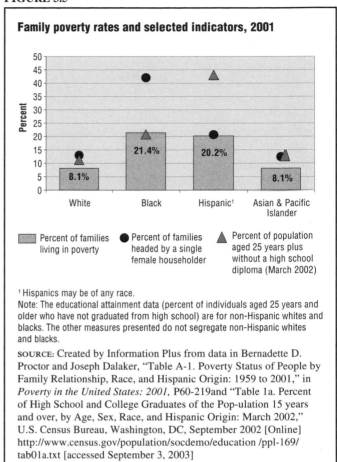

FIGURE 3.5

Family poverty rates and selected indicators, 2001

Percent of families living in poverty

Percent of families headed by a single female householder

Percent of population aged 25 years plus without a high school diploma (March 2002)

[1] Hispanics may be of any race.
Note: The educational attainment data (percent of individuals aged 25 years and older who have not graduated from high school) are for non-Hispanic whites and blacks. The other measures presented do not segregate non-Hispanic whites and blacks.

SOURCE: Created by Information Plus from data in Bernadette D. Proctor and Joseph Dalaker, "Table A-1. Poverty Status of People by Family Relationship, Race, and Hispanic Origin: 1959 to 2001," in *Poverty in the United States: 2001*, P60-219 and "Table 1a. Percent of High School and College Graduates of the Pop-ulation 15 years and over, by Age, Sex, Race, and Hispanic Origin: March 2002," U.S. Census Bureau, Washington, DC, September 2002 [Online] http://www.census.gov/population/socdemo/education /ppl-169/ tab01a.txt [accessed September 3, 2003]

both employment and wages are an essential part of the determination of poverty.

Household Income

Median annual household income in 2001 was $42,228, which means that half of all American households earned less than this amount and half earned more. (See Table 3.3.) Not surprisingly, median household income varies greatly according to the composition of the household. The median income for married-couple families in 2001 was $60,471, but for female-headed families with no husband present, it was only $28,142, less than half that of a couple-headed family. Race and ethnicity were also factors. In 2001 Asian and Pacific Islander households had the highest median income ($53,635). The median income for white households was $44,517; for Hispanics, $33,565; and for blacks, $29,470.

An analysis of median household income, of course, does not shed much light on those whose wages are lowest and therefore are most likely to fall below the poverty threshold. A look at the shifting nature of jobs available to those earning the minimum federal hourly wage will refocus the discussion more squarely on those most vulnerable to poverty and in the worst cases, to homelessness.

FIGURE 3.6

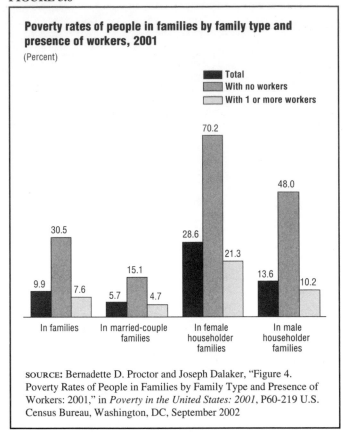

Poverty rates of people in families by family type and presence of workers, 2001

(Percent)

SOURCE: Bernadette D. Proctor and Joseph Dalaker, "Figure 4. Poverty Rates of People in Families by Family Type and Presence of Workers: 2001," in *Poverty in the United States: 2001*, P60-219 U.S. Census Bureau, Washington, DC, September 2002

Educational Attainment and Income Level

A strong correlation exists between income level and educational attainment. The poor tend to be those with less education and fewer of the well educated are poor. Table 3.4 presents family income data for the year 2000 by highest level of education completed by the head of family, the primary provider. The data are divided into seven income ranges and the percentage of families with incomes in each of these ranges is presented. For all families, regardless of educational level, 8.7 percent earned under $15,000 in 2000 and 17.6 percent earned $100,000 or more.

When educational attainment is added to the comparison of family income distribution a clear and predictable pattern emerges. Those with the least education predominantly earn at the lowest ranges of income while the majority of those with the most education earn at the highest income range. (See Figure 3.7.) Of heads of households with less than a ninth-grade education, one-half earn under $25,000—24 percent earn under $15,000, and 26 percent earn between $15,000 and $24,999. On the other extreme are the heads of households with a doctoral degree. More than half of these households (53.6 percent) earned $100,000 or more in 2000.

A lack of education leaves a person ill equipped to support him or herself comfortably, much less be responsible financially for others. Education opens doors and opportunities that are simply not available to the under educated,

especially in an economy that is transitioning from a reliance on manufacturing to a reliance on the information and service industries.

Growth of Jobs in Low Wage Industries

During the 1970s manufacturing industries began closing down plants and moving their production facilities to cheaper labor markets at home and abroad. For much of the 20th century the United States had been primarily an industrial economy, certainly from the mid-1930s to the mid-1980s. The last two decades of the century saw the beginning of the nation's transition to what has now been dubbed the information or service economy.

Figure 3.8 shows the change in employment between 1980 and 2001 by industrial sector. The industry that grew most was the service industry. In 1980 the service sector employed 28.8 million people; by 2001 it had grown to employ 50.5 million, a growth rate of 75.6 percent. Industries that pay higher wages than those offered in the services, like mining and manufacturing, shrank during this same period, 42.1 percent and 13.5 percent respectively.

The shift in employment from production work to service work has shifted workers from higher to lower paying jobs. The jobs available in an economy that is ever more strongly led by services are lower paying jobs. According to the U.S. Bureau of Labor Statistics average hourly wages earned by those employed in the service industries are much lower than average hourly wages earned in the fields of manufacturing, mining, and construction.

Minimum Wage Jobs

The Bureau of Labor Statistics provides data on where minimum wage jobs are most prevalent. Table 3.5 shows the total number of wage and salary workers by occupation and by industry. It also shows the number and percent of those workers who, in 2002, earned at or below the prevailing minimum wage of $5.15 per hour.

The occupations with the highest percentage of workers at or below minimum wage were in the service occupations where 10.2 percent of workers earned minimum wage or below. Within the service sector several occupations were notable for high percentages of low-wage workers. They were food service workers (29.5 percent) and those employed in private households (17.0 percent). (See Table 3.5.)

By industrial sector a similar outcome is seen. The service sector as a whole offered 2.3 percent of its workers minimum wages or below in 2002. (See Table 3.5.) The wholesale and retail trades as a whole employed 7.5 percent of their wage and salary workers at an hourly wage equal to or below the federal minimum. The wholesale trade had only 0.6 percent at or below minimum wage while the retail portion of this industrial sector paid

TABLE 3.3

Comparison of summary measures of income by selected characteristics, 2000 and 2001

(Households and people as of March of the following year)

Characteristic	Number in 2001 (thousands)	Median income in 2001 (in current dollars) Value (dollars)	Median income in 2001 (in current dollars) 90-percent confidence interval[2] (±) (dollars)	Median income in 2000[1] (in 2001 dollars) Value (dollars)	Median income in 2000[1] (in 2001 dollars) 90-percent confidence interval[2] (±) (dollars)	Percent change in real income 2000 to 2001	90-percent confidence interval[2] (±) of percent change
HOUSEHOLDS							
All households	109,297	42,228	212	43,162	223	*−2.2	0.6
Type of household							
Family households	74,329	52,275	290	53,155	304	*−1.7	0.6
Married-couple families	56,747	60,471	342	60,926	453	−0.7	0.8
Female householder, no husband present	13,143	28,142	475	29,053	516	*−3.1	1.9
Male householder, no wife present	4,438	40,715	860	43,332	854	*−6.0	2.2
Nonfamily households	34,969	25,631	278	26,012	279	*−1.5	1.2
Female householder	19,390	20,264	347	21,052	323	*−3.7	1.8
Male householder	15,579	32,312	395	32,358	358	−0.1	1.3
Race and Hispanic origin of householder							
All races [3]	109,297	42,228	212	43,162	223	*−2.2	0.6
White	90,682	44,517	344	45,142	328	*−1.4	0.8
Non-Hispanic white	80,818	46,305	316	46,896	309	*−1.3	0.8
Black	13,315	29,470	571	30,495	665	*−3.4	2.3
Asian and Pacific Islander	4,071	53,635	2,106	57,313	1,608	*−6.4	3.7
Hispanic origin [4]	10,499	33,565	701	34,094	808	−1.6	2.1
Age of householder							
Under 65 years	86,821	49,227	327	49,990	338	*−1.5	0.8
15 to 24 years	6,391	28,196	799	28,624	656	−1.5	2.9
25 to 34 years	18,988	45,080	614	45,654	712	−1.3	1.7
35 to 44 years	24,031	53,320	689	55,263	619	*−3.5	1.3
45 to 54 years	22,208	58,045	801	59,251	747	*−2.0	1.5
55 to 64 years	15,203	45,864	699	46,105	742	−0.5	1.8
65 years and over	22,476	23,118	314	23,727	294	*−2.6	1.4
Nativity of the householder							
Native born	95,884	42,917	339	43,578	250	*−1.5	0.8
Foreign born	13,413	37,948	943	40,055	977	*−5.3	2.7
Naturalized citizen	6,069	43,968	1,513	46,492	1,409	*−5.4	3.5
Not a citizen	7,344	34,812	872	36,345	827	*−4.2	2.6
Region							
Northeast	21,128	45,716	615	44,971	720	1.7	1.7
Midwest	25,755	43,834	574	45,496	560	*−3.7	1.4
South	39,151	38,904	507	39,460	473	*−1.4	1.4
West	23,263	45,087	740	46,169	666	*−2.3	1.7
Residence							
Inside metropolitan areas	88,112	45,219	309	45,942	342	*−1.6	0.8
Inside central cities	32,540	36,731	347	37,741	387	*−2.7	1.1
Outside central cities	55,572	50,697	337	51,606	358	*−1.8	0.8
Outside metropolitan areas	21,185	33,601	604	33,832	692	−0.7	2.2
EARNINGS OF YEAR-ROUND, FULL-TIME WORKERS							
Male	58,712	38,275	424	38,292	171	-	-
Female	41,639	29,215	271	28,228	172	*3.5	1.0
PER CAPITA INCOME							
All races [3]	282,082	22,851	174	22,970	193	−0.5	1.9
White	230,071	24,127	202	24,240	230	−0.5	1.0
Non-Hispanic white	194,822	26,134	234	26,242	265	−0.4	1.1
Black	36,023	14,953	308	15,209	348	−1.7	2.4
Asian and Pacific Islander	12,500	24,277	1,124	24,002	1,146	1.1	5.2
Hispanic origin [4]	37,438	13,003	326	13,004	402	-	-

*Statistically significant change at the 90-percent confidence level.

[1] Consistent with 2001 data through implementation of Census 2000-based population controls and a 28,000 household sample expansion.

[2] For an explanation of confidence levels, see "standard errors and their use" at www.census.gov/hhes/income/income01/sa.pdf.

[3] Data for American Indians and Alaska Natives are not shown separately in this table because of the small sample of those households.

[4] Hispanics may be of any race.

SOURCE: Carmen DeNavas-Walt and Robert Cleveland, "Table 1. Comparison of Summary Measures of Income by Selected Characteristics: 2000 and 2001," in *Money Income in the United States: 2001,* P60-218, U.S. Census Bureau, Washington, DC, 2002

TABLE 3.4

Family income by educational attainment of the householder, 2000

Characteristics	Number of families (000)	Percent of families by income level							Median income (dollars)
		Under $15,000	$15,000 to $24,999	$25,000 to $34,999	$35,000 to $49,999	$50,000 to $74,999	$75,000 to $99,999	$100,000 and over	
Number of families (000)	72,388	6,910	8,308	8,704	11,521	15,543	9,118	12,282	50,890
Educational attainment of householder[1]									
Total	68,899	8.7	11.0	11.8	15.9	21.9	13.0	17.6	52,166
Less than 9th grade	4,178	24.0	26.0	17.9	14.6	11.1	4.0	2.3	24,946
9th to 11th grade (no diploma)	6,026	21.4	21.2	17.3	16.6	15.6	4.7	3.2	28,878
High school graduate [2]	21,502	9.6	13.2	14.7	19.2	23.7	11.3	8.3	44,248
Some college, no degree	12,593	7.0	10.2	12.5	18.4	24.6	13.4	13.8	51,642
Associate degree	5,869	4.4	8.5	11.0	17.1	25.5	17.2	16.3	57,814
Bachelor's degree or more	18,732	2.7	3.3	5.2	10.2	21.1	18.1	39.4	84,172
Bachelor's degree	12,016	2.7	3.7	6.2	11.9	23.2	18.0	34.3	77,245
Master's degree	4,518	2.7	2.4	3.6	8.0	19.3	19.8	43.9	91,126
Professional degree	1,161	2.3	1.6	3.7	5.1	11.1	14.1	62.0	100,000
Doctorate degree	1,036	2.5	3.3	1.7	6.7	16.3	16.0	53.6	100,000

[1] Persons 25 years old or over.

[2] Includes equivalency.

SOURCE: Adapted from "No. 660. Money Income of Families–Distribution by Family Characteristics, and Income Level: 2000," in *Statistical Abstract of the United States: 2002*, U.S. Census Bureau, Washington, DC, December 2002

FIGURE 3.7

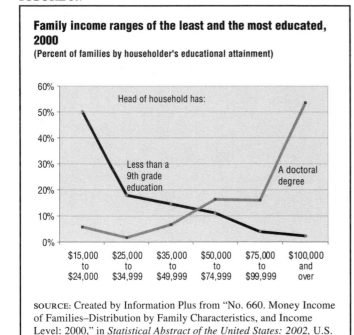

Family income ranges of the least and the most educated, 2000

(Percent of families by householder's educational attainment)

SOURCE: Created by Information Plus from "No. 660. Money Income of Families–Distribution by Family Characteristics, and Income Level: 2000," in *Statistical Abstract of the United States: 2002*, U.S. Census Bureau, Washington, DC, December 2002

8.4 percent of its workers minimum wages. Those working in eating and drinking establishments were most likely to make minimum wage or below, to a large extent because many earn a good part of their incomes from tips or gratuities left for them by customers.

The shift from a primarily industrial economy to one primarily engaged in providing services has been one of the leading factors in a shift in the distribution of wealth in the United States.

THE DISTRIBUTION OF WEALTH

While most discussions of poverty focus simply on people who are below the poverty line versus those who are above it, it is important to keep in mind that even among the poor, there are those who are worse off than others. An analysis of changes in the distribution of wealth helps to explain why homelessness and poverty can remain level, even when the economy performs well.

During the 1980s and 1990s the poverty rate declined for the most part. In the first years of each of these decades the number of people in poverty rose but during the rest of the 20-year period the numbers of people in poverty declined. (See Figure 3.3.) However, the patterns seen in the distribution of wealth underwent a change. Table 3.6 breaks the U.S. population down into five groups based on income, ranging from the fifth of the population with the lowest incomes to the fifth with the highest incomes. It then displays the percent of total income earned by each fifth of the population in a particular year, as well as the amount earned by those in the top five percent of all Americans (the highest fifth of the highest fifth).

From 1991 to 2001, the highest fifth or quintile of the population increased its share of total income from 44.2 percent to 47.7 percent, an increase of 7.9 percent. (See Table 3.6.) In each of the other, lower income quintiles the share of aggregate income received declined over the same

FIGURE 3.8

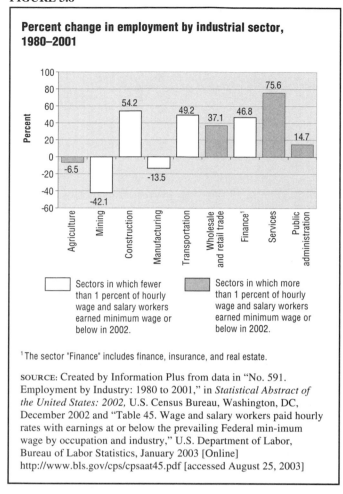

Percent change in employment by industrial sector, 1980–2001

Sectors in which fewer than 1 percent of hourly wage and salary workers earned minimum wage or below in 2002.

Sectors in which more than 1 percent of hourly wage and salary workers earned minimum wage or below in 2002.

[1] The sector "Finance" includes finance, insurance, and real estate.

SOURCE: Created by Information Plus from data in "No. 591. Employment by Industry: 1980 to 2001," in *Statistical Abstract of the United States: 2002,* U.S. Census Bureau, Washington, DC, December 2002 and "Table 45. Wage and salary workers paid hourly rates with earnings at or below the prevailing Federal min-imum wage by occupation and industry," U.S. Department of Labor, Bureau of Labor Statistics, January 2003 [Online] http://www.bls.gov/cps/cpsaat45.pdf [accessed August 25, 2003]

time period, 1991—2001. The lowest fifth went from 4.5 percent of all income in 1991 down to 4.2 percent in 2001. The top five percent of Americans saw their percentage of aggregate income rise 23 percent during the 1990s, from 17.1 percent to 21.0 percent. What all of this means is that as the U.S. economy went through a period of historic growth during the 1990s, every quintile fifth of the population also saw its income rise. (See Figure 3.9.) The richest fifth of the population, however, gained the largest share of the new wealth and increased their overall share of aggregate income while each of the other fifths lost some of its share of the aggregate income. Although it is not accurate to say that the poor got poorer, since their incomes grew, it is true that they became poorer relative to the rich. The 1990s resulted in increased disparity between the rich and the poor.

SAVINGS ARE DOWN, BANKRUPTCIES ARE UP

One of the risk factors for becoming homeless is the lack of a financial safety net upon which individuals can fall back should something unexpected occur. The loss of a job, and in many cases the concomitant loss of health insurance, is one such occurrence. An accident resulting in the need for expensive medical treatment is another

example of the sort of incident that requires a financial safety net. Financial experts stress the importance of maintaining savings that can help see people through this sort of eventuality. Yet in the United States over the past two decades (1980–2000), the rate at which Americans have been saving has declined.

Figure 3.10 provides an overview of the personal savings rate over the period 1960–2002. The Bureau of Economic Analysis defines personal savings as the rate at which we save our disposable income, the income remaining after obligatory taxes have been paid. Disposable income grew over this period from $13,761 in 1960 to $25,754 in 2002 (based on constant, inflation adjusted 2000 dollars). The rate at which we saved in 1960 was 7.2 percent but by 2002 it had dropped to just over half that rate (3.7 percent) and this was up from the low reached in 2001 of 2.3 percent. As people save less, they become ever more vulnerable to the unplanned expenditures that periodically arise in life.

Exacerbating the problem of low savings is the rise in consumer credit debt. In an article by Catherine Valenti ("Living on Credit, As the Economy Slows and Layoffs Increase, Debt Levels Become a Problem," *ABCNEWS.com,* October 18, 2001) the author points out that the nation heavily depends on credit and is getting in over its head. "Most of us are never taught about credit and how to use it," according to Joy Thormodsgard, vice president of the National Foundation of Credit Counseling. "We don't plan ahead, we get what we want now and figure out how we're going to pay for it later."

Of particular concern, explains the author, is the high number of homeowners who are over-leveraged. They have taken out second and third mortgages on their homes, and if they fall upon hard times and are unable to pay their loans, they run the risk of loosing their homes.

The rise in number of bankruptcy filings during the late 1990s, a period of strong economic growth, is likely the result of low savings and high credit debt. According to the Federal Reserve, the typical family filing for bankruptcy in 1997 owed more than one and a half times its annual income in short-term, high-interest debt. For example, a family earning $24,000 had an average of $36,000 in credit card and similar debt. Figure 3.11 presents data on the personal savings rate and the number of personal bankruptcy filings over the period 1980–2002. Over this period the number of personal bankruptcy filings rose by an astonishing 435 percent, from 287,580 in 1980 to 1,539,111 in 2002.

Controversial proposed changes to the bankruptcy laws (pending passage through the Congress as of August 2003), if passed, would make it more difficult for many to file personal bankruptcy. One of the proposed changes addresses what is seen as part of the problem of growth in

TABLE 3.5

Wage and salary workers paid hourly with earnings at or below the prevailing federal minimum wage by occupation and industry, 2002

(Numbers in thousands)

Occupation and industry	Total	Workers paid hourly rates		Total at or below prevailing federal minimum wage	
		Below prevailing federal minimum wage	At prevailing federal minimum wage	Number	Percent of hourly-paid workers
Occupation					
Managerial and professional specialty	10,744	48	25	73	0.7
Executive, administrative, and managerial	4,531	28	6	34	0.8
Professional specialty	6,212	20	19	36	0.6
Technical, sales, and administrative support	22,594	157	174	331	1.5
Technicians and related support	2,801	5	6	12	0.4
Sales occupations	7,467	97	108	204	2.7
Administrative support, including clerical	12,326	54	61	115	0.9
Service occupations	14,235	1,191	263	1,454	10.2
Private household	371	58	5	63	17.0
Protective service	1,655	15	3	18	1.1
Service, except private household and protective	12,209	1,119	254	1,373	11.2
Food service workers	5,839	975	166	1,141	29.5
Health service workers	2,416	32	12	44	1.8
Cleaning and building service workers	2,439	46	34	80	3.3
Personal service workers	1,514	67	42	108	7.2
Precision production, craft, and repair	9,535	43	12	55	0.6
Operators, fabricators, and laborers	14,170	137	80	216	1.5
Machine operators, assemblers, and inspectors	5,610	30	17	47	0.8
Transportation and material moving occupations	3,745	38	11	49	1.3
Handlers, equipment cleaners, helpers, and laborers	4,815	69	52	121	2.5
Farming, forestry, and fishing	1,443	22	15	38	2.6
Industry					
Private wage and salary workers	63,670	1,518	509	2,026	3.2
Agriculture	1,220	19	10	29	2.4
Nonagricultural industries	62,449	1,498	499	1,997	3.2
Mining	286	1	-	1	0.5
Construction	5,049	34	5	39	0.8
Manufacturing	11,355	35	31	66	0.6
Durable goods	6,833	21	17	38	0.5
Nondurable goods	4,521	14	14	29	0.6
Transportation and public utilities	4,209	31	8	39	0.9
Transportation	2,684	26	5	32	1.2
Communications and other public utilities	1,525	5	3	7	0.5
Wholesale and retail trade	18,105	1,055	298	1,353	7.5
Wholesale trade	2,230	9	4	13	0.6
Retail trade	15,874	1,046	294	1,340	8.4
Eating and drinking places	5,601	929	180	1,109	19.8
Finance, insurance, and real estate	3,010	14	8	22	0.7
Services	20,436	328	148	477	2.3
Private households	414	60	6	66	15.8
Other service industries	20,022	269	143	411	2.1
Personal services, except private households	1,829	72	42	114	6.2
Entertainment and recreation services	1,391	52	17	69	5.0
Government workers	9,050	81	61	142	1.6
Federal	1,786	15	7	22	1.2
State	2,382	27	23	50	2.1
Local	4,882	39	30	70	1.4

Note: The prevailing federal minimum wage was $5.15 per hour in 2002. Data are for wage and salary workers, excluding the incorporated self-employed. They refer to a person's earnings on their sole or principal job, and pertain only to workers who are paid hourly rates. Salaried workers and other nonhourly workers are not included. The presence of workers with hourly earnings below the minimum wage does not necessarily indicate violations of the Fair Labor Standards Act, as there are exceptions to the minimum wage provisions of the law. In addition, some survey respondents might have rounded the hourly earnings to the nearest dollar, and, as a result, reported hourly earnings below the minimum wage even though they earned the minimum wage or higher.

SOURCE: "Table 45. Wage and salary workers paid hourly rates with earnings at or below the prevailing Federal minimum wage by occupation and industry," U.S. Department of Labor, Bureau of Labor Statistics, January 2003 [Online] http://www.bls.gov/cps/cpsaat45.pdf [accessed August 25, 2003]

bankruptcy filing, namely the uninformed and un-educated use of consumer credit by large numbers of Americans. The proposed changes include a new require-ment that in order to successfully conclude any personal

bankruptcy case the filer must participate in a credit coun-seling course. Such courses are designed to help the filer of personal bankruptcy learn a range of techniques for managing personal finances more successfully.

Homeless in America: How Could It Happen Here?

TABLE 3.6

Share of aggregate income received by each fifth and top five percent of families, 1947–2001

(Percent)

	Lowest fifth	Second fifth	Middle fifth	Fourth fifth	Highest fifth	Top 5 percent
1947	5.0	11.9	17.0	23.1	43.0	17.5
1948	4.9	12.1	17.3	23.2	42.4	17.1
1949	4.5	11.9	17.3	23.5	42.7	16.9
1950	4.5	12.0	17.4	23.4	42.7	17.3
1951	5.0	12.4	17.6	23.4	41.6	16.8
1952	4.9	12.3	17.4	23.4	41.9	17.4
1953	4.7	12.5	18.0	23.9	40.9	15.7
1954	4.5	12.1	17.7	23.9	41.8	16.3
1955	4.8	12.3	17.8	23.7	41.3	16.4
1956	5.0	12.5	17.9	23.7	41.0	16.1
1957	5.1	12.7	18.1	23.8	40.4	15.6
1958	5.0	12.5	18.0	23.9	40.6	15.4
1959	4.9	12.3	17.9	23.8	41.1	15.9
1960	4.8	12.2	17.8	24.0	41.3	15.9
1961	4.7	11.9	17.5	23.8	42.2	16.6
1962	5.0	12.1	17.6	24.0	41.3	15.7
1963	5.0	12.1	17.7	24.0	41.2	15.8
1964	5.1	12.0	17.7	24.0	41.2	15.9
1965	5.2	12.2	17.8	23.9	40.9	15.5
1966	5.6	12.4	17.8	23.8	40.5	15.6
1967	5.4	12.2	17.5	23.5	41.4	16.4
1968	5.6	12.4	17.7	23.7	40.5	15.6
1969	5.6	12.4	17.7	23.7	40.6	15.6
1970	5.4	12.2	17.6	23.8	40.9	15.6
1971	5.5	12.0	17.6	23.8	41.1	15.7
1972	5.5	11.9	17.5	23.9	41.4	15.9
1973	5.5	11.9	17.5	24.0	41.1	15.5
1974	5.7	12.0	17.6	24.1	40.6	14.8
1975	5.6	11.9	17.7	24.2	40.7	14.9
1976	5.6	11.9	17.7	24.2	40.7	14.9
1977	5.5	11.7	17.6	24.3	40.9	14.9
1978	5.4	11.7	17.6	24.2	41.1	15.1
1979	5.4	11.6	17.5	24.1	41.4	15.3
1980	5.3	11.6	17.6	24.4	41.1	14.6
1981	5.3	11.4	17.5	24.6	41.2	14.4
1982	5.0	11.3	17.2	24.4	42.2	15.3
1983	4.9	11.2	17.2	24.5	42.4	15.3
1984	4.8	11.1	17.1	24.5	42.5	15.4
1985	4.8	11.0	16.9	24.3	43.1	16.1
1986	4.7	10.9	16.9	24.1	43.4	16.5
1987	4.6	10.7	16.8	24.0	43.8	17.2
1988	4.6	10.7	16.7	24.0	44.0	17.2
1989	4.6	10.6	16.5	23.7	44.6	17.9
1990	4.6	10.8	16.6	23.8	44.3	17.4
1991	4.5	10.7	16.6	24.1	44.2	17.1
1992	4.3	10.5	16.5	24.0	44.7	17.6
1993	4.1	9.9	15.7	23.3	47.0	20.3
1994	4.2	10.0	15.7	23.3	46.9	20.1
1995	4.4	10.1	15.8	23.2	46.5	20.0
1996	4.2	10.0	15.8	23.1	46.8	20.3
1997	4.2	9.9	15.7	23.0	47.2	20.7
1998	4.2	9.9	15.7	23.0	47.3	20.7
1999	4.3	9.9	15.6	23.0	47.2	20.3
2000	4.3	9.8	15.4	22.7	47.7	21.1
2001	4.2	9.7	15.4	22.9	47.7	21.0

SOURCE: "Table F-2. Share of aggregate income received by each fifth and top 5 percent of families, 1947–2001," in *Historic Income Tables – Families*, U.S. Census Bureau, Washington, DC, September 2002 [Online] http://www.census.gov/hhes/income/histinc/f02.html [accessed August 25, 2003]

UNEMPLOYMENT

The official unemployment rate has been the subject of considerable scrutiny and criticism over the years. Many social and economic researchers believe that the rate misrepresents the actual number of people who cannot find work to support themselves and their families. For example, the official unemployment figures do not count those who have given up searching for work because of failure to find work over a long period of time. The figures also leave out those who are underemployed, such as the college graduate who takes a low-paying job or part-time job until he or she finds adequate employment. It is likely, then, that the true number of people who cannot find adequate employment is higher than official statistics indicate.

The U.S. Bureau of Labor Statistics reported that in 2002 the official number of unemployed persons in the United States was almost 8.4 million, 5.8 percent of the labor-aged population wishing to work. In 2000 the

FIGURE 3.9

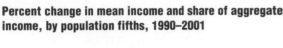
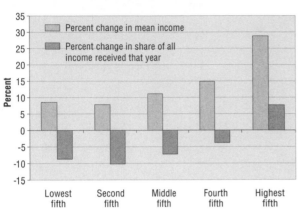

Percent change in mean income and share of aggregate income, by population fifths, 1990–2001

SOURCE: Created by Information Plus from "Table F-2. Share of Aggregate Income Received by Each Fifth and Top 5 Percent of Families, 1947-2001," and "Table F-3. Mean Income Received by Each Fifth and Top 5 Percent of Families (All Races): 1966 to 2001," in *Historical Income Tables – Families,* U.S. Census Bureau, Washington, DC, 2002 [Online] http://www.census.gov/ hhes/income/histinc/incfamdet.html [accessed August 26, 2003]

FIGURE 3.10

National per capita savings rate as percent of disposable income, 1960–2002

SOURCE: Created by Information Plus from data in "Monthly and Annual Personal Saving as a Percentage of Disposable Personal Income," in *Personal Income and Outlays,* Bureau of Economic Analysis, Washington, DC, August 2003 [Online] http://www.bea.gov/bea/dn/ home/personalincome.htm [accessed September 9, 2003]

unemployment rate was 4.0 percent. The rise in unemployment between 2000 and 2002 (31 percent) reflected the down turn in the economy that began in 2001.

Unemployment is a permanent feature of the economy. It can never be entirely eliminated since there will always be people who lose their jobs for various reasons. The transition between a lost job and the next job takes time even in the best of economic times.

The 1990s were a period of economic growth. The decade began with an unemployment rate in 1990 of 5.6 percent. The rate rose to a high of 7.5 percent in 1992 and then fell to a low of 4.0 percent in 2000. By the end of 2001 it has risen to 4.7 percent and by the end of 2002 it was 5.8 percent. The first two quarters of 2003 saw the unemployment rate continue to rise. By June 2003 it was 6.5 percent on a seasonally adjusted basis. By August 2003 the unemployment rate had fallen slightly to 6.0 percent but there were signs of a growing number of people dropping off the unemployment registers. It is speculated that the decline in unemployment rate experienced in the summer of 2003 was the result of a growing number workers who had given up the search for a new job.

UNEMPLOYMENT RATES BY POPULATION SEGMENT. Some segments of American society have experienced more unemployment than other segments. According to the U.S. Bureau of Labor Statistics in 2002, of the nation's 74.2 million families, 7.8 percent reported having an unemployed member at some time during the average week.

The proportion of black families with an unemployed member (13.1 percent) was higher than the proportion for either Hispanic (11.2 percent) or white families (7.0 percent). (See Figure 3.12.) However, between 1999 and 2002 it was white families who saw the largest increase in their unemployment rate (32 percent) compared with black families whose unemployment rate rose 24 percent and Hispanic families who saw a rise of 16 percent.

Underemployed and Discouraged Workers

The U.S. Census Bureau's *Current Population Survey* regularly reports unemployment figures as well as figures for those who are not in the labor force and a subgroup of those not in the labor force, namely those who are discouraged and have stopped looking for work.

Discouraged workers give up looking for work specifically because they believe no jobs are available for them. In July 2003 the number of discouraged workers was reported as 470,000, up 65,000 over the number of discouraged workers reported one year earlier (U.S. Census Bureau, *Current Population Survey,* August 2003).

WELFARE REFORM AND THE POOR

In 1996 the passage of the Personal Responsibility and Work Opportunity Reconciliation Act (PL 104-193), the most sweeping welfare legislation since the 1960s, ended Aid to Families with Dependent Children (AFDC) and gave the states control over the administration of benefits for previous AFDC recipients in the form of Temporary

FIGURE 3.11

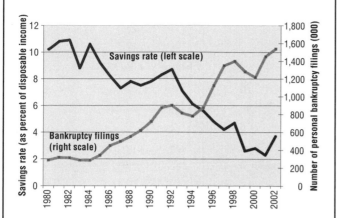

Personal savings rates and bankruptcy filings, 1980–2002

SOURCE: Created by Information Plus from data in "Monthly and Annual Personal Saving as a Percentage of Disposable Personal Income," in *Personal Income and Outlays,* Bureau of Economic Analysis, Washington, DC, August 2003 [Online] http://www.bea.gov/bea/dn/ home/personalincome.htm [accessed September 9, 2003] and bank-ruptcy data from various databases produced by the U.S. Department of Justice, U.S. Courts [Online] http://www.uscourts.gov/ bankruptcycourts.html [accessed September 9, 2003]

FIGURE 3.12

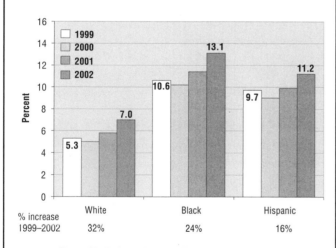

Percent of all families with an unemployed member, by race and Hispanic origin, 1999–2002

SOURCE: Created by Information Plus from data in "Families with unemployed member(s), 1999–2000," in *Monthly Labor Review,* vol. 124, no. 4, April 2001, and "Table 1. Employment and unemployment in families by race and Hispanic origin, 2001–02 annual averages," U.S. Department of Labor, Bureau of Labor Statistics, Washington, DC, 2003 [Online] http://www.bls.gov/news.release/famee.t01.htm [accessed August 8, 2003]

Assistance for Needy Families (TANF) grants. In addition, the Personal Responsibility and Work Opportunity Reconciliation Act made changes to Supplemental Security Income (SSI) and Medicaid.

Returning Local Control

The Temporary Assistance for Needy Families (TANF) block grant legislation (the welfare reform initiative) was designed to fulfill two primary objectives:

- Return more control of relief assistance programs to the state governments—this grants the states great flexibility to design whatever mix of services and benefits they think will reduce dependency and provide for the needy.

- Limit the amount of time a person spends on public assistance—specifically, the 1996 law contains a five-year lifetime limit on receipt of federally funded cash assistance; authorizes states to impose shorter time limits at their discretion; and requires that, by the year 2002, 50 percent of all recipients who have received cash aid for two years work at least 30 hours a week in order to continue receiving benefits.

Many people agree that these are worthy goals. Local authorities are clearly better equipped to determine the needs of the people in their area than a distant federal government. Each state has specific needs; geography, climate, and ethnicity all vary from state to state, and all deserve individual consideration. The second focus, to encourage work instead of public assistance, is also respectful of the needs of the individual and society to advance themselves. Many critics of the old system felt that it unintentionally discouraged welfare recipients from working. Working brings in money, but it also creates new expenses, such as commuting to and from work and childcare. Since most welfare recipients were qualified only for low-paying jobs, they often found that these expenses left them with less money than they would have had if they simply stayed on welfare, even though that meant they had no prospect of ever leaving poverty. The welfare-to-work initiative has another, residual benefit as well: not only does it aim to benefit the recipient, but the chances that the children of the recipient will be impoverished as an adult are lowered.

Both these objectives reflect the attitudes of the English Poor Laws of feudal times. The first, local responsibility for the poor, has historically proven to result in discriminatory practices—from medieval England through colonial times. It lends itself to subjective and/or punitive practices. The second objective resembles the deserving/undeserving moral judgments of the poor. It was in applying these same qualifications that the poorhouses were born.

These historical attitudes and their results continue to provide a basis for concern regarding welfare reform. While local control makes it easier to address the specific needs of the poor in particular areas, it also makes it possible for localities to restrict benefits in ways that a nationwide program would never be able to. The welfare reform laws do place some limits on local authorities, but it remains necessary for people concerned with equal justice to remain alert to possible violations. There is also an inherent assumption that anyone who really wants work will be able to find it, and that anyone who cannot find work within a specified period must not really be trying and therefore does not deserve government aid. This ignores the fact that many people on welfare, and poor people in general, lack the skills or education necessary for most jobs. The homeless, who do not even have a fixed address or telephone number and may not have clean clothes for an interview, are especially vulnerable in this system.

President George W. Bush, in an address at St. Luke's Catholic Church in Washington, D.C., in February 2003, proposed that the Welfare Reform Act should be changed by Congress to require that 70 percent of former welfare recipients be required to spend 40 hours a week working or training for work by 2007. The U.S. House of Representatives passed the Personal Responsibility, Work, and Family Promotion Act of 2002 (HR 4737), increasing the required working hours as recommended by the president; however, as of early 2003 the U.S. Senate had not taken definitive action on the issue.

LIFE AFTER WELFARE REFORM. By 2001 welfare reform had been more successful than its many critics expected. Welfare rolls had declined by roughly half since the early 1990s and employment rates had risen for most former (and many current) welfare recipients. How much of these positive results were due to the economic boom of the 1990s, with the accompanying increase in jobs, remains to be determined. Since the economic downturns in 2001, when the most recent recession began, the number of welfare recipients continued to decline from 5.3 million to 5.0 million between October 2001 and September 2002, according to the Administration for Children and Families of the U.S. Department of Health & Human Services.

Researchers know that there have been declines in the welfare rolls. But as of yet, they don't know what happened to the people who are missing from the files. Major studies are now underway. To get a look at what information is available and what the welfare reform act meant to people whose lives were directly affected, Sheila Zedlewski and Donald Alderson of the Urban Institute analyzed current data and presented the following preliminary results of the AFDC-to-TANF reform measures in April 2001:

- The proportion of single mothers on welfare who reported living with partners increased

- The proportion of African Americans on welfare who reported living with partners increased

- The proportion of adults on welfare who worked for pay rose

- The proportion of recipients who were new entrants to the welfare system was about the same, despite some

new state programs that attempt to divert adults from enrolling in TANF

- Adults on TANF in 1999 were no more disadvantaged than those on TANF in 1997

- Longer-term welfare recipients were significantly more disadvantaged than the new entrants

- The proportion of recipients blocked from access to the workforce due to less than high school education was the same (29 percent) in 1997 and 1999.

This analysis is based on a comparison of 1,831 families on Temporary Assistance for Needy Families (TANF) in 1997 and 850 families in 1999, representing 2.2 million and 1.5 million families, respectively. The characteristics and work activities presented were obtained from interviewing the adult most knowledgeable about the children in the family, usually the mother. (Sheila Zedlewski and Donald Alderson, *Families on Welfare in the Post-TANF Era: Do They Differ from Their Pre-TANF Counterparts?* Paper presented at the American Economics Association meeting, New Orleans, January 2001.)

EMPLOYMENT AND THE HOMELESS

It is extremely difficult for the homeless to escape their condition without a job. Yet it is equally difficult for the homeless to find and keep good jobs. Health Care for the Homeless Information Resource Center's newsletter "Employment for Homeless People: What Works, Fall 2000" listed the following barriers:

- Lack of transportation

- Medical and dental problems

- Housing instability

- Mental Illness

- Substance abuse

- Domestic violence

- Lack of job skills

- Criminal record

- Lack of childcare

- Lack of education

- Diminished self confidence

To these barriers must be added one more, namely the state of the labor market. The availability of jobs and the wages paid for the available jobs often determined whether or not people could remove themselves from homelessness.

Wage Barriers to Exiting Homelessness

Of the homeless respondents from the Urban Institute's 1996 study, 44 percent reported working in the previous month (see Table 3.7). Two percent earned income as self-employed entrepreneurs—by peddling or selling belongings—leaving 42 percent of the homeless respondents who worked for and were paid by an employer. Since 96 percent of the employed homeless people in the Urban Institute study earned their wages in a manner that gave others control over their income, it underscores the strong dependency working homeless people have on the wages and conditions of the labor market.

Advocates for the homeless are concerned that this dependency, combined with the current labor market conditions, actually supports continued homelessness. Since the majority of homeless people do not have more than a high-school education, and since a majority of the low-paying jobs go to those without more than a high-school education, advocates worry that the available job opportunities for homeless people provide an insufficient base for exiting homelessness.

WORK FOR THE HOMELESS

It costs money to live. Even homeless people have needs that can only be met with money. From needing something as simple as a toothbrush or a meal, to money for a newspaper and to call job prospects, homeless people need money to begin to improve their lives. Out of the need to survive, homeless people have come up with a number of ways to earn money, weaving their ventures among local ordinances, public opinion, and the labor market.

Street Newspapers: Bootstrap Initiatives

In the United States, as well as overseas, homeless people are publishing, writing for, and selling their own newspapers. *The 2002 North American Directory of Street Newspapers,* published by the National Coalition for the Homeless in April 2002 reported on 47 homeless newspapers in the United States and 6 in Canada.

Many street newspaper publishers belong to a professional organization, the North American Street Newspaper Association (NASNA), organized in Chicago in 1996. NASNA holds an annual conference, offers business advice and services, and supports street newspaper publishers in the same way that any professional organization supports its membership. They also lobby the government on homeless issues.

Generally, the street newspapers are loaned on credit to homeless vendors who then sell them for one to two dollars apiece. At the end of the workday, the vendor pays the publisher the agreed-upon price and pockets the remainder as profit. For example, Boston's *Spare Change* newspaper publishes 12,000 copies every two weeks. Vendors purchase newspapers for 25 cents apiece and resell them for $1.00, pocketing $.75 for each paper sold. New York

City's *Street News* gives the vendors ten free copies and allows them to earn $1.40 from each paper sold at $2.00.

This cooperative arrangement between publishers, vendors, and consumers has many benefits:

- Creation of jobs
- Supports the work ethic
- Accommodates the mobility of homeless people
- Provides reliable employment despite crisis living conditions
- Informs the public about homelessness
- Erases stereotypes of the lazy, drunken, illiterate, "unworthy" homeless person
- Gives the writers and vendors a sense of accomplishment
- Provides immediate cash to those who need it most.

Most of the homeless newspaper vendors have not been able to earn enough just from selling newspapers to move themselves from homelessness, but as the quality and availability of these publications grow, homeless people envision the street newspaper industry becoming a means of moving tens of thousands from homelessness.

THE STREET NEWS, NEW YORK CITY. The earliest known homeless publication, *The Street News,* was launched in 1989 by *The New York Times* and the New York Metropolitan Transportation Authority. By 1991, when the publication suffered from a scandal involving misuse of funds, *The Street News* was boasting some 25,000 copies per issue, which then fell to 8,000. By 2000 circulation was back up to 20,000. The paper is known for its radical political stance and unusual stories.

SPARE CHANGE, BOSTON. Begun in 1992 as one of the nation's first street newspapers to benefit the homeless, *Spare Change* is published every other week by the Homeless Empowerment Project (HEP) in Cambridge, Massachusetts. Its stated mission is to "play a role in ending homelessness in our community by providing income, skill development and self-advocacy opportunities to people who are homeless or at risk of homelessness." The newspaper provides a forum for creative expression and advocacy for homeless individuals. Along with the production, distribution, and sale of the street newspaper, HEP operates a training center for teaching computer skills to the homeless. They also sponsor a writer's workshop and promote a speaker's bureau.

Day Labor

Regular work, characterized by a permanent and ongoing relationship between employer and employee, does not figure significantly in the lives and routines of most homeless, as it is usually unavailable or inaccessible.

TABLE 3.7

Income levels, income sources, and employment, by homeless status, 1996

	Currently homeless clients (N = 2938)	Formerly homeless clients (N = 677)	Other service users (N = 518)
Mean income from all sources (last 30 days) [1]	$367	$470	$575
Median income from all sources (last 30 days) [1]	300	462	514
Income from all sources over last 30 days			
None	13(%)	5(%)	5(%)
Less than $100	17	9	6
$100 to $299	19	16	10
$300 to $499	18	30	25
$500 to $699	14	20	21
$700 to $799	4	6	7
$800 to $999	5	6	7
$1,000 to $1,199	3	2	3
$1,200 or more	4	5	12
No answer	3	1	2
Did any paid work at all in last 30 days	44	34	28
Sources of earned income in last 30 days			
Job lasting 3 or more months	13	14	16
Job expected to last 3 or more months	7	7	4
Temporary job, nonfarm work	8	6	3
Temporary job, farm work	3	*	1
Day job or pick-up job	14	5	5
Peddling or selling personal belongings	2	2	*
Received money/benefits from government sources in last 30 days			
Aid to Families with Dependent Children (AFDC)	10	8	10
Aid to Families with Dependent Children (AFDC) only families with children	52	45	45
General Assistance	9	16	7
Supplemental Security Income	11	29	26
Social Security Disability Insurance (SSDI)	8	16	10
Social Security	3	6	33
Veteran's disability payments (veterans only)	6	14	23
Veteran's pension (not disability related—veterans only)	2	1	16
Food stamps	37	48	37
Received means-tested government benefits [2]			
Any including food stamps	45	70	56
Any other than food stamps	28	57	47
Other sources of income over the last 30 days			
Parents	9	4	6
Friends (includes boyfriends or girlfriends)	12	9	5
Asking for money on the streets	8	3	*

* Denotes values that are less than 0.5 but greater than 0 percent.
[1] If an income range was reported by client, mid-point of range was used in calculating mean.
[2] AFDC, GA, SSI, food stamps, housing assistance.

SOURCE: Martha R. Burt, et al, "Table 3.8: Income Levels, Income Sources, and Employment, by Homeless Status," in *Homelessness: Programs and the People They Serve: Findings of the National Survey of Homeless Assistance Providers and Clients*, Urban Institute, Washington, DC, December 1999

Homelessness makes getting and keeping regular work difficult due to the lack of a fixed address, communication, and, in many cases, the inability to get a good night's sleep, clean up, and dress appropriately. Studies have found that the longer a person is homeless, the less likely he or she is to pursue wage labor and the more likely that person is to engage in some other form of work. For those who do participate in regular jobs, in most cases the wages received are not sufficient to escape from living on the street.

Day labor, wage labor secured on a day-to-day basis, typically at lower wages and changing locations, is somewhat easier for the homeless to secure. Day labor may involve unloading trucks, cleaning up warehouses, cutting grass, or washing windows. Day labor often fits the abilities of the homeless because transportation may be provided to the work site, and appearance, work history, and references are less important. Equally attractive to a homeless person, day labor usually pays cash at quitting time, thus providing immediate pocket money. Day labor jobs are, however, by definition, without a future. They can provide survival on the street, but are not generally sufficient to get a person off the street. Consequently, many homeless turn to shadow work.

Shadow Work

Shadow work refers to methods of getting money that are outside the normal economy, some of them illegal.

FIGURE 3.13

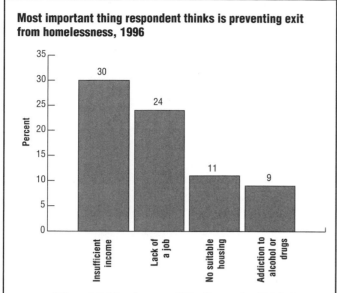

Most important thing respondent thinks is preventing exit from homelessness, 1996

SOURCE:"Figure 2.8: Most Important Thing Respondent Thinks Is Preventing Exit from Homelessness," in *Homelessness: Programs and the People They Serve: Findings of the National Survey of Homeless Assistance Providers and Clients*, Urban Institute, Washington, DC, December 1999

These methods include panhandling, scavenging, selling possessions, picking up cans and selling them, theft, selling one's blood or plasma, or peddling illegal goods, drugs, or services. A homeless person seldom engages in all of these activities consistently but may turn to some of them, as needed. Researchers estimate that 60 percent of the homeless engage in some shadow work. Shadow work is more common for homeless men than homeless women. Theft is more common for younger homeless persons.

A mixture of institutionalized assistance, wage labor, and shadow work are necessary for survival on the streets. Studies have found that many homeless people are very resourceful in surviving the rigors of street life and recommend that this resourcefulness be somehow channeled into training that can lead to jobs paying a living wage. Some observers suggest, however, that homeless people who have adapted to street life may likely need transitional socialization programs as much as programs that teach them a marketable skill.

Institutionalized Assistance

Institutionalized assistance refers to "established or routine monetary assistance patterned in accordance with tradition, legislation, or organizations" (David Snow, Leon Anderson, Theron Quist, and Daniel Cress, *Material Survival Strategies on the Street: Homeless People as Bricoleurs, Homelessness in America*, edited by the National Coalition for the Homeless, Oryx Press, 1996). This would include institutionalized labor, such as that provided by soup kitchens, shelters, and rehabilitation programs that sometimes pay the homeless for work related to facility operation. The number of people employed by these agencies is a small percentage of the homeless population. In addition, the pay—room, board, and a small stipend—tends to tie the homeless to the organization rather than providing the means to get off the street.

Institutionalized assistance also includes income supplements provided by government, family, and friends. According to the *Homelessness in America* study, while a considerable number of the homeless may receive some financial help from family or friends, it is usually small. Women seem to receive more help from family and friends and to remain on the streets for shorter periods of time than men. Cash from family and friends seems to decline with the amount of time spent on the street and with age.

EXITING HOMELESSNESS

The further down someone has fallen in his or her life circumstances, the harder it is to get up. This is particularly true of the homeless. The 1996 Urban Institute study revealed that homeless people say that the primary reason they cannot exit homelessness is insufficient income (see Figure 3.13). Of those clients surveyed, 54 percent cited employment-related reasons for why they remained homeless. Nearly a third (30 percent) cited insufficient income and nearly a quarter (24 percent) cited lack of a job.

Table 3.7 illustrates the lack of income experienced by the homeless. Eighty-one percent of the "currently" homeless had incomes of less than $700 in the 30 days before the study. Most of the homeless in the study were receiving their income from Aid to Families with Dependent Children (now referred to as TANF). Of formerly homeless people surveyed, the median income of $470 would amount to an annual income of $5,640, an amount well below even the lowest poverty level limit.

These income levels clearly demonstrate the financial difficulty a homeless person encounters in trying to permanently exit homelessness or poverty. Just as government spending on elderly programs can be argued to have made the lives of those over 65 significantly better, government spending applied to programs for the poor might raise them out of poverty, making their lives easier as well. The Housing and Urban Development (HUD) study shows that families with the benefit of government sponsored tenant assistance had an easier time moving in all regions of the nation in 1997 as compared to 1991 when less funding was available (*Rental Housing Assistance—The Worsening Crisis, A Report to Congress on Worst Case Housing Needs*, 2000).

In order to sustain life away from homelessness and poverty all of the problems that led a person into homelessness must be addressed, not only the financial ones. Persistent medical assistance, sometimes for an entire lifetime, has to be available for the mentally ill, including many of those with addiction and substance abuse problems. Furthermore without programs such as job training, assistance with general education, help with socialization skills, and in many instances counseling, the maintenance of a degree of independent life for the long term will be very difficult.

CHAPTER 4
THE HOUSING PROBLEM

A home was at one time defined as a place where a family resided, but as American society changed, so did the definition of home. A home is now considered a place where one or more people live together, a private place to which they have legal right and where strangers may be excluded. It is the place where people keep their belongings and where they feel safe from the outside world. For housing to be considered a home it should be permanent with an address. Furthermore, in the best of circumstances a home should not be substandard but should still be affordable. Most people would agree that a place to call home is a basic human right.

Those people who have no fixed address and no private space of their own, however temporary, are the homeless. The obvious solution to homelessness would be to find a home for everyone who needs one. There is plenty of housing available in the United States, certainly enough to shelter every single soul. The problem lies in the affordability of that housing. Most of the housing in the United States costs far more than the very poor can afford to rent or buy. According to the Census 2000, the median monthly gross rent for the nation's 35.7 million renter-occupied housing units (one-third of the nation's 105.5 million occupied housing units) was $602, a 5.4 percent increase over the $571 median for 1990. (See Table 4.1.) Renters in California led the nation in the share of their incomes spent on rent (27.7 percent). According to the Census Bureau, 9 of the nation's 10 highest-rent cities are in California, with median gross rents ranging from $985 to $1,272.

In June 2003 the National Association of Realtors reported $223,200 as the average price of an existing single-family home, which is less costly than a new home.

THE PRIMARY REASON FOR HOMELESSNESS

Research indicates that the primary cause of most homelessness is a simple inability to pay for housing, caused by some combination of low income and high housing costs. While many other factors may contribute to homelessness, such as a low level of educational achievement or mental illness, addressing these problems will seldom bring someone out of homelessness by itself. The underlying issue of not being able to afford housing will still need to be addressed.

New York University (NYU) researchers conducted a study that showed no real difference exists between homeless people and the rest of society, other than housing affordability issues. Funded by the National Institute of Mental Health (NIMH), the NYU team conducted a five-year study of 564 homeless families. In *Predictors of Homelessness Among Families in New York City: From Shelter Request to Housing Stability* (November 1998), they presented their results.

The research team found that when homeless families were provided with subsidies that allowed them to afford housing, 80 percent remained housed in their own residence for at least a year. This was true regardless of their social or personal attributes, such as their education level, race, or sex. This confirms the idea that while many homeless people face difficulties due to their personal backgrounds, these problems are not what drove most of them into homelessness. Furthermore, if they are given access to affordable housing, most will be able to take advantage of it.

HOUSING THE POOR

Broadly speaking, low-income housing is housing that is affordable to those in poverty. The federal government's official standard for low-income housing is that it should cost no more than 30 percent of the annual income of someone in poverty. This includes the cost of utilities. In 2002 a family of two people with an annual income of less than $12,047 was in poverty; a family of four with two

TABLE 4.1

Median gross rent and median gross rent as percent of household income, 1990 and 2000

Area	1990 Median gross rent	1990 Median gross rent as percent of household income (1989)	2000 Median gross rent	2000 Median gross rent as percent of household income (1999)
United States	$571	26.4	$602	25.5
Region				
Northeast	$638	26.4	$651	25.9
Midwest	$506	25.4	$533	24.0
South	$517	25.7	$559	25.0
West	$684	27.9	$694	27.1
State				
Alabama	$415	24.8	$447	24.8
Alaska	$714	23.8	$720	24.8
Arizona	$560	27.5	$619	26.6
Arkansas	$418	26.5	$453	24.4
California	$792	29.1	$747	27.7
Colorado	$533	26.1	$671	26.4
Connecticut	$764	26.6	$681	25.4
Delaware	$634	24.7	$639	24.3
District of Columbia	$612	25.4	$618	24.8
Florida	$613	28.0	$641	27.5
Georgia	$553	25.8	$613	24.9
Hawaii	$830	27.4	$779	27.2
Idaho	$422	23.8	$515	25.3
Illinois	$569	25.9	$605	24.4
Indiana	$477	24.3	$521	23.9
Iowa	$429	24.1	$470	23.2
Kansas	$474	24.5	$498	23.4
Kentucky	$408	24.9	$445	24.0
Louisiana	$450	27.9	$466	25.8
Maine	$535	26.8	$497	25.3
Maryland	$700	25.4	$689	24.7
Massachusetts	$741	26.8	$684	25.5
Michigan	$540	27.2	$546	24.4
Minnesota	$539	26.7	$566	24.7
Mississippi	$394	27.1	$439	25.0
Missouri	$470	25.2	$484	24.0
Montana	$396	25.0	$447	25.3
Nebraska	$445	23.7	$491	23.0
Nevada	$650	26.8	$699	26.5
New Hampshire	$701	26.4	$646	24.2
New Jersey	$756	26.3	$751	25.5
New Mexico	$473	26.5	$503	26.6
New York	$620	26.3	$672	26.8
North Carolina	$488	24.4	$548	24.3
North Dakota	$400	23.9	$412	22.3
Ohio	$483	25.3	$515	24.2
Oklahoma	$434	25.4	$456	24.3
Oregon	$521	25.5	$620	26.9
Pennsylvania	$516	26.1	$531	25.0
Rhode Island	$625	27.5	$553	25.7
South Carolina	$482	24.4	$510	24.4
South Dakota	$391	24.6	$426	22.9
Tennessee	$456	25.0	$505	24.8
Texas	$505	24.6	$574	24.4
Utah	$471	23.8	$597	24.9
Vermont	$570	27.1	$553	26.2
Virginia	$632	25.8	$650	24.5
Washington	$569	25.7	$663	26.5
West Virginia	$387	26.8	$401	25.8
Wisconsin	$510	24.9	$540	23.4
Wyoming	$425	23.7	$437	22.5
Puerto Rico	$261	29.4	$297	27.0

Note: The dollars have been adjusted to 2000 dollars using the government's Consumer Price Index (CPI). This means that the effect of inflation has been eliminated.

SOURCE: "Table 2. Median Gross Rent and Median Gross Rent as Percentage of Household Income for the United States, Regions, and States, and for Puerto Rico: 1990 and 2000," in "Housing Costs of Renters: 2000," *Census 2000 Brief,* U.S. Census Bureau, May 2003 [Online] http://www.census.gov/prod/2003pubs/c2kbr-21.pdf [accessed September 9, 2003]

children under age 18 was in poverty if their income was less than $18,244. Thus in 2002, low-income housing for a family of two should cost no more than $301 a month; for a family of four it should cost no more than $456 a month.

Not Enough Affordable Units Available

Researchers from every discipline agree that the number of housing units that are affordable to the poor is insufficient to meet needs. The poor essentially have two rental options: low-income housing units operated by local public housing authorities and privately-owned housing, whose owners accept Section 8 rental assistance vouchers issued by the federal government. In 2002 about 1.5 million families took advantage of the Section 8 vouchers. However, the rents permitted under the voucher program have not kept pace with actual rents in many markets. In his testimony before the House Subcommittee on Housing & Community Opportunity on April 23, 2002, Roy Ziegler of the National Leased Housing Association reported that many Section 8 vouchers go unused because there are not enough rental units available to which the vouchers can be applied.

According to a 1999 report from the U.S. Department of Housing and Urban Development (HUD) (*Waiting In Vain: An Update On America's Housing Crisis,* Washington, D.C.), in 1998 a family spent an average of 33 months on a waiting list for HUD-assisted housing operated by the largest public housing authorities. In some large cities the waiting period was even longer, ranging from five years in Washington, D.C. and Cleveland to six years in Oakland, California, and eight years in New York City. The average waiting period for a Section 8 rental assistance voucher was five years in Memphis and Chicago, seven years in Houston, eight years in New York City, and 10 years in Los Angeles and Newark.

In December 2000 Congress established the bipartisan Millennial Housing Commission (MHC) to examine the role of the federal government in meeting the nation's housing needs. In *Meeting Our Nation's Housing Challenges* (Washington, D.C., May 2002), the commission stated that "there is simply not enough affordable housing. The inadequacy of supply increases dramatically as one moves down the ladder of family earnings. The challenge is most acute for rental housing in high-cost areas, and the most egregious problem is for the very poor."

The report presented data from the Census Bureau's 1999 American Housing Survey showing that in 1999, one in four American households (nearly 28 million) spent more on housing than the federal government considers affordable and appropriate (more than 30 percent of income). One-quarter (25 percent) of renter households (8.5 million) spent 58 percent of their income on housing, while 9 percent of owner households (6.4 million) spent 50 percent of their income for housing. The actual monthly housing cost for the 8.5 million renter households was $426; $175 was considered affordable. The 6.4 million owner households paid $300 a month for housing; $163 was considered affordable.

The National League of Cities, in its seventeenth annual opinion survey of municipal elected officials (*The State of America's Cities,* 2001), found that 28 percent of city officials believed that President George W. Bush should devote the most attention to increasing the availability of affordable housing (see Table 4.2). In response to a similar question two years earlier, only 3 percent of those officials said they would want to address Congress about housing in their cities.

The Joint Center for Housing Studies of Harvard University reported in *The State of the Nation's Housing: 2003* that in 2002, 3 in 10 households had housing affordability problems. More than 14.3 million owner and renter households spent more than half their income on housing and an additional 17.3 million owner and renter households spent 30 to 50 percent. More than 9 million households faced the additional burdens of living in overcrowded and substandard houses. These households earned around $10,000 a year in jobs that paid minimum wage or below. When 30 percent or more of a meager income is spent on housing, hardship is the result.

At Risk of Becoming Homeless

In January 2001 the HUD Office of Policy Development and Research released the results of an in-depth study (*A Report on Worst Case Housing Needs in 1999—New Opportunity Amid Continuing Challenges*). The report found that in the two years between 1997 and 1999, a time of economic prosperity, the number of renter households with worst-case housing needs declined at least 8 percent (440,000 households), reversing the preceding 10-year trend of growing worst-case needs. However, there were still nearly 5 million households in serious need of housing assistance. HUD defines families with "worst-case needs" as those who:

- Are renters.

- Do not receive housing assistance from federal, state, or local government programs.

- Have incomes below 50 percent of their local area median family income (AMI), as determined by HUD.

- Pay more than one-half of their income for rent and utilities, or live in severely substandard housing.

In other words, these are extremely impoverished people who do not own their housing and can barely afford to pay their housing costs, or can only afford to stay in the very worst housing. Of all the people who had housing, they are the ones closest to being forced into

TABLE 4.2

Opinions of city officials polled by the National League of Cities, October 2000

In which of the priority areas listed below do you think the federal government and the new presidential administration should devote the most new attention and significant resources toward helping American communities achieve their true potential? (List your top 3.)

Investing in regional economic and workforce development	67%
Increasing the availability of affordable housing	28%
Revitalizing and redeveloping neighborhoods	28%
Supporting local and regional "smart growth" or growth management strategies	34%
Investing in infrastructure (roads/transit, water, sewer)	67%
Investing in public education and other supports for children, youth, and families	65%
Protecting natural resources and local environmental quality	2%

SOURCE: "12. In which of the priority areas listed below do you think the federal government and the new Presidential Administration should devote the most new attention and significant resources toward helping American communities achieve their true potential?," in *The State of America's Cities: The Seventeenth Annual Opinion Survey of Municipal Elected Officials,* National League of Cities, Washington, DC, January 2001

homelessness. HUD found that 10.9 million people inhabited the 4.9 million households in the worst-case housing classification in 1999. This number included 1.4 million elderly and 3.6 million children.

The reduction in the number of worst-case households between 1997 and 1999 was attributed to income growth among low-income renters rather than to growth in the number of affordable rental housing units. The report stated that the number of units affordable and available to renters with extremely low income fell, and also predicted that in the event of an economic slowdown, income growth among low-income renters could very well be reversed. (According to the U.S. Census Bureau, the nation entered a period of recession in 2001 from which it had not fully recovered as of late 2003.)

For as long as worst-case needs have been reported, affordability rather than housing quality has been the main problem facing renters. A household that spends more than 50 percent of its income on housing is considered severely cost-burdened. Using data from the 2001 American Housing Survey, *The State of the Nation's Housing, 2003* found that in 2001 the largest group of households (75 percent) experiencing serious cost burdens was from the bottom income quintile (the lowest of five income classes). With a median annual income of $10,500, this group had less than $500 a month left after paying rent to cover all other expenses (data are not shown).

Working Families Struggle to Keep Up

Even those with higher incomes face housing affordability problems. Included in the group of severely cost-burdened households was 16 percent of the lower-middle income quintile and 9 percent of the top three income quintiles. Working hard no longer guarantees decent, affordable housing. In 2001 there were 5.2 million households that were moderately to severely cost-burdened despite having incomes that were one to three times the full-time, minimum-wage equivalent (between $10,713 and $36,136 in 2003).

According to *Rental Housing for America's Poor Families: Farther Out of Reach Than Ever, 2002,* a report by the National Low Income Housing Coalition (NLIHC), 2002 marked the fourth year in a row in which there was not a single place in the United States where a family with one full-time worker earning the minimum wage could afford the local fair-market rent for a two-bedroom apartment. The problem of housing affordability is particularly acute in large metropolitan areas on the east and west coasts, where even a one-bedroom apartment is out of the reach of the working poor. Using NLIHC data relative to a "housing wage," *The State of the Nation's Housing, 2003* reported that: "[T]he amount it takes to afford an apartment at 30 percent of income—is two to three times the minimum wage in 92 metropolitan areas and 63 nonmetropolitan counties, and more than triple the minimum wage in 24 metro areas and 12 nonmetro counties."

Reasons for the Lack of Low-Income Housing

The major reasons for the lack of low-income housing are declining federal support; bureaucratic red tape, fraud, and waste; and a variety of local factors that affect new construction.

DECLINING FEDERAL SUPPORT. The development and operation of low-income housing units depends on the government funding administered by HUD. In "The Rise and Fall of Public Housing" (*Regulation,* Summer 2002), Michael A. Stegman, the MacRae Professor of Public Policy and Business at the University of North Carolina, chronicled the decline of federal investment in low-income housing since 1976. According to Stegman, spending on subsidized housing fell 80 percent, from about 5 percent of the federal budget in 1976 to 1 percent in 2000. (In subsidized housing, HUD pays money to local housing authorities to cover the difference between rent payments and operating expenses.) Stegman contended that while federal spending was declining, the need for housing assistance was rising. Current political realities do not bode well for increased spending on low-income housing. HUD's proposed fiscal year 2004 budget was $31.3 billion, 7 percent lower than in 2001. In a press release announcing the proposed budget, HUD acknowledged that national defense and homeland security now take precedence in federal spending.

FRAUD, WASTE, DELAYS HAMPER REHABILITATION. A major HUD goal is to increase the supply of affordable, decent, and safe rental housing, but it has not been particularly successful in this regard. In *Department of Housing and Urban Development: Status of Achieving Key Outcomes and Addressing Major Management Challenges* (Washington, D.C., July 2001), the U.S. General Accounting Office (GAO), the watchdog arm of Congress, noted that HUD programs have been plagued by fraud, waste, and errors.

One of the few federal housing production programs administered by HUD in recent years is the Urban Revitalization Demonstration Program, commonly known as HOPE VI. This program provides grants to local public housing authorities, who contract with private developers to rehabilitate public housing. Between fiscal years 1993 and 2001, HUD awarded about $4.5 billion in HOPE VI revitalization grants to 98 public housing authorities for 165 sites. In 2002 Congress charged the GAO with investigating and reporting on progress and HUD's oversight of the projects. In *Public Housing: HUD's Oversight of HOPE VI Sites Needs to Be More Consistent* (Washington, D.C., May 2003), the GAO reported that as of December 31, 2002, construction was complete on only 15 of the 165 sites. About one-quarter (27 percent) of the planned rehabilitation work had been done but nearly half (47 percent, or $2.1 billion) of the grant money had been spent. Work had been completed by the deadline on only three of the grants and the construction deadlines had expired on 42 grants. For fiscal year 2004 the Bush administration proposed eliminating the HOPE VI program; as of September 2003 Congress's counter-proposal was to fund the program at $50 million, down 91 percent from the $574 million funded in fiscal year 2003.

LOW PROFIT MARGINS BRING NEGLECT. As of 2001 HUD assisted nearly 30,000 privately owned and operated multifamily properties through subsidies, financing, or mortgage insurance. The contracts with private owners limit profits and often limit the monies put back into the property for repairs. The existing housing available to renters at the lowest income levels often suffers from lack of upkeep. Neglected maintenance results in deterioration and sometimes removal from the housing inventory altogether.

According to *The State of the Nation's Housing, 2003,* about 705,000 tenants receiving government housing assistance lived in substandard conditions. HUD data show that between 1997 and 1999 more than 1 million very-low-income residential units were lost as old buildings were torn down or owners opted out of low-income programs; also lost were 750,000 units available to the next income level (30% of area median income).

FACTORS THAT INHIBIT CONSTRUCTION. Construction of low-income units is hampered by community resistance, regulations that increase the cost of construction, and limits on tax credits that make new construction unprofitable.

In his "Dissenting Statement to the Report of the Millennial Housing Commission" (May 30, 2002), Commissioner Robert Rector complained: "It is a simple fact that those cities that have the greatest 'affordability' problems are those that have 'smart growth' or other regulatory policies that severely limit new housing growth. Policies such as restrictive zoning, antiquated building codes, and high impact fees for new construction reduce housing supply and greatly increase costs for everyone in a community."

To many people, the prospect of low-income subsidized housing is synonymous with rising crime, falling property values, and overcrowded classrooms, and it is cause for protest. Resistance to the construction of low-income housing is said to be evidence of a not-in-my-backyard (NIMBY) way of thinking. *From NIMBY to Good Neighbors: Recent Studies Reinforce that Apartments Are Good for a Community,* a 2003 report from the National Multi Housing Council/National Apartment Association, summarizes research showing that smart growth may depend on the development of more high-density housing, such as apartments.

Developers complain that there is no profit to be made from building and operating low-income housing. The 1986 Low-Income Housing Tax Credit program gave the states $1.25 per capita in tax credits toward the private development of low-income housing. In "A New Era for Affordable Housing" (*National Real Estate Investor,* March 1, 2003), H. Lee Murphy reported National Council of State Agencies' data indicating that construction peaked in 1994, when 117,100 apartment units were built with the credits. Skyrocketing construction costs brought a decline in new construction, which reached a low of 66,900 units in 2000. In 2001, Congress raised the per capita allotment to $1.75 and provided that the formula would rise each year with inflation. The tax credits financed the construction of 75,000 new units in 2001.

AN EXAMPLE: ST. PAUL, MINNESOTA. A housing research project was conducted in 2000, a time of economic prosperity, by the Wilder Research Center of St. Paul, Minnesota. The study illustrated how many trends converged to limit the supply of low-income housing in the region:

- The regional economic boom—The strong economy drew people to the area for work, creating a higher demand for housing and driving up prices.

- All-time-high home ownership—Low mortgage rates led to increased home ownership and an increased demand for new homes, at the expense of further construction of apartments and rental units.

- Decline in federal housing subsidies—With government cutbacks, housing developers who once relied on outside funding preferred to compete in the hot housing market.

- Suburban growth—New housing was in the suburbs and focused on upscale, not affordable, housing.

- Property taxes—led to higher rents. Renters pay more taxes per square foot than homeowners, absorbing the higher tax burden passed on through rent costs.

- Aging housing stock—A large portion of affordable housing money goes towards maintenance, repair, and renovation, which is less for new units.

Affordable Housing for the Homeless

In testimony before the House Subcommittee on Housing and Community Opportunity, Committee on Financial Services, on June 21, 2003, Nan P. Roman, President of the National Alliance to End Homelessness, spoke about affordable housing and the homeless. She claimed that for 80 percent of the homeless, "homelessness is a housing affordability issue." Roman also testified that for the remaining 20 percent—the chronically homeless who suffer from a variety of disabilities ranging from mental illness to substance abuse, HIV/AIDS, and physical problems—200,000 units of supportive housing such as group homes, multi-family units, or individual homes with programs to address their needs "could end chronic homelessness."

HABITAT FOR HUMANITY

One group dedicated to solving the housing problem one house at a time was the brainchild of Millard and Linda Fuller, who formed Habitat for Humanity International with a group of supporters in 1976. The purpose of this worldwide Christian service organization is to provide simple housing for the needy, built by volunteers assisted by the future homeowner. The homeowner assumes an interest-free, 30-year mortgage, and materials are funded through donations and fund-raising activities. The idea is to give people assistance accompanied by responsibility.

As of July 2003 Habitat for Humanity International had built 150,000 houses in 3,000 communities worldwide. More than 625,000 people have benefited. Homes in developing countries may cost less than $1,000 to build while the average house in the United States can cost up to $46,600. Not all houses are new; the organization also restores older homes. Many volunteers travel to other countries to build homes. The most famous volunteers, former President Jimmy Carter and his wife, Rosalynn, made their first work trip in 1984 to New York City, sparking widespread interest in the movement. In the week of June 7 to 13, 2003, the Jimmy Carter Work Project 2003 built 92 homes.

WHERE THE HOMELESS LIVE

When faced with high rents and low housing availability, many poor people become homeless. What happens to them? Where do they live? Research shows that after becoming homeless, many people move around, staying in one place for a while, then in another place. Many homeless people take advantage of homeless shelters at some point. Such shelters may be funded by the federal government, by religious organizations, or by other private homeless advocates.

Emergency Housing: Shelters and Transitional Housing

Typically, a homeless shelter provides dormitory-style sleeping accommodations and bathing facilities, with varying services for laundry, telephone calls, and other needs. Residents are often limited in the length of their stays and must leave the shelter during the day under most circumstances. Transitional housing, on the other hand, is intended to bridge the gap between the shelter or street and permanent housing, with appropriate services to move the homeless into independent living. It may be a room in a hotel or motel, or it may be a subsidized apartment.

Counting the Homeless in Shelters

According to the U.S. Conference of Mayors, in 2000 the number of demands for emergency shelter beds in the 25 major cities surveyed increased overall by an average of 19 percent, compared to a 12 percent increase in 1999. Of all the cities surveyed, 88 percent reported an increase in demand, compared to 69 percent in 1999.

The 2000 census, however, showed a decline in the number of people living in homeless shelters since the 1990 census. The Census Bureau counted 170,706 people living in shelters in March 2000, down 4 percent from the 178,638 people counted 10 years earlier. Based on their own experience, advocates for the homeless denied that there could have been a decline in the numbers. They criticized the Census Bureau's count as flawed, complaining that the survey excluded shelters with fewer than 100 beds and could not provide a full picture of homelessness because it was conducted over only three nights. In its report, *Emergency and Transitional Shelter Population: 2000: Census 2000 Special Reports* (Washington, D.C., October 2001), the Census Bureau cautions that its count is not "representative of the entire population that could be defined as living in emergency and transitional shelters."

Homeless Youth

In 2002 an attempt to count the number of homeless people in Monterey County, California, was undertaken. Researchers focused on what was called "the fastest growing segment of the homeless population," homeless youth ("Homeless Census and Homeless Youth/Foster Teen Study" [Online] http://www.appliedsurveyresearch.org/products/MC_Homeless02_report.pdf [accessed September 8, 2003]). Based on an actual count and interviews with 2,681 homeless individuals, the researchers estimated that somewhere between 8,686 and 11,214 people were

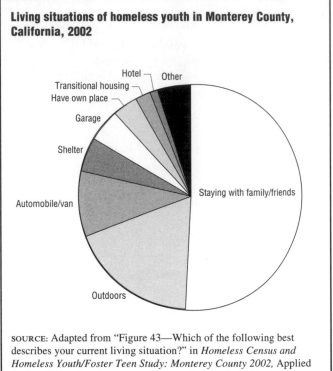

FIGURE 4.1

Living situations of homeless youth in Monterey County, California, 2002

SOURCE: Adapted from "Figure 43—Which of the following best describes your current living situation?" in *Homeless Census and Homeless Youth/Foster Teen Study: Monterey County 2002,* Applied Survey Research and Monterey County, Department of Social Services, Monterey, CA, 2002

homeless in Monterey County at some time during 2002. The majority of those interviewed (65 percent) were found on the street and 14 percent were in transitional housing, while another 6 percent were in emergency shelters.

Of the individuals counted, more than one-fifth (21 percent) were between the ages of 14 and 18. The youths were asked to describe their current living situation. The majority (61 percent) reported staying temporarily with family or friends. (See Figure 4.1.) More than one-fifth (22 percent) reported they were living outdoors, 6.1 percent were living in a shelter, and 11.5 percent were living in an automobile/van. This particular segment of the homeless tended to shy away from shelters, especially if they were underage and feared interference from the authorities.

Homeless Children

In accordance with the provisions of the Education for Homeless Children and Youth program, Title VII-B of the McKinney-Vento Homeless Assistance Act (42 USC 11431 et seq.), every three years the states that are receiving funds under the act must submit a report to the U.S. Department of Education regarding the estimated number of homeless children in the state. According to the *Report to Congress Fiscal Year 2000* (Washington, D.C., 2000), in 2000 there were an estimated 866,899 homeless children in 46 reporting states, up 176 percent from the 314,449 homeless children reported in 48 states in 1997. (See Table 4.3.) About two-thirds (67 percent) were enrolled in

TABLE 4.3

Primary nighttime residence of homeless children, by state, 2000

State	Primary nighttime residence					
	Shelter	Doubled-up	Un-sheltered	Other	Unknown	Total
Alabama	2,984	3,243	105	-	-	6,332
Alaska	1,057	548	160	723	3,178	5,666
Arizona[1]	1,288	6,225	841	1,408	1,416	11,178
Arkansas	2,629	1,442	127	190	1,136	5,524
California	61,182	80,058	17,640	130,145	-	289,025
Colorado	1,773	1,976	436	1,326	893	6,404
Connecticut	3,151	-	-	-	-	3,151
Delaware	1,100	-	-	-	-	1,100
Florida	-	-	-	-	-	-
Georgia	14,717	3,287	-	1,619	1	19,623
Hawaii	563	80	388	-	-	1,031
Idaho	218	452	13	45	28	756
Illinois	1,547	14,567	260	-	-	16,374
Indiana	14,060	11,200	1,400	840	1,500	29,000
Iowa	-	-	-	-	-	-
Kansas	2,075	1,175	43	61	20	3,374
Kentucky	1,294	5,798	702	250	292	8,336
Louisiana	10,438	4,873	565	-	-	15,876
Maine	4,913	-	-	-	-	4,913
Maryland	3,618	820	-	1,086	229	5,753
Massachusetts	-	-	-	-	-	-
Michigan	28,900	11,376	2,054	3,043	2,528	47,901
Minnesota	2,396	-	-	-	303	2,699
Mississippi[2]	-	-	-	-	-	-
Missouri	7,264	6,741	5,094	2,277	207	21,583
Montana	1,113	1,127	168	157	170	2,735
Nebraska	5,119	786	94	719	445	7,163
Nevada	192	992	35	485	-	1,704
New Hampshire[3]	4	-	-	-	-	4
New Jersey	6,435	1,064	5	8,940	71	16,515
New Mexico	682	1,264	-	269	-	2,215
New York	9,165	-	-	-	-	9,165
North Carolina	-	-	-	-	-	-
North Dakota	93	130	-	8	1	232
Ohio	7,124	17,809	2,968	-	1,780	29,681
Oklahoma	2,998	3,793	127	-	-	6,918
Oregon	12,540	4,390	2,900	12,000	920	32,750
Pennsylvania	17,000	3,000	1,000	-	-	21,000
Puerto Rico	649	100	100	858	500	2,207
Rhode Island	1,286	53	1	1	2	1,343
South Carolina	1,731	4,219	33	196	36	6,215
South Dakota	2,968	1,245	381	-	379	4,973
Tennessee	2,300	2,600	275	443	-	5,618
Texas	29,910	90,728	-	29,975	-	150,613
Utah	1,668	3,845	282	2,402	581	8,778
Vermont	-	-	-	-	276	276
Virginia	12,631	2,649	174	572	952	16,978
Washington	15,703	-	-	-	-	15,703
West Virginia	402	2,061	-	355	651	3,469
Wisconsin	2,718	1,220	244	617	55	4,854
Wyoming	150	550	-	-	108	808
Totals	306,404	301,195	38,732	201,313	19,255	866,899

- Data were not provided.
[1] Only 34 school districts responded.
[2] Data were reported by percentage: shelters, 23 percent; doubled-up, 75 percent; un-sheltered, 2 percent.
[3] Data were requested but not consistently reported by school district.

SOURCE: "Table 2. Primary Nighttime Residence of Homeless Children and Youth," in *Education for Homeless Children and Youth Program, Report to Congress, Fiscal Year 2000*, U.S. Department of Education, Washington, DC, December 2000

school, and the greatest number of those were in preschool and elementary school. More than one-third (35 percent) of these children lived in shelters; 35 percent stayed doubled up with others, presumably family or friends; 25 percent lived in motels and the like. Most distressing for those concerned about the health and well-being of children is that 38,732 children lived unsheltered. By far the greatest number of unsheltered children (17,640) lived in California. (See Figure 4.2.)

Proper and permanent housing is essential to the well-being of children. The same might be said for adults.

Illegal Occupancy

Poor neighborhoods are often full of abandoned buildings. Even the best-intentioned landlords cannot afford to maintain their properties in these areas. Many have let their buildings deteriorate or have simply walked away, leaving the fate of the building and its residents in the hands of the government. Despite overcrowding and unsafe conditions, many homeless people move into these dilapidated buildings illegally, glad for what shelter they can find. Municipal governments, overwhelmed by long public-housing waiting lists and a lack of funds and personnel, are often unable or unwilling to strictly enforce housing laws, allowing the homeless to become "squatters" rather than forcing them into the streets. Some deliberately turn a blind eye to the problem, knowing they have no better solution for the homeless.

The result is a multitude of housing units with deplorable living conditions—tenants bedding down in illegal boiler basements or sharing beds with children or in-laws, bathrooms with strangers. The buildings may have leaks and rot, rusted fire escapes, and rat and roach infestations. Given the alternative, many homeless people feel lucky to be sheltered.

THE RISK OF SQUATTING. These situations can leave the homeless vulnerable to legal remedies or public criticism. In December of 1999, in Worcester, Massachusetts, a homeless couple had taken up residence in an abandoned building. One of them allegedly knocked over a candle during an argument and the building caught fire. The Worcester fire department was called, and six firefighters were killed. The homeless man and woman were each charged with involuntary manslaughter. The public outcry against the homeless couple, and against homeless people in general, reached national proportions. Frustration ran rampant in the ranks of homeless advocates. Most believed the Worcester couple was guilty of nothing more than trying to stay alive. In an Associated Press story dated December 8, 1999, Nicole Witherbee, policy coordinator for the Massachusetts Coalition for the Homeless, voiced her frustration: "We make laws all the time, they can't panhandle, they can't loiter, we don't have enough

FIGURE 4.2

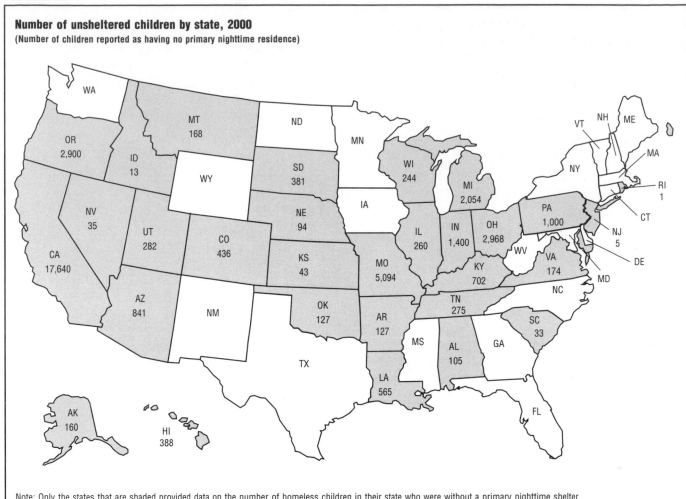

Number of unsheltered children by state, 2000
(Number of children reported as having no primary nighttime residence)

Note: Only the states that are shaded provided data on the number of homeless children in their state who were without a primary nighttime shelter.

SOURCE: Created by Information Plus from data in "Table 2. Primary Nighttime Residence of Homeless Children and Youth," in *Education for Homeless Children and Youth Program, Report to Congress, Fiscal Year 2000,* U.S. Department of Education, Washington, DC, December 2000

shelter beds, so when they go into abandoned buildings it's trespassing. So where is it they're supposed to be?"

STUDIES OF HOMELESSNESS IN THE WELFARE REFORM ERA

The Personal Responsibility and Work Opportunity Reconciliation Act of 1996 (PRWORA) (also called the welfare reform law; PL 104-193) placed a five-year time limit on families receiving cash assistance, after which they would be cut off. In April 2001 the National Welfare Monitoring and Advocacy Partnership Agency published its findings on the status of 4,988 former or current recipients of either welfare checks or some other form of public assistance (such as food stamps) (*Welfare to What? Part II,* National Coalition for the Homeless/Los Angeles Coalition to End Hunger & Homelessness/National Welfare Monitoring and Advocacy Partnership, 2001). The study did not claim a causal relationship between welfare reform and hardship, but it did find that many of the families affected by welfare reform were enduring hardship.

Only half (50 percent) of the survey respondents had living conditions that could be described as stable (rental unit, owned a home). (See Figure 4.3.) The other half were either homeless or staying with family/friends.

In *Housing Strategies to Strengthen Welfare Policy and Support Working Families* (Center on Urban & Metropolitan Policy, The Brookings Institution, and The Center on Budget and Policy Priorities, Washington, D.C., April 2002) Barbara Sard and Margy Waller reported that work did not solve the housing problems of families forced to leave welfare. Their analysis showed that the average total monthly income of households that previously received welfare benefits and had at least one working member was only $1,261 (in 2002 dollars). (In 2002 the federal poverty threshold for a family of three with two children under age 18 was $1,208 per month). According to the authors, "a family with this income would have to pay 58 percent of its total income to rent a two-bedroom unit at the Fair Market Rent in jurisdictions with rental costs at the national median."

FIGURE 4.3

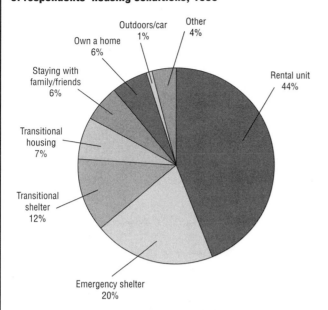

National Welfare Monitoring and Advocacy Partnership survey of respondents' housing conditions, 1999

Outdoors/car 1%

Other 4%

Own a home 6%

Staying with family/friends 6%

Transitional housing 7%

Transitional shelter 12%

Emergency shelter 20%

Rental unit 44%

SOURCE: Maura Rozell, et al., "Figure 6: Respondents Housing Conditions: Almost 50% living homeless in one form or another," in *Welfare to What? Part II: Laying the Groundwork for the 2002 Congressional TANF Reauthorization Debate,* National Coalition for the Homeless, Los Angeles Coalition to End Hunger & Homelessness, on behalf of the National Welfare Monitoring and Advocacy Partnership, Washington, DC, April 19, 2001

Library
Academy of the Holy Cross
4920 Strathmore Avenue
Kensington, MD 20895

CHAPTER 5
FEDERAL GOVERNMENT AID FOR THE HOMELESS

When there is a problem as widespread as homelessness, many people in the United States expect the government to step in. Exactly what the government's role in combating homelessness should be is a topic for debate. Some people believe it is the duty of the government to look out for the citizen in every way. Others point out that government help has often been misdirected or inadequate; in some instances, it has even added to the problem. Some feel that people are better served by working things out for themselves. Federal programs for the homeless reflect a consensus that is somewhere between the two extremes.

A TIMELINE OF GOVERNMENT INVOLVEMENT

Since 1860 the federal government has been actively involved with the housing industry, specifically the low-income housing industry. In 1860 the government conducted the first partial census on housing—by counting slave dwellings. Twenty years later the U.S. Census focused on the living quarters of the rest of the population, conducting a full housing census. Since then the federal government has played an increasingly larger role in combating housing problems in the United States:

- 1892—Congress designated $20,000 for a Labor Department study on slum conditions in Baltimore, New York, Chicago, and Philadelphia, the four cities with populations over 200,000 at that time. The study revealed that 14 percent of the cities' populations lived in slums under crowded conditions and were mostly foreign immigrants. Most spent one-third or more of their income on rent.

- 1908—President Theodore Roosevelt appointed a Housing Commission to study the problems in American slums; among the suggestions made by the panel were broad federal acquisition of slum properties and direct loans from the federal government to finance the renovation and construction of decent, sanitary housing which the poor could buy or occupy at low interest rates or rents.

- 1925—Borrowing and mortgaging properties reached their highest levels ever to that date. The rate of foreclosures also started to rise, leading to increased homelessness. Although no one knew it at the time, the debts that Americans had run up for their housing would be a major problem just a few years later.

- 1929—Stocks trading at the New York Stock Exchange suffered a tremendous crash in prices. The Great Depression had begun.

- 1932—As many Americans lost their jobs and failing banks called in their loans, homelessness skyrocketed. The Emergency Relief and Construction Act authorized the Reconstruction Finance Corporation to lend government money to corporations to build housing for low-income families.

- 1933—The National Industrial Recovery Act allowed the Public Works Administration (a government-sponsored work program) to use federal funds for slum clearance, low-cost housing, and subsistence homesteads; close to 40,000 units were produced that year.

- 1937—The United States Housing Act of 1937 established the Public Housing Administration (which was later merged into the Federal Housing Administration [FHA] and the Department of Housing and Urban Development [HUD]) to create low-rent housing programs across the country through the establishment of local public housing agencies.

- 1938—The National Housing Act Amendments were implemented. They allowed the FHA to insure low-income rental projects built for profit.

- 1940—The U.S. Census, reporting on the first comprehensive survey of the nation's housing stock, showed that 18 percent of the housing units needed major repairs, 31 percent lacked running water, 44 percent had neither a bathtub nor a shower, and 35 percent lacked a flush toilet. The worst conditions generally were found in inner-city slums and in the South.

- 1941—The United States entered World War II (1939–45). The economy surged to meet wartime needs, and millions of young men entered the military. As a result, the Great Depression came to a close.

- 1946—The Farmers Home Administration (FmHA) was created under the Department of Agriculture to provide low-income housing assistance in rural areas.

- 1949—The Housing Act of 1949 set the goals of "a decent home and a suitable environment" for every family and authorized an 810,000-unit public housing program over the next six years. Title I created the Urban Renewal program; Title V created the basic rural housing program under the FmHA, which put the federal government directly into the mortgage business.

- 1961—President John F. Kennedy called for action to accelerate urban renewal projects, make more mortgage funds available to those seeking housing, and provide decent housing for low-income and minority households. He made decent housing for all Americans a national objective. Congress passed the Housing Act of 1961, creating a new program for FHA-insured, low-income rental housing. This was the FHA's first direct subsidy program.

- 1965—Congress established the Department of Housing and Urban Development (HUD). Its goal was to create a new rent supplement program for low-income households in private housing.

- 1968—The Housing and Urban Development Act was passed in response to President Johnson's Message to Congress on Housing and Cities. The president declared that America's cities were in crisis and set a national housing goal of 26 million new units (6 million targeted to low- and moderate-income households) over the next 10 years. Congress provided two new options for low- and moderate-income rent subsidy programs and mortgage insurance for low- and moderate-income families with poor credit histories.

- 1970—A massive reorganization of federal housing organizations was completed. FHA was merged into HUD. With this reorganization, the FHA began to provide support for lower-priced housing and directed home ownership and rental opportunities to low-income households in inner cities.

- 1973—President Nixon declared a moratorium on housing and community development assistance, suspending all subsidized housing programs.

- 1974—The Housing and Community Development Act of 1974 created a new leased-housing program that included a certificate (voucher) program, expanding housing choices for low-income tenants, and fair-market rent ceilings to control the cost of the program. The voucher program soon became known as Section 8, after the section of the act that established it.

- 1981—The Housing and Community Development Amendments of 1981 required subsidized tenants to pay up to 30 percent of their income for rent before qualifying for assistance under Section 8 and further targeted the Section 8 and public housing programs to limit their benefits to the neediest households.

- 1983—The Housing and Urban-Rural Recovery Act of 1983 established rental rehabilitation programs and modified components of the Section 8 program to limit its benefits. Under Section 8, an experimental housing voucher program was established, and new rehabilitation grants and housing development grants were created.

- 1987—The Stewart B. McKinney Homelessness Assistance Act was passed. This was the first federal act aimed directly at helping the homeless. It established new programs and funding for HUD to provide emergency shelter to the homeless and eventually help secure permanent housing for them.

- 1989—The HUD Reform Act of 1989 was enacted. Its intent was to clean up HUD and prevent the misuse of funds that had been plaguing the agency.

- 1990—The National Affordable Housing Act renewed the federal government's commitment to home ownership, tenant-based assistance, and subsidized housing. The Low-Income Housing Preservation and Residential Home Ownership Act demonstrated a federal commitment to permanent preservation of assisted low-income, multi-family housing; the act also repealed the rental rehabilitation grant and the rehabilitation loan program. A special homeless assistance component of the moderate rehabilitation program was retained.

THE MCKINNEY-VENTO HOMELESS ASSISTANCE ACT

Widespread public outcry over the plight of the homeless in the early 1980s prompted Congress to pass the Stewart B. McKinney Homeless Assistance Act of 1987. The act was renamed by Congress the McKinney-Vento Homeless Assistance Act in 2000 (H.R. 5417) to honor Representative Bruce Vento's service to the homeless. The range and reach of the act has broadened over the years. Money authorized by the act went, initially, toward the funding of homeless shelters. Amendments to the act later enabled funding and other services to support permanent housing and other programs to help the homeless. HUD administers most McKinney-Vento funds.

Program Structure

Programs administered under the McKinney-Vento Act as of 2003 fall into three distinct categories. The first, a cluster of activities known as the Continuum of Care programs, are competitive grants intended to help communities and organizations provide comprehensive services to the homeless. The second is a single formula grant program, meaning that it is not competitive. This program is handled as part of community development planning and is targeted to states, large cities, counties, and territories to provide funds for emergency shelters. The third program, authorized under Title V of McKinney-Vento and called, for that reason, the Title V program, makes available properties to be used to house the homeless.

Continuum of Care

HUD's website (*Homeless Assistance Programs*, HUD, Washington, D.C., August 26, 2003 [Online] http://www.hud.gov/offices/cpd/homeless/programs/index.cfm) describes the concept behind these programs as follows: "A continuum of care system is designed to address the critical problem of homelessness through a coordinated community-based process of identifying needs and building a system to address those needs. The approach is predicated on the understanding that homelessness is not caused merely by a lack of shelter, but involves a variety of underlying, unmet needs—physical, economic, and social."

Those applying for funds under these programs are expected to survey and assess local needs and to fashion suitable answers to needs to combat homelessness comprehensively. Three major programs and some additional demonstration and rural efforts have developed over the years.

SUPPORTIVE HOUSING PROGRAM (SHP). The aim of SHP is to provide housing to the homeless as well as services that will enable clients of the program to reach economic independence and control over their lives. SHP provides up to $200,000 for the acquisition, construction, or refurbishing of buildings to house people (ranging up to $400,000 in high-cost areas). The program underwrites 75 percent of the operating cost, including administration. Support programs may take almost any form so long as they help the homeless achieve independence, including skills training, childcare, education, transportation assistance, and job referrals. Elements of the program include transitional housing for 24 months, permanent housing for the disabled, supportive services without housing, havens

for the hard-to-reach and the mentally ill, and innovative programs to solve problems of homelessness.

SHELTER PLUS CARE (S+C). This program, initiated in 1990, helps agencies that specifically target the hardest to serve homeless: those with mental and physical disabilities living on the street or in shelters, including drug addicts and AIDS sufferers. The program provides for rental assistance funded by HUD and other sources. Housing in this program can be in the form of group homes or individual units delivered with supportive services. Grant funds must be matched with local dollars. Rental assistance includes four types of contracts: (1) direct contract with a low-income tenant (Tenant-Based Rental Assistance); (2) building owner contracts (Project-Based Rental Assistance); (3) contracts with non-profit organizations (Sponsor-Based Rental Assistance); and (4) single room occupancy contracts provided by public housing authorities (PHAs) (SRO-Based Rental Assistance). Subsidies for projects are available for 10 years; assistance to sponsors and tenants is available for 5 years.

SINGLE ROOM OCCUPANCY (SRO). Single-room-occupancy housing is housing in a dormitory-style building where each person has his or her own private room but shares kitchens, bathrooms, and lounges. SRO housing is generally the cheapest type of housing available. Funding is intended to encourage the establishment and operation of such housing. Subsidy payments fund a project for a period of 10 years in the form of rental assistance in amounts equal to the rent, including utilities, minus the portion of rent payable by the tenants.

OTHER PROGRAM COMPONENTS. Other programs folded under the Continuum of Care designation by HUD include demonstration programs for safe havens for the homeless and innovative homeless programs as well as rural homeless housing programs.

Emergency Shelter Grants Program (ESG)

The Emergency Shelter Grants program provides homeless persons with basic shelter and essential supportive services. It can assist with the operational costs of the shelter facility, and for the administration of the grant. ESG also provides short-term homeless prevention assistance to persons at imminent risk of losing their own housing due to eviction, foreclosure, or utility shutoffs.

Emergency Shelter Grants (ESG) Program, HUD, May 30, 2003 [Online] http://www.hud.gov/offices/cpd/homeless/programs/esg/index.cfm [accessed October 2, 2003]

The ESG is HUD's formula grant program administered as a part of its community planning and development grant program. Recipients of funding are states, large cities, urban counties, and U.S. territories that have filed consolidated community development plans with HUD. ESG is called a formula program because the amounts

TABLE 5.1

Requirements of four Housing and Urban Development (HUD) McKinney programs

Program requirement	Emergency shelter grants program	Supportive housing program	Shelter plus care program	Single-room occupancy program
Types of funds	Formula grant	Competitive grant	Competitive grant	Competitive grant
Eligible applicants	States Metropolitan cities Urban counties Territories	States Local governments Other governement agencies Private nonprofit organizations Community mental health centers that are public nonprofit organizations	States Local governments Public housing authorities	Public housing authorities Private nonprofit organizations
Eligible program components	Emergency shelter Essential social services	Transitional housing Permanent housing for people with disabilities Supportive services only Safe havens Innovative supportive housing	Tenant based rental assistance Sponsor based rental assistance Project based rental assistance SRO based rental assistance	Single-room occupancy housing
Eligible activities	Renovation/conversion Major rehabilitation Supportive service Operating costs Homelessness prevention activities	Acquisition Rehabilitation New construction Leasing Operating and administrative costs Supportive services	Rental assistance	Rental assistance
Eligible population	Homeless individuals and families People at risk of becoming homeless	Homeless individuals and families for transitional housing and supportive services Disabled homeless individuals for permanent housing Hard-to-reach mentally ill homeless individuals for safe havens	Disabled homeless individuals and their families	Homeless individuals
Initial term of assistance	1 year	Up to 3 years	5 or 10 years	10 years
Matching funds	States: no match for first $100,000 and dollar-for-dollar match for rest of funds Local governments: dollar-for-dollar match for all funds	Dollar-for-dollar match for acquisition, rehabilitation, and new construction grants Operating costs must be shared by 25 percent in the first 2 years and 50 percent in the third year A 25 percent match for supportive service grants No match for grants used for leasing or administrative costs	Dollar-for-dollar match of the federal shelter grant to pay for supportive services	No match required

SOURCE: "Table 1.1: Requirements of Four HUD McKinney Programs," in *Homelessness: Consolidating HUD's McKinney Programs*, U.S. General Accounting Office, Washington, DC, May 23, 2000

allocated are based in part on population and poverty levels within the planning entities that participate. ESG funds flow from governmental entities to organizations that actually operate shelters and provide services. Money may be used to help individuals avoid homelessness by providing emergency funds.

Title V

HUD maintains information about and publishes listings of federal properties categorized as unutilized, underutilized, in excess, or in surplus. States, local governments, and non-profit organizations can apply to use such properties to house the homeless. Title V does not provide funding; it provides properties to agencies for housing use. Other programs, such as those shown under Continuum of Care, may be used to modify, refurbish, and to adapt such structures for residential uses.

Consolidations, New Initiatives, and Reorganizations

HUD's programs, particularly those under Continuum of Care, have overlapping objectives yet operate under separate rules and requirements. (See Table 5.1.) The U.S. General Accounting Office (GAO), an investigative body of the U.S. Congress, studied the McKinney programs in 1999 and concluded that the number of programs and the differences between them create barriers to their efficient use (*Homelessness: Coordination and Evaluation of Programs Are Essential*, GAO, Washington, D.C., 1999).

HOMELESS ASSISTANCE GRANTS. HUD's program administrators evidently reached much the same conclusions as GAO. In its FY 2004 budget request to Congress (*Fiscal Year 2004 Budget Summary*, HUD, Washington, D.C., February 3, 2003), HUD proposed consolidating its three major programs under Continuum of Care, along with the demonstration and rural assistance programs, into

TABLE 5.2

HUD budget authority for homeless and public housing programs, FY 2002–04

(In millions of dollars)

	FY 2002 Actual	FY 2003 Budget	FY 2004 Estimate	Percent of total 2004
Homeless programs				
Homeless assistance grants	1,123	1,130	1,325	5.2
Samaritan Homeless Program	...	...	50	0.2
Emergency Food and Shelter		153	153	0.6
Total - homeless	1,123	1,283	1,528	6.0
Public and Indian Housing				
Housing Assistance for Needy Families (HANF)[1]	...	...	12,535	49.2
Project-Based Rental Assistance (PBRA)[2]	14,052	16,427	4,523	17.8
Public Housing Capital Fund	2,843	2,426	2,641	10.4
Public Housing Operating Fund	3,495	3,530	3,574	14.0
Native-American Housing Block Grants	649	647	647	2.5
Indian Housing Loan Guarantee Fund	6	5	1	0.0
Native Hawaiian Loan Guarantee Fund	1	1	1	0.0
Native Hawaiian Housing Block Grants	...	10	10	0.0
Total - housing	21,609	23,620	23,932	94.0
Total, homeless assistance and housing	22,732	24,903	25,460	100.0

Note: ... stands for no funds allocated.
[1] New program intended to replace PBRA shown immediately below.
[2] PBRA funds for FY 2004 represent renewals and amendments under the old program structure.

SOURCE: Adapted from "Budget Authority by Program," *Fiscal Year 2004 Budget Summary*, U.S. Department of Housing and Urban Development, Washington, DC, February 3, 2003

a single Homeless Assistance Grants program in order to achieve more comprehensive delivery of services and to reduce administrative expenses, both at HUD and on the part of grants recipients. HUD requested $1.325 billion for these programs for FY 2004, up from $1.13 billion in FY 2003.

The federal fiscal year begins October 1 and ends on September 30. The number of the year is that of the calendar year in which the fiscal year ends. FY 2004 moneys, therefore, are expended in the fall of 2003 and the first nine months of 2004. FY 2005 funding will be proposed by federal agencies in the early months of 2004.

THE SAMARITAN INITIATIVE. HUD also proposed that Congress fund a new program in FY 2004 called the Samaritan Initiative. The new program would be targeted to an estimated 150,000 individuals HUD believes to make up the nation's "chronically homeless." HUD's requested funding for this initiative was $70 million, of which $50 million would be from HUD's funds and earmarked for providing housing for the chronically homeless. The U.S. Department of Health and Human Services (DHHS) and the U.S. Department of Veterans Affairs (VA) would provide $10 million each in services for drug abuse and health

treatment. The new program is structurally similar to the S+C program described above.

EMERGENCY FOOD AND SHELTER PROGRAM. HUD's budget document also proposed that the Emergency Food and Shelter Program, currently administered by the Federal Emergency Management Agency (FEMA), be transferred to HUD and merged with HUD's ESG program. Funding for this program would be at a level of $153 million in FY 2004, unchanged from the previous year.

All told, HUD's budget request in FY 2004 was $1.528 billion, up from $1.283 in FY 2003, representing a 19 percent increase in expenditures. HUD's FY 2002 request had been $1.123 billion.

FEDERALLY SUBSIDIZED HOUSING

The national effort to provide housing for those in need is far more massive than would be indicated by the expenditure of about $1.5 billion on assistance to the homeless. HUD's expenditures on public and Indian housing were projected to be $23.9 billion in FY 2004. (See Table 5.2.) If these funds are added to projected expenditures on homeless programs, total spending on subsidized housing in FY 2004 will be $25.6 billion. As Table 5.2 shows, of this total 6 percent is allocated to helping the homeless and 94 percent to ensuring that people do not become homeless. A closer look at the government's housing programs provides the background to the housing problem for poor and low-income people.

Households in Subsidized Housing

In 2000 nearly 4.7 million households in the United States lived in subsidized housing, equivalent to 4.4 percent of total U.S. households. (See Table 5.3.) Of those in subsidized housing, 2.4 million households had income below the officially-defined poverty level; these households were 2.3 percent of all households and just over half of all subsidized households (51.1 percent).

Bureau of the Census statistics on those living in poverty provide estimates of families living in poverty but not on households as households are defined in recent time; households include families as well as non-family households, e.g., singles living alone. In 2000 there were 72.4 million families in the U.S. (in contrast with 106.4 million households). Of total families, 6.4 million or 8.8 percent were living in poverty (*Current Population Reports*, P60-219, U.S. Census Bureau, Washington, D.C., September 2002). By contrast, 2.3 percent of households living in poverty were living in subsidized housing. Housing programs are, thus, not targeted exclusively to the elimination of poverty.

TABLE 5.3

Households occupying subsidized housing, 1990–2000

(In thoussands and percent)

	1990	1991	1992	1993	1994	1995	1996	1997	1998	1999	2000
Total households	94,312	95,669	96,391	97,107	98,990	99,627	101,018	102,528	103,874	104,705	106,418
Total in subsidized housing	4,339	4,511	4,478	5,183	4,946	4,846	4,981	4,778	4,808	4,447	4,689
Below poverty level	2,637	2,765	2,616	2,909	2,686	2,546	2,622	2,728	2,709	2,488	2,397
Subsidized as % of all households	4.6	4.7	4.6	5.3	5.0	4.9	4.9	4.7	4.6	4.2	4.4
Below poverty as % of all households	2.8	2.9	2.7	3.0	2.7	2.6	2.6	2.7	2.6	2.4	2.3
Below poverty as % of subsidized	60.8	61.3	58.4	56.1	54.3	52.5	52.6	57.1	56.3	55.9	51.1

SOURCE: Adapted from "Households Receiving Means-Tested Noncash Benefits," *Current Population Reports*, P-60 Reports, reproduced in *Statistical Abstract of the United States*, U.S. Census Bureau, 1992–2001

FIGURE 5.1

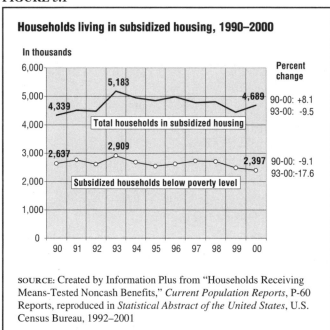

Households living in subsidized housing, 1990–2000

SOURCE: Created by Information Plus from "Households Receiving Means-Tested Noncash Benefits," *Current Population Reports*, P-60 Reports, reproduced in *Statistical Abstract of the United States*, U.S. Census Bureau, 1992–2001

Data on the number of individuals living in subsidized housing are available for 1999. That year 10.65 million people lived in subsidized housing; of these 6.35 million were below poverty. In 1999 a total of 32.26 million people were in poverty; of these, therefore, 19.7 percent had housing with government funding, suggesting that most of the households below poverty are in fact family units as conventionally defined, including families headed by a woman only or a man only.

The data in Table 5.3 are charted in Figure 5.1 to show trends more graphically. In the 1990–2000 period, those in subsidized housing peaked in 1993, trending downward from that year. Total households living in subsidized housing increased 8.1 percent in the period but decreased 9.5 percent between 1993 and 2000. Between 1990 and 2000, households living below poverty in subsidized housing declined by 9.1 percent; between 1993 and 2000, they declined by 17.6 percent; this suggests that housing support is actually diminishing as a means of fighting poverty.

Types of Programs

Virtually all government housing programs are targeted to poor or low-income households. For this reasons subsidized housing is "means-tested," meaning that the income of those receiving help must be below a threshold. The qualifying income level—much like the definition of poverty—changes over time. Beneficiaries of housing assistance never receive cash outright, a policy that echoes ancient prejudices against those with minimal means. The benefits are therefore labeled "means-tested noncash benefits."

HUD has operated many different kinds of housing programs, but these can be classified under three headings: public housing owned by the government, tenant based programs that provide people vouchers to subsidize rent, and project-based programs that underwrite the costs of private owners who, in turn, pledge to house low-income people.

Public housing and voucher programs account for roughly equal proportions of subsidized units. Project-based programs, also known as "private subsidized projects," account for the most units (see Figure 5.2), but these "private subsidies" take many forms, some quite complicated. A look at the major programs follows.

PUBLIC HOUSING

HUD's FY 2004 budget anticipated funding for 1.24 million public housing units. Public housing has been decreasing in numbers (1.37 million in 1998, for example), in part because of an initiative to remove, modernize, and refurbish many poorly constructed and dilapidated public housing units. An estimated 3,050 public housing authorities manage 14,000 housing projects. Federal costs

FIGURE 5.2

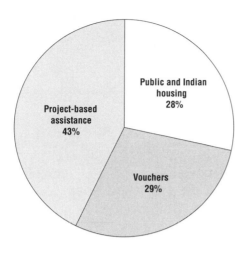

Distribution of subsidized housing units by project type, 1998

Note: Data shown represent 4.839 million available housing units; not all were occupied in 1998. Public housing represented 1.373 million, vouchers 1.392 million, and project based units 2.074 million units.

SOURCE: Created by Information Plus from "Basic Counts," in *A Picture of Subsidized Households in 1998*, U.S. Department of Housing and Urban Development, Washington, DC, August 28, 1998

in FY 2004 were estimated to be $6.215 billion, 57.5 percent for operations and 42.5 percent for capital outlays. Expenditures per unit in FY 2004 project to $5,180 or about $432 per month.

Public Housing Residents

HUD analysts have estimated based on HUD records that 1.1 million households were living in public housing in 2000 (Jeffrey M. Lubell, et al., "Work Participation and Length of Stay in HUD-Assisted Housing," *Cityscape* vol. 6, no. 2, HUD, 2003). Based on HUD data for 2003, the average occupancy per unit of public housing was 2.2 persons. Using this ratio, the total public housing population was around 2.5 million in 2000. Of the households surveyed in 2000, half (50.4 percent) were headed by nonelderly and nondisabled persons. Of these slightly over half (51.6 percent) worked, 22 percent received only welfare, and 26.4 percent had reported neither income nor government support of any kind to the PHA. (HUD's analysts note that underreporting of income is common for a number of reasons.) Median income of such households (nonelderly, nondisabled) was $11,648. (Median means that half earned less and half earned more.) The highest earnings were $24,900 a year, the lowest $2,832. According to the U.S. Census Bureau, median income in 2000 for a family of four was $62,228.

More recent data for the public housing population as a whole, not just the nonelderly and nondisabled, confirm the 2000 data. On its web site HUD provides a data server

on public housing residents called *Resident Characteristics Report* (http://www.hud.gov/offices/pih/systems/pic/50058/rcr/index.cfm). Some highlights from the server, generated on September 18, 2003:

- Average annual income was $10,440. Only 6 percent of the public housing population earned more than $25,000 a year.

- Among residents, 30 percent had wage income, 15 percent had welfare income, 55 percent had Social Security income, and 16 percent had other income (the same person could have income from more than one source).

- The average rental payment was $236 per month.

- Females with children were 38 percent of families, 20 percent were elderly and not disabled, 12 percent were elderly with a disability. A number of other, overlapping, categories were shown as well but not a category for male-headed families with children.

- Half (50 percent) of heads of households were white, 46 percent were black, 2 percent were Asian, and 1 percent were American Indians or Alaska Natives. By ethnic origin, 80 percent were non-Hispanic, 20 percent Hispanic.

- Nearly half (46 percent) of households consisted of one person, 20 percent of two, 15 percent of three, 10 percent of four, 5 percent of five, 2 percent of six, and 1 percent of seven persons, the highest.

- The 884,780 units reporting data had 1,972,723 household members, with an average household size of 2.2 persons. (1998 data from HUD showed a ratio of 2.24 persons per household.)

- Of units occupied, 7 percent had no bedroom, 34 percent had one, 30 percent had two, 23 percent had three, 5 percent had four, and 1 percent had more than five bedrooms.

- Twelve percent of the population had been in public housing for more than 20 years, 16 percent for 10 to 20 years, 21 percent for 5 to 10 years, 24 percent for 2 to 5 years, 12 percent for a year or two, and 11 percent had moved in during the past year. The rest did not report on length of stay.

Public Housing Agencies

Management of public housing is handled by housing agencies (sometimes called authorities) established by local governments to administer HUD housing programs. The Housing Act of 1937 requires that PHAs submit annual plans to HUD but also declares it to be the policy of the United States "… to vest in public housing agencies that perform well the maximum amount of responsibility and flexibility in program administration, with appropriate

TABLE 5.4

Public Housing Assessment System (PHAS) designations under partial and full implementation, fiscal year 2001

PHAS designation	Number of authorities designated under one indicator	Number of authorities that could be designated under four indicators
Overall troubled[1]		90
Troubled in one area[1]		442
Substandard physical		169
Substandard financial		249
Substandard management[2]	45	24
Standard performer	3,122	1,808
High performer[1]		827
Total	**3,167**	**3,167**

[1] HUD designated no high performers for fiscal year 2001. The only troubled performers were those that were troubled in the management area.

[2] When performance is assessed using all four indicators, housing authorities that are troubled in more than one area become overall troubled. Some of the 45 housing authorities that were troubled in the management area alone under one indicator moved into the overall troubled category when their physical and financial condition were taken into account. As a result, only 24 housing authorities remained troubled in the management area alone under all four indicators.

SOURCE: "Table 1: PHAS Designations for Fiscal Year 2001 under Partial and Full Implementation," in *Public Housing: New Assessment System Holds Potential for Evaluating Performance*, GAO-02-282, U.S. General Accounting Office, Washington, DC, March 2002

accountability to public housing residents, localities, and the general public."

PHAs thus operate under plans approved by HUD and under HUD supervision, but they are expected to operate with some independence accountable to their residents, local (or state) governments, and the public. Not all PHAs have "performed well," and HUD has been accused of lax supervision. PHAs and public housing generally reflect the distressed conditions of the population living in government-owned housing. PHAs have been charged with neglecting maintenance, tolerating unsafe living conditions for tenants, and with fraudulent or careless financial practices.

Responding to such accounts, Congress created the National Commission on Severely Distressed Public Housing in 1990. In its report, released in August 1992, the commission concluded that severely distressed public housing was a national problem. The commission reported that 86,000 (or 6 percent) of the nation's public housing units were plagued by crime and deteriorated physical conditions in violation of HUD standards. Five years later the National Housing Institute, a not-for-profit advocacy group, charged that HUD still did not know how much, or which parts, of its public housing inventory met its own "troubled housing" definition despite the fact that these troubled properties represent a significant portion of the available low-income housing in the United States

(J. Atlas and E. Shoshkes, *Saving Affordable Housing, What Community Groups Can Do and What Government Should Do,* National Housing Institute, Montclair, NJ, 1997).

Troubled housing refers to low-income projects that are badly deteriorated, are located in unsafe neighborhoods, or are in danger of being lost to market-rate housing conversion or foreclosure. In an effort to improve its accountability for the conditions of low-income housing, HUD began to implement a new Public Housing Assessment System (PHAS) in January 2000. PHAS is used to measure the performance of public housing agencies. The four primary PHAS components are:

1. Physical Inspection Indicator—ensures that PHAs meet the minimum standard of being decent, safe, sanitary, and in good repair.

2. Financial Condition Indicator—oversees the finances of PHAs.

3. Management Operations Indicator—evaluates the effectiveness of PHA management methods.

4. Resident Satisfaction and Service Indicator—allows public housing residents to assess PHA performance.

A March 2002 GAO report commissioned by Congress studied the implementation of PHAS and its progress. The study found that HUD had also formed the Public and Indian Housing Information Center (PIC), a database that collected additional information not addressed by PHAS, such as compliance and funding. The findings indicated that as of 2002, PHAS's method of evaluation considered only component three, managerial deficiencies, to declare PHAs as troubled. The plans were to incorporate all four components. Table 5.4 shows the number of the then existing 3,167 authorities investigated that would have been be classified as troubled if all four PHAS components had been applied instead of just one ("New Assessment System Holds Potential for Evaluating Performance," GAO, Washington, D.C., March 2002).

The table shows that 532 PHAs were "troubled" (16.8 percent), 827 were high performers (26.1 percent) and 1,808 were standard performers (57 percent).

HOPE VI

As a result of the 1992 recommendations of the National Commission on Severely Distressed Public Housing, Congress authorized $300 million for an urban revitalization demonstration program in the FY 1993 Appropriations Act. The program came to be named HOPE VI. The acronym stands for Housing Opportunities for People Everywhere. HUD had had, until then, four different HOPE initiatives. For some reason no HOPE V was ever launched (James Bovard, "HUD's Biggest Farce?" *Free Market*, vol. 18, no. 11, November 2000).

The aim of HOPE VI was to eliminate or upgrade the 86,000 deteriorated units identified by the Commission. In the FY 1993–2002 period, HUD reported revitalization grants totaling $5.04 billion and expended $335.6 million on demolitions. In its FY 2004 Budget Summary, HUD reported budget authority for FY 2003 of $574 million. HUD reported that 55,000 housing units had been demolished and 140,000 approved for demolition under HOPE VI and other programs, and no new funding was required for FY 2004 as the agency worked through its existing backlog.

Critiques and Implications

The findings of the National Commission in 1992 and the launch of an initiative like HOPE VI (aimed at demolishing public housing) illustrates the sometimes troubled history of public housing. HOPE VI itself has been severely criticized by advocacy groups. A 2002 report entitled *False Hope* (prepared by the National Housing Law Project, the Poverty & Race Research Action Council, Sherwood Research Associates, and Everywhere and Now Public Housing Residents Organizing Nationally Together, issued in June 2002 [Online] http://www.nhlp. org/html/pubhsg/FalseHOPE.pdf) found that HOPE VI (1) appeared headed toward eliminating twice the number of units found to have been "severely distressed" by the National Commission, (2) has eliminated rather than increased units available to the lowest income population, (3) has made it very difficult for residents to participate in program decisions, (4) has not improved the "living environment" of those in HOPE VI sites, and (5) has failed to provide data on project outcomes.

Data on the number of public housing units available to house low income people bear out the general charge that the number of units has declined from nearly 1.37 million in 1998 to 1.24 million in 2003, a drop of 130,000 units. If those who inhabit such units are not able to find accommodation under HUD Section 8 Voucher programs, they are at greater risk of becoming homeless.

VOUCHERS

How Voucher Programs Work

Voucher programs pay a portion of the rent for qualifying families. Only low-income families are eligible, namely those with incomes lower than half of an area's median income. Under some circumstances, families with up to 80 percent of the local median income may also qualify; such cases may involve, for instance, families displaced by public housing demolition. The family pays 30 percent of its income in rent. Vouchers are issued by the Public

Housing Agency, which executes assistance contracts with the landlord, who must also qualify.

Two major voucher programs are available: tenant-based and project-based. In tenant-based programs, the voucher "follows" the tenant when the tenant moves to another qualifying unit. In project-based programs, the voucher "attaches" to a project; families are directed to participating projects after they qualify. Tenants cannot automatically transfer their voucher in a project-based dwelling to another—but they may qualify for tenant-based vouchers after they move.

In addition to these two basic programs, HUD also has five other voucher programs. Conversion vouchers are used when public housing is demolished to help tenants relocate. Family unification vouchers are used to help families stay together. Homeownership vouchers assist families in purchasing a first home or another home if the family has not lived in a house in the past three years. Participants must be employed and have an income of at least minimum wage. Vouchers for people with disabilities and welfare-to-work vouchers assist the elderly or non-elderly disabled and families transitioning from welfare to work.

In all of these programs, the housing supplied is privately owned and operated and rents paid are at or below fair market rent (FMR). HUD determines the FMR in every locality of the nation by an annual survey of new rental contracts signed in the past 15 months. The FMR is set as the 40th percentile of rents paid, meaning that 40 percent paid a lower and 60 percent a higher rent. HUD has chosen the 40th percentile to increase housing choices while keeping budgets at reasonable levels. Table 5.5 presents fair market rentals used by HUD in 2003 and those proposed for 2004. Rentals for certain cities are calculated at the 50th percentile under new HUD rules that went into effect in 2001 for 39 markets.

The highest projected FMR for 2004 was in San Jose, CA ($1,821 per month), the lowest in Aguadilla, Puerto Rico ($329) and, on the mainland, in the counties of Tennessee ($375).

Voucher Growth

Subsidized housing units created under Section 8 of the Housing Act of 1974 increased from a total of 2.39 million units in 1998 to 2.89 million in 2003, as shown in Table 5.6. The two parts of the program, however, had uneven growth. Tenant voucher units increased 49.3 percent in the 1998–2003 period while Section 8 program-based units declined by 18.4 percent. During this same period, public housing units declined 4.5 percent. Other rental assistance program units, managed under a number of different programs, increased by 1.8 percent.

TABLE 5.5

Fair market rental rates for selected metropolitan areas, 2003–04

	2003	2004		2003	2004
Albuquerque, NM[1]	671	673	Little Rock-North Little Rock, AR	536	538
Anchorage, AK	842	885	Louisville, KY-IN	581	583
Atlanta, GA[1]	927	944	Los Angeles-Long Beach, CA PMSA	967	1021
Baltimore, MD	844	888	Madison, WI	711	716
Billings, MT	554	563	Memphis, TN-AR-MS	624	626
Birmingham, AL	557	559	Miami, FL[1]	813	842
Bismarck, ND	556	565	Minneapolis-St. Paul, MN-WI	912	951
Boise City, ID	580	593	New Orleans, LA	659	661
Boston, MA-NH	1343	1419	New York, NY	1031	1073
Bridgeport, CT	868	900	Newark, NJ	949	987
Buffalo-Niagara Falls, NY[1]	623	624	Norfolk-Virginia Beach-Newport News, VA-NC	743	748
Burlington, VT	836	850	Oklahoma City, OK	581	561
Casper, WY	519	527	Omaha, NE-IA	621	626
Chicago, IL[1]	928	951	Philadelphia, PA-NJ	871	892
Cincinnati, OH-KY-IN	662	672	Pittsburgh, PA	608	615
Cleveland-Lorain-Elyria, OH[1]	748	752	Portland, ME	845	859
Columbia, SC	586	588	Portsmouth-Rochester, NH-ME	882	930
Dallas, TX[1]	850	871	Providence-Fall River-Warwick, RI-MA	667	678
Denver, CO[1]	945	964	Raleigh-Durham-Chapel Hill, NC	796	799
Des Moines, IA	649	655	St. Louis, MO-IL	691	695
Detroit, MI[1]	771	801	Salt Lake City-Ogden, UT	744	756
Eugene-Springfield, OR	661	675	San Francisco, CA	1940	1775
Honolulu, HI	844	858	Seattle-Bellevue-Everett, WA	899	923
Houston, TX[1]	747	760	Sioux Falls, SD	655	665
Indianapolis, IN	588	592	Topeka, KS	531	536
Jackson, MS	587	589	Washington, DC-MD-VA	1154	1218
Kansas City, MO-KS[1]	701	713	Wheeling, WV-OH	454	457
Las Vegas, NV-AZ[1]	827	856	Wilmington-Newark, DE-MD	752	771

Note: Fair market rentals are set at the 40th percentile of surveyed new rent contracts in an area, meaning that 40 percent of rents are below levels shown, 60 percent are above. In 2001 HUD introduced a 50th percentile measure in 39 markets; not all are included above; those that are are marked with a footnote.
[1] Based on 50th percentile.

SOURCE: Adapted from "FMR History1983–Present: Data in MS EXCEL," in *Fair Market Rents*, U.S. Department of Housing and Urban Development, Washington, DC, June 10, 2003 [Online] http://www.huduser.org/datasets/fmr.html [accessed September 22, 2003]

Project-based Section 8 housing has been in decline because funding for new construction stopped in 1983 with some minor exceptions (including construction/rehabilitation aimed at supporting homeless programs). Support of housing in such units continues, but the housing stock is going out of use through demolitions and conversions. Other housing units have been added under other authorities and show a slight increase.

Characteristics of Voucher Residents

Tenant-voucher residents are fractionally better off than public housing residents, as shown in Table 5.7. Voucher users have slightly higher incomes and larger households. Both populations, however, have minimal income. The shift of the subsidized population from public housing toward voucher housing represents not an improvement so much as a shift in policy, whereby the provision of housing, in the future, appears to be headed for privatization.

Proposed Reorganization

In its FY 2004 budget, HUD has proposed a division of the Section 8 program into two parts. The tenant-voucher program would become a block grant to states, with states administering the funds and channeling them to PHAs. Section 8 now deals with some 2,600 housing agencies directly. Under the new program, to be called Housing for Needy Families (HANF), HUD would be dealing with 60 grant recipients instead, thus achieving administrative efficiencies.

HUD intends to retain direct control over the Section 8 project-based programs and anticipates that, in FY 2004, funding for 870,000 units (up about 50,000 units from 2003 levels), will be managed under this program.

OTHER HOUSING ASSISTANCE PROGRAMS

The two biggest low-income housing programs in the U.S. are public housing and the Section 8 programs, but

TABLE 5.6

Subsidized units available under public housing and voucher programs, 1998 and 2003

	1998	2003	% Change
Public housing[1]	1,300,493	1,241,466	-4.5
S8 tenant vouchers	1,391,526	2,077,336	49.3
S8 project-based vouchers	1,001,939	817,274	-18.4
Other rental assistance[2]	1,072,135	1,091,502	1.8

Note: S8 stands for Section 8 of the Housing Act of 1937.
[1] Excludes Indian housing.
[2] Includes low interest loans and interest subsidy, special population programs, property disposal program housing, housing tax credits, and other FHA supported programs.

SOURCE: For 1998 data, "Basic Counts," in *A Picture of Subsidized Households in 1998*, U.S. Department of Housing and Urban Development, Washington, DC, August 28, 1998. For 2003 public housing data, *Resident Characteristics Report*, U.S. Department of Housing and Urban Development, Washington, DC [Online] http://www.hud.gov/offices/pih/systems/pic/50058/rcr/index.cfm [accessed September 23, 2003]. For other 2003 data, Fiscal Year 2003 Budget Summary, HUD, Washington, DC [Online] http://www.hud.gov/about/budget/fy03/bugsum.pdf [accessed September 23, 2003]

these do not account for all of the housing units supported by HUD; and housing assistance is also available from other agencies. The last line of Table 5.6, labeled "other rental assistance," shows about a million units of housing supported by HUD under a diversity of programs. Section 8 funds are distributed under HUD's Housing Certificate Fund (HCF). In addition to vouchers and project-based programs, another 560,000 units are supported under HCF. These include housing for AIDS victims, the elderly, Indian housing, housing for Native Hawaiians, and persons with disabilities.

The Self-Help Homeownership Opportunity Program (SHOP) supported 3,800 homes for low-income people. Section 8 funds were also used to help low-income people buy homes. FHA provides mortgage insurance for multi-family projects and helped to lower costs on 135,000 units in 2003. The Low-Income Housing Tax Credit program in 2003, available to developers who provide a portion of their projects at low rents, added an estimated 100,000 low-income units according to HUD's FY 2003 budget.

In 2003 HUD also supported 296,000 units under the Section 236 Rental Housing Assistance Program. Although this program terminated in 1973, a substantial number of units were still eligible for support in 2003. Between 2002 and 2003, 21,000 units lost eligibility; between 2003 and 2004, 76,000 went off the rolls. Eventually this program will disappear, replaced by new initiatives.

Funding under HUD's Community Development Block Grant program also has money available for low-income housing.

TABLE 5.7

Selected characteristics of subsidized housing populations, 2003

	Public housing	Tenant vouchers
Average income	$10,440	$10,583
Percent with income of–		
$0	5	5
$1-5,000	15	13
$5,001-10,000	43	41
$10,001-15,000	18	20
$15,001-20,000	8	11
$20,001-25,000	4	6
Above $25,000	6	5
Percent below 30% of median income	45	43
Average monthly payment	$236	$241
Race		
White	50	53
Black	46	43
American Indian/Alaska Native	1	1
Asian	2	3
Ethnicity		
Hispanic	20	16
Not-Hispanic	80	84
Average household size	2.2	2.6
Percent with 4 or more people	18	25
Percent with 2 bedrooms	30	39

SOURCE: Adapted from *Resident Characteristics Report*, U.S. Department of Housing and Urban Development, Washington, DC [Online] http://www.hud.gov/offices/pih/systems/pic/50058/rcr/index.cfm [accessed September 23, 2003]

HUD maintains demographic and income data only on participants in the major programs. For that reason, information on the characteristics of participants in many other HUD subsidy programs aimed at low-income people are unavailable. The programs cited above do, not include mortgage insurance and other FHA programs aimed to assist the more affluent general population to own a home.

Federal Home Loan Bank

Federal law requires each of the twelve District Federal Home Loan Banks to establish an Affordable Housing Program (AHP). Member banks then provide grants and below-market loans to organizations for the purchase, construction, and/or rehabilitation of rental housing. Only 20 percent of the units created with these funds have to be occupied and affordable to very low-income households.

In addition, the Federal Home Loan Bank offers a loan program called the Community Investment Program (CIP). This provides long-term funding at fixed rates to develop rental housing or finance first-time home purchases for families and individuals with incomes up to 115 percent of the area's median income. This means that middle-income people can build or buy homes using these funds, but the

TABLE 5.8

Data on Rural Housing Service's (RHS's) housing programs, 1979–99

(Dollars in millions)

RHS housing program	Total dollars spent, fiscal year 1979	Total dollars spent, fiscal year 1994	Total dollars spent, fiscal year, 1999	Number of households helped, fiscal year 1999	Type of assistance
Single-Family Housing Direct Loans (sec. 502)	$2,870.0[1]	$1,656.8[1]	$966.9[1]	15,000	Loans subsidized as low as 1 percent interest
Single-Family Housing Guaranteed Loans (sec. 502)		$725.9[1]	$2,980.0[1]	38,600	No money down, no monthly mortgage insurance loans
Single-Family Home Repair Grants and Loans (sec. 504)	$33.7	$52.7	$46.8	9,021	Grants for elderly and loans subsidized as low as 1 percent interest
Single-Family Housing Mutual Self-Help Grants (sec. 523)	$5.6	$12.8	$25.4	1,350	Grants to nonprofit and public entities to provide technical assistance
Multifamily Direct Rural Rental Housing Loans (sec. 515)	$869.5[1]	$512.4[1]	$114.3[1]	2,181	Loans to developers subsidized as low as 1 percent interest
Multifamily Housing Guaranteed Loans (sec. 538)			$74.8[1]	2,540	Guaranteed loans for developing monderate-income apartments
Multifamily Housing Farm Labor Grants and Loans (secs. 516/514)	$68.8	$56.3	$33.2	622	Grants and loans subsidized at 1 percent interest
Multifamily Housing Preservation Grants (sec. 533)		$23.0	$7.2	1,800	Grants to nonprofit organizations, local governments, and Native American tribes, usually leveraged with outside funding
Multifamily Housing Rental Assistance (sec. 521)	$423.0	$446.7	$583.4	42,000	Rental assistance to about one-half the residents in RHS rental and farm labor units

[1] Dollar amounts represents private-sector loan levels guaranteed by RHS or loans made directly by RHS during the year. Actual federal outlays are much lower because they cover the subsidy cost, not the face value of the loans or guaranteed loans. The subsidy cost is the estimated long-term cost to the government of a direct or guaranteed loan calculated on a net present value basis, excluding administrative costs.

SOURCE: William B. Shear, "Table 1: Data on RHS's Housing Programs," in *Rural Housing Service: Opportunities to Improve Management*, GAO-03-911T, U.S. General Accounting Office, Washington, DC, June 19, 2003

expenses are considered part of the low-income housing assistance budget.

Rural Housing Programs

The Rural Housing Programs are administered by the U.S. Department of Agriculture and make federal money available in an effort to increase both the amount and the quality of housing in rural areas of the country. Rural areas are places with a population of 50,000 or less. Eligibility for rural housing programs is similar to that of subsidized urban programs. The requirements vary from region to region, and applicants must meet minimum and maximum income guidelines. The subsidies came in the form of grants or low-interest loans to repair substandard housing, subsidized mortgages for low-income home ownership, and grants to cover down payment and purchasing costs of low-income homes.

Rural area homeownership is 8 percent higher (76 percent) than the national rate (68 percent), but affordable housing is in short supply in rural areas. Much of the rural low-income housing where renters, migrant workers, and a high population of minorities live is substandard. There are four major areas affected by housing inadequacies:

the Mississippi Delta, Indian trust lands, the Colonias bordering Mexico, and Appalachia. The June 19, 2003 GAO Report "Rural Housing Services, Opportunity to Improve Management, June 2003" (U.S. General Accounting Office, Washington, D.C.), found that the Rural Housing Service (RHS) could be improved by reducing costs and centralizing administration. Table 5.8 shows the various programs that were available under RHS funding in millions of dollars and the number of households helped in 1999. In 2003, $1.6 billion was appropriated; of that, $721 million went to assist renters and $4.2 million toward single-family home loan guarantees.

Projects for Transition from Homelessness (PATH)

This federally funded program is administered by the federal Center for Mental Health Services through grants to state mental health agencies. These state agencies provide PATH-funded services to homeless people with mental illness primarily through local or regional mental health service providers. PATH funds can be used for outreach, screening, diagnostic treatment, habilitation, rehabilitation, community mental health services, case management, supportive and supervisory services in residential settings, and other housing-related services.

Education for Homeless Children and Youth

In response to reports that over 50 percent of homeless children were not attending school regularly, Congress enacted the McKinney Education for Homeless Children and Youth (EHCY) program in 1987. The program ensures that homeless children and youth have equal access to the same free, appropriate education, including preschool education, provided to other children. EHCY also provides funding for state and local school districts to implement the law. States are required to report estimated numbers of homeless children and the problems encountered in serving them. The No Child Left Behind Act of 2001 reauthorized the program and included the following new guidelines.

- Homeless children cannot be segregated.

- Transportation has to be provided to and from schools of origin if requested (a school of origin is the school the student attended when permanently housed, or the school in which the student was last enrolled).

- In case of a placement dispute, immediate enrollment is required pending the outcome.

- Local education agencies (LEAs) must put the "best interest of the child" first in determining the feasibility of keeping children in their school of origin.

- LEAs have to designate a local liaison for homeless children and youth.

- States have to subgrant 50 to 75 percent of their allotments under EHCY competitively to LEAs.

Unaccompanied Youth Services

The Runaway and Homeless Youth Program (RHYA), administered by the Department of Health and Human Services, began in 1974 and provides financial assistance to community-based crisis and referral centers that serve runaway and homeless youth and their families. Transitional Living Program for Older Homeless Youth (TLP) was created in 1988 as part of RHYA to assure long-term assistance to this segment of the homeless ("Family and Youth Services Bureau—Transitional Living Program for Older Homeless Youth," U.S. Department of Health and Human Services [Online] http://www.acf.dhhs.gov/programs/fysb/tlp.htm). Services are geared to the following areas:

- Living accommodations that are safe and stable.

- Skill building on two levels: life-skills such as housekeeping, budgeting, and food preparation, and interpersonal skills such as relationship-building, decision-making, and stress management.

- Education area addresses furthering secondary and post secondary achievement, job preparation, and substance abuse education.

- Mental and physical healthcare, which includes counseling, health assessment, and treatment in emergencies.

- Available funds in fiscal year 2003 for new grants under this program totaled $7.9 million and an additional $27.8 million for the continued funding of existing grants according to the Administration for Children and Families, DHHS.

CHAPTER 6

THE LAW, THE COURTS, AND THE HOMELESS

The widening gap between the haves and the have-nots in American society is perhaps nowhere more evident than in the plight of homeless people. As more and more privately owned, federally subsidized apartment buildings and former "skid rows" were gentrified during the economic boom of the 1990s, more of the poorest people were forced into homelessness. Merriam-Webster Online defines gentrification as "the process of renewal and rebuilding accompanying the influx of middle-class or affluent people into deteriorating areas that often displaces earlier usually poorer residents." When a neighborhood is gentrified, the visible homeless come to be seen as a blight on the quality of life of the new residents. The homeless can drive away tourists and frustrate the proprietors of area businesses.

Recent years have seen an increase in the enactment of laws and ordinances intended to regulate the actions of homeless people. Moreover, in some areas homeless children have found themselves placed outside the regular public school system, segregated in special schools for the homeless. Advocates for the homeless contend that these practices deny the homeless their most basic human, legal, and political rights.

There may not be enough shelter beds to accommodate every homeless person every night, but local ordinances prevent the homeless from sleeping on the streets or in parks. The homeless may be turned out of shelters to fend for themselves during the day, yet local ordinances prevent them from loitering in public places or resting in bus stations, libraries, or public buildings. Begging or picking up cans for recycling may help the homeless to support themselves, yet often there are restrictions against panhandling (begging) or limits on the number of cans they can redeem. To see the homeless bathe or use the toilet in public makes people uncomfortable; consequently, a law is passed to prohibit such activities.

The homeless are . . .

Are the homeless singled out by these laws and consequently denied their civil rights? Do such ordinances criminalize homelessness by singling out the minority (the unhoused) but not the majority (the housed)? For example, drinking in public is illegal, but the police may selectively enforce the law against street people while ignoring other drinkers, such as tourists. Ordinances disallowing life-sustaining activities performed by homeless individuals may be said to exclude the homeless from equal protection under the law.

Most measures regulating the behavior of the homeless are enacted at the community level. Sometimes the most restrictive of these laws have been challenged in federal court as violating the rights of the homeless people they seek to regulate. For example, a federal court may be asked to determine whether begging or panhandling is considered protected conduct under the First Amendment (freedom of speech).

A LAW CONCERNING THE EDUCATION OF HOMELESS CHILDREN

The 1987 McKinney-Vento Homeless Assistance Act (42 U.S.C. 11431 et seq.) is the federal law that entitles children who are homeless to a free, appropriate public education, for which federal funding is provided to the states under Subtitle VII-B, the Education for Homeless Children and Youth Program. At the time the legislation was passed, an estimated 57 percent of homeless children were enrolled in school. By 2000 the percentage had increased to 88 percent.

In implementing the legislation, school districts found that barriers arose in areas such as residency, guardian requirements, a lack of immunization records and birth certificates, and transportation. Consequently, some school districts established separate schools for homeless children. As of August 2002 there were an estimated

41 separate schools for the homeless nationwide (Marjorie Coeyman, "Homeless Kids Steered Into Regular Schools: A New Law Encourages 'Mainstreaming' and Sets Up Public-School Liaisons to Assist Homeless Students," *The Christian Science Monitor*, August 20, 2002). Proponents of separate schools argue they provide badly needed supportive services such as showers, clothing, hygiene items, dental and medical care, psychological counseling, and birthday parties and gifts. The schools also shield children from the embarrassment and ridicule they might expect to encounter in regular public schools.

A January 2000 report from the National Law Center on Homelessness and Poverty (*Separate and Unequal: A Report on Education Barriers for Homeless Children and Youth*, Washington, D.C.) found that such programs violated the McKinney-Vento Act and were "vastly inferior" to regular public schools in terms of resources and curricula. For example, some of the schools were located in shelters or churches that violated health and safety codes, and some were not staffed by certified teachers. Walter Varner, President of the National Association for the Education of Homeless Children and Youth, testified before Congress on September 5, 2000, that in his opinion, "separate [education] is never equal." (The landmark Supreme Court decision in *Brown v. Board of Education* [347 U.S. 483 (1954)] found that "the 'separate but equal' doctrine . . . has no place in the field of public education.") Varner pointed out that thousands of schools across the country had successfully eliminated barriers to the education of homeless children. Furthermore, he stated that it is "unacceptable to accommodate the prejudices of housed children against their homeless peers. . . . As the Supreme Court has said, 'private biases may be outside the reach of the law, but the law cannot, directly or indirectly, give them effect.'"

When Congress reauthorized the Homeless Children and Youth Program in January 2002 (through the enactment of the No Child Left Behind Act [PL 107-110]), it sought to express its belief that "Homelessness alone is not sufficient reason to separate students from the mainstream school environment." The new law required that homeless children be placed in mainstream schools, and it cut off federal aid to 41 separate schools for the homeless. Just before the bill was signed, however, six schools were exempted from the new law.

One unintended consequence of the new law was documented in a study by Homes for the Homeless and the Institute for Children and Poverty. The study found that 34 percent of 226 students in a New York homeless shelter faced commutes of longer than an hour because their parents had opted to keep their children in the same schools they had attended before they became homeless, a right guaranteed by the new law (Nicole Brode,

"New York's School Choice Leaves More Homeless Children with Hour-Plus Commutes," *Knight-Ridder/Tribune Business News*, February 10, 2003).

RESTRICTIVE ORDINANCES
Not in My Backyard (NIMBY)

To many people, the prospect of low-income, subsidized housing is synonymous with rising crime, falling property values, and overcrowded classrooms, and therefore cause for protest. Because of these fears, local governments often use zoning requirements to block the establishment of group-living homes and shelters for the homeless in all or part of their city. Zoning requirements are local laws regulating what kinds of buildings can be placed in different parts of a city. The use of zoning requirements to block particular developments is often called the "Not In My Backyard" (NIMBY) effect. The people in the neighborhoods are essentially saying that they do not want to have services for the homeless near them, even if they do not oppose them on principle.

In 1997 the city of Springfield, Missouri, passed a zoning ordinance that is typical of the NIMBY effect. The ordinance imposed new restrictions on the operation of emergency and transitional shelters and soup kitchens. No such facility was allowed to be located within two thousand feet of another similar facility. Among other restrictions, the ordinance limited the capacity of emergency shelters to 50 beds, prohibited shelters from serving meals to nonshelter residents unless the shelter obtains city authorization, and required shelters to have at least one off-street parking space for every three beds. The overall effect was to keep services for the homeless small and scattered, with none of them able to provide for all of the needs of a homeless person at once.

CRIMINALIZING THE HOMELESS LIFE. Homeless people live in and move about public spaces and many Americans feel society has a right to control or regulate what homeless people can do in those shared spaces. A city or town may introduce local ordinances or policies designed to restrict homeless people's activities, remove their belongings, or destroy their nontraditional living places. In many cities, municipal use of criminal sanctions to protect public spaces has come into conflict with efforts by civil rights and homeless advocates to prevent the criminalization of the homeless.

There have been other approaches. Several cities have proposed or created community courts specifically to handle "public nuisance" crimes. Other cities have implemented plans to privatize public property as a way of restricting the access of homeless people to certain areas.

VIOLATING HUMAN RIGHTS. The National Coalition for the Homeless (NCH) produced two reports (2002 and

2003) documenting what they termed "the widespread trend of the violations of the basic human rights of people experiencing homelessness in 147 communities in 42 states, Puerto Rico, and the District of Columbia." The 2003 report (*Illegal to Be Homeless: The Criminalization of Homelessness in the United States,* Washington, DC, 2003) noted that nearly all of the communities surveyed lacked sufficient shelter space to accommodate the homeless and suggested that the effort and money spent on bringing the homeless into the courthouse might better be directed toward addressing the nation's lack of affordable housing.

The NCH reported that in the brief time between the issuance of the two reports, many of the cities examined had passed new ordinances that criminalized certain behaviors of the homeless. Table 6.1 illustrates the anti-homeless laws that existed in 50 of the cities surveyed for the 2003 report. Prohibited or restricted behaviors fell under the categories of sanitation, begging, sleeping/camping, sitting/lying, loitering/loafing, and vagrancy. The report declared Las Vegas, San Francisco, New York, Los Angeles, and Atlanta the five "meanest cities" for the number of anti-homeless laws passed or pending, the enforcement and severity of their laws, and the "general political climate" with regard to the homeless, among other criteria. The "meanest states" were California and Florida.

The report noted that in Las Vegas, behavior that is tolerated in tourists is cause for jailing the city's "undesirables." The report described how downtown Los Angeles became the focus of revitalization efforts, drawing attention to the thousands of homeless people who live in a 50-block area called Skid Row. The Los Angeles Police Department launched "Operation Enough," a three-day "sweep" that netted nearly 200 arrests of parole violators and people in possession of drugs or weapons. The American Civil Liberties Union filed a suit against the city of Los Angeles, the police department, and its chief, charging that sidewalk sleepers were rousted but no beds were provided. A federal judge issued a temporary restraining order that prohibited the police from conducting sweeps to look for parole violators. The city subsequently agreed to pay nearly $170,000 to dozens of homeless people who were caught up in the sweeps.

The NCH report asserted that the San Francisco police issued more than 27,000 citations to homeless people in 2000 and 2001 for offenses "such as urinating in public, sleeping or camping in the park, trespassing, disobeying park signs, and drinking in public," in other words, "doing what they need to do to survive." The NCH report described a policy of "arrest and harassment" designed to keep homeless New Yorkers out of sight, which is said to be a top priority of the Bloomberg administration. In Atlanta, the NCH report stated, a systematic police campaign ensures public safety through the aggressive enforcement of "quality-of-life" ordinances. (In 1996, nine thousand homeless people were arrested in Atlanta just prior to the Olympic Games for violating quality-of-life ordinances that make sleeping or lying in public an offense punishable by jail.)

USE OF FORCE. Just as force was used against striking coal miners at the turn of the 20th century and against homeless and poor World War I veterans who marched on Washington during the Great Depression, violence and force have often been used to deal with the "homeless problem." In 1995 the New York City police used an armored personnel carrier and riot gear to retake two East Village tenements from a group of squatters who had resisted city efforts for nine months. Homeless people had occupied the city-owned buildings for as long as a decade and claimed that their continuous use of the buildings without the formal objection of the city gave them rights to the building, under a legal principle known as "adverse possession."

The Rationale for Restrictive Laws

Local officials often restrict homeless people's use of public space to protect public health and safety—either of the general public, the homeless themselves, or both. Dangers to the public have included tripping over people and objects on sidewalks, intimidation of passersby caused by aggressive begging, and the spreading of diseases. Many people believe the very presence of the homeless is unsightly and their removal improves the appearance of public spaces. Other laws are based on the need to prevent crime. New York's campaign is based on the "broken windows" theory of criminologists James Q. Wilson and George Kelling (*Atlantic Monthly*, March 1982). Their theory argues that allowing indications of disorder, such as a broken window, or street people, to remain unaddressed shows a loss of public order and control, as well as apathy in a neighborhood, which breeds more serious criminal activity. Therefore, keeping a city neat and orderly should help to prevent crime.

All of these are legitimate concerns to some degree. The problem is that rather than try to eliminate or reduce homelessness by helping the homeless find housing and jobs, most local laws try to change the behavior of the homeless by punishing them. They target the homeless with legal action if they do not change their behavior, ignoring the fact that many would gladly stop living in the streets and panhandling if they had any feasible alternatives. While these laws may be effective in the sense that the shanties are gone and homeless people no longer bed down in subway tunnels or doorways, the fact remains that

TABLE 6.1

Prohibited conduct in selected cities, 2002–03

City	Sanitation		Begging			Sleeping/camping			
	Bathing in public waters	Urination/ defecation in public	Begging in public places city-wide	Begging in particular public places	"Aggressive" panhandling	Sleeping in public city-wide	Sleeping in particular public places	Camping in public city-wide	Camping in particular public places
Albuquerque, NM		X			X				X
Atlanta, GA		X		X	X		X	X	
Austin, TX		X	X		X		X	X	
Baltimore, MD		X		X	X		X		
Boston, MA				X	X	X			
Buffalo, NY	X		X				X	X	
Charlotte, NC		X		X	X		X		
Chicago, IL					X				
Cincinnati, OH	X	X		X	X				
Cleveland, OH				X			X		
Columbus, OH				X	X			X	
Dallas, TX	X	X		X	X	X	X		X
Denver, CO	X	X		X	X		X		X
Detroit, MI			X	X					
El Paso, TX		X		X					X
Fort Worth, TX			X	X					
Fresno, CA	X	X		X	X		X		X
Honolulu, HI									X
Houston, TX		X			X		X		X
Indianapolis, IN	X		X	X	X		X		
Jacksonville, FL	X		X	X	X	X	X	X	X
Kansas City, MO				X	X				X
Long Beach, CA		X	X					X	X
Los Angeles, CA	X			X	X		X		X
Memphis, TN				X	X				
Miami, FL	X				X	X	X		
Milwaukee, WI	X				X		X		X
Minneapolis, MN	X		X	X				X	X
Nashville, TN	X			X					X
New Orleans, LA			X			X			
New York, NY	X	X		X	X		X		X
Oakland, CA	X		X	X		X	X	X	
Oklahoma City, OK	X		X	X			X		X
Omaha, NE			X				X		
Philadelphia, PA		X		X	X				
Phoenix, AZ		X	X	X	X	X	X	X	X
Pittsburgh, PA	X			X	X				X
Portland, OR	X	X		X			X	X	
Sacramento, CA		X		X	X			X	X
San Antonio, TX	X			X					
San Diego, CA	X		X	X	X		X		X
San Francisco, CA			X		X		X		X
San Jose, CA		X		X					
Seattle, WA	X	X			X				X
St. Louis, MO					X				
Toledo, OH			X	X					
Tucson, AZ	X	X		X	X		X		X
Tulsa, OK				X	X		X	X	X
Virginia Beach, VA		X	X			X	X		
Washington, DC				X	X				

the homeless have not disappeared. They have simply been forced to move to a different part of town, hide, or else they have been imprisoned. Furthermore, many of these laws have been challenged in court as violating the legal rights of the homeless people they target.

AN ARGUMENT AGAINST CRIMINALIZATION AS PUBLIC POLICY. In "Downward Spiral: Homelessness and Its Criminalization" (*Yale Law & Policy Review*, vol. 14, no. 1, 1996), Maria Foscarinis, founder of the National Law Center on Homelessness & Poverty, argued that criminalization of the homeless is poor public policy for several reasons:

- It may be constitutionally unsound, especially in cities that are unable to offer adequate resources to their homeless residents.

- It leads to legal challenges, which may take years to resolve, regardless of outcome.

TABLE 6.1

Prohibited conduct in selected cities, 2002–03 [CONTINUED]

| City | Sitting/lying | Loitering/loafing | | Vagrancy | | |
	Sitting or lying in particular public places	Loitering/ loafing/ vagrancy city-wide	Loitering/ loafing in particular public places	Obstruction of sidewalks/ public places	Closure of particular public places	Other (see footnotes)
Albuquerque, NM				X	X	2,11,15
Atlanta, GA	X		X	X	X	1,2,6,7,12
Austin, TX	X		X		X	2
Baltimore, MD		X	X	X	X	1,3,14
Boston, MA	X		X	X		9
Buffalo, NY			X	X	X	1,2,6,7,14,17
Charlotte, NC	X		X	X	X	5,14
Chicago, IL				X	X	1,3,4,6
Cincinnati, OH	X			X	X	1,2,14
Cleveland, OH			X	X	X	
Columbus, OH	X		X	X	X	1,2,4
Dallas, TX			X	X	X	2
Denver, CO			X	X	X	1,2,4,14
Detroit, MI		X	X	X	X	1,2,5,7,14
El Paso, TX			X	X	X	1,2,6,10
Fort Worth, TX		X		X		2,4,8,14
Fresno, CA	X		X	X		2
Honolulu, HI			X		X	
Houston, TX	X			X	X	2,9
Indianapolis, IN		X		X	X	1,2,4
Jacksonville, FL	X		X	X	X	1,2,4,7,11,16,17
Kansas City, MO			X	X	X	1,2,4,14
Long Beach, CA				X		2
Los Angeles, CA	X		X	X	X	2,3,7,17
Memphis, TN				X	X	
Miami, FL	X		X	X	X	4,11
Milwaukee, WI	X	X		X	X	1,2,3,5
Minneapolis, MN	X		X	X	X	1,2,5,10,11,14
Nashville, TN	X		X	X	X	1
New Orleans, LA					X	
New York, NY	X			X	X	
Oakland, CA	X		X	X	X	1,4
Oklahoma City, OK			X	X	X	2,8,14,15
Omaha, NE				X		4,8,17
Philadelphia, PA	X		X	X	X	1,2,3,4
Phoenix, AZ	X	X	X	X	X	2
Pittsburgh, PA				X	X	1,2
Portland, OR	X			X	X	1,2,4,5,6,8,9,11,12,15
Sacramento, CA			X	X	X	1,2,5
San Antonio, TX			X	X	X	1,2,9
San Diego, CA			X	X		1,2,8
San Francisco, CA			X	X		2,3,4,11,14
San Jose, CA	X			X		2
Seattle, WA	X			X	X	4
St. Louis, MO		X		X	X	1,2,3,6,13
Toledo, OH			X	X	X	2,4,9
Tucson, AZ	X		X	X	X	2,8,14
Tulsa, OK				X	X	1,2,11,14
Virginia Beach, VA	X		X	X		2,4,11
Washington, DC		X				2,7,8

[1] Spitting.
[2] Minor curfew.
[3] Having/abandoning merchandise carts away from premises of owner.
[4] Failure to disperse.
[5] Maintaining junk/storage of property.
[6] Making music on the street/street performers.
[7] Washing automobile windows.
[8] Prohibition to enter vacant building.
[9] Rummaging.
[10] Creating odor.
[11] Vehicular residence.
[12] Walking on highway.
[13] Bringing paupers/insane persons into city.
[14] Peddling.
[15] Public nuisance.
[16] Charging for car wash.
[17] Washing cars.

SOURCE: "Prohibited Conduct," in *Illegal to Be Homeless: The Criminalization of Homelessness in the United States,* The National Coalition for the Homeless, Washington, DC, August 2003 [Online] http://www.nationalhomeless.org/civilrights/crim2003/report.pdf [accessed September 2, 2003]

- Legal battles are costly and will deplete already scarce municipal resources that could be used on solutions to homelessness.

- Criminalization responses do not reflect public sentiment, but rather the will of a vocal, politically influential minority.

- Criminalization fosters divisiveness, pitting "us" (the housed) against "them" (the homeless).

- Like emergency relief, criminalization addresses the visible symptom of homelessness—the presence of homeless people in public space—and neglects the true causes of homelessness.

- Finally there is the fact that, in the long-term, criminalization does not and cannot work. Like all humans, homeless people must eat, sleep, and occupy space. If they are prohibited from occupying one area, they must go somewhere else.

As an alternative to criminalization, Maria Foscarinis suggested the following:

- Police advocacy programs, in which "sweeps" are replaced by outreach units—officers assigned to go out, with service providers, to homeless people to refer them to necessary services. Unless criminal activity is involved, the police remain in the background to provide security, and the presence of service providers prevents police from being too heavy-handed or harassing.

- Standing committees composed of homeless people, advocates, a police captain, and a representative of the city government to respond to complaints about "camping" of homeless residents. The committee outreach team attempts to make alternative arrangements for the homeless. The police act only if criminal activity is involved, or if homeless people refuse alternative arrangements.

- Day-labor centers—buildings where homeless people can meet with employers to get jobs.

- One-stop access centers, which offer medical services, mental health services, social services, and job training at one location.

IMPLEMENTED ALTERNATIVES

Alternatives to criminalizing homeless behavior can be implemented with help from community leadership and homeless advocates, who have intimate knowledge from close contact with homelessness. In *Constructive Alternatives To Criminalization: Models to Replicate and Useful Tips to Consider,* the National Law Center on Homelessness and Poverty (NLCHP) reports what some cities have done about homeless problems (October 2002 [Online] http://www.nlchp.org/FA_CivilRights/CR_con-alt_booklet.pdf [accessed September 19, 2003]).

Miami

After 10 years in litigation, a class action suit brought by homeless persons, *Michael Pottinger, Peter Carter, Berry Young, et al. v. City of Miami* (810 F. Supp. 1551 [1992]), resulted in a financial settlement and the "no bed/no arrest" policy that other cities have adopted as a model. (No bed/no arrest means that if a person is to be arrested for an action that is a result of being homeless, that person must first be referred to an appropriate, available, and accessible shelter bed. If the person declines that bed, then he or she may be arrested.) The city of Miami used some of the settlement money to build two large shelters. Funds were raised to provide programs for the homeless, and police officers were required to undergo training on interacting with the homeless.

Philadelphia

When Philadelphia proposed a "Sidewalk Behavior Ordinance" in 1998, homeless people and the mental health community formed a coalition, staged sit-ins, lobbied, and testified at city council meetings to increase public awareness of homelessness. In the end nearly $6 million was appropriated for the necessary social services in the event the ordinance was passed by voters (it was). A no bed/no citation policy (for violation of the ordinance) was adopted, and additional shelter beds and other housing opportunities were provided, with the result that there was a noticeable decline in the homeless population.

Washington, D.C.

In Washington, D.C., a 1-cent-per-square-foot tax levied on business property built the DC Downtown Day Center. Support came from those most affected by the homeless situation and resulted in services and solutions rather than fines and jail time for those in need.

In analyzing the actions taken by cities to deal with homelessness, the NLCHP noted the downside to the no bed/no arrest policy: Any type of bed space can be offered to a homeless person and if that space is refused, cities often permit an arrest "rather than focusing on other more constructive long-term solutions to homelessness such as outreach or building of affordable housing."

CONSTITUTIONAL RIGHTS

The U.S. Constitution and its amendments, especially the Bill of Rights, guarantee certain freedoms and rights to all citizens of the United States, including the homeless. As more and more cities move to deal with homelessness by aggressively enforcing public place restrictions, the restrictions are increasingly being challenged in court as unconstitutional. Sometimes a city ordinance has been declared unconstitutional; at other times, the courts have found that there were special circumstances that allowed the ordinance to stand.

There are numerous ways in which ordinances affecting the homeless can in effect violate their rights. Many court challenges claimed that the law in question was unconstitutionally broad or vague. Others claimed that a particular law denied the homeless equal protection under the law or violated their right to due process, as guaranteed by the Fifth and Fourteenth Amendments. There have also been cases based on a person's right to travel, and others that claimed restrictions on the homeless constituted "cruel and unusual punishment," which is prohibited by the Eighth Amendment. Many cities have ordinances against panhandling, but charitable organizations freely solicit in public places. As a result, say those challenging the ordinances, the right to free expression under the First Amendment is available to organizations but denied to the homeless.

The appearance of poverty should not deny an individual's right to be free from unreasonable search and seizure, as guaranteed by the Fourth Amendment. Often homeless people's property has been confiscated or destroyed (camping gear, personal possessions) without warning because they were found on public property. Unfortunately the state of homelessness is such that even the most personal living activities have to be performed in public. Denying these activities necessary for survival may infringe on an individual's rights under the Eighth Amendment.

The Fourteenth Amendment right to equal protection under the law may be at issue when the homeless are cited for sleeping in the park, but others lying on the grass sunning themselves or taking a nap during a picnic, for instance, are not.

Testing the Laws in Court

Some court cases test the law through civil suits and others challenge the law by appealing convictions in criminal cases. Many advocates for the homeless, or the homeless themselves, have challenged laws that they felt infringed on the rights of homeless people.

NO BED, NO ARREST. The concept of "no bed, no arrest" first arose out of a 1988 class action suit filed by the Miami Chapter of the American Civil Liberties Union on behalf of about 6,000 homeless people living in the city of Miami. The city had a practice of "sweeping" the homeless from the areas where the Orange Bowl Parade and other related activities were held. The complaint alleged that the city had

> a custom, practice and policy of arresting, harassing and otherwise interfering with homeless people for engaging in basic activities of daily life—including sleeping and eating—in the public places where they are forced to live. Plaintiffs further claim that the City has arrested thousands of homeless people for such life-sustaining conduct under various City of Miami ordinances and Florida Statutes. In addition, plaintiffs assert that the city routinely seizes and destroys their property and has failed to follow its own inventory procedures regarding the seized personal property of homeless arrestees and homeless persons in general.

In *Michael Pottinger, Peter Carter, Berry Young, et al. v. City of Miami* (810 F. Supp. 1551 [1992]), the U.S. District Court for the Southern District of Florida ruled that the city's practices were "cruel and unusual," in violation of the Eighth Amendment's ban against punishment based on status. (Only the homeless were being arrested.) Furthermore, the court found the police practices of taking or destroying the property of the homeless to be in violation of Fourth and Fifth Amendment rights of freedom from unreasonable seizure and confiscation of property.

The city appealed the district court's judgment. Ultimately, a settlement was reached in which the city of Miami agreed that a homeless person observed committing a "life-sustaining conduct" misdemeanor may be warned to stop, but if there is no available shelter, no warning is to be given. If there is an available shelter, the homeless person is to be told of its availability. If the homeless person accepts assistance, no arrest is to take place.

USING LIBRARIES. Richard Kreimer, a homeless man in Morristown, New Jersey, often visited the Joint Free Library of Morristown. The library personnel objected to his presence, claiming his behavior was disruptive, and his body odor so offensive that it kept patrons from using some of the areas of the library. After the librarians documented the problems for a period of time, the Library Board of Trustees passed a Library Patron Policy that, among other things, allowed librarians to ask people to leave if their hygiene was unacceptable to community norms.

In 1990 Kreimer filed suit in the Federal District Court for New Jersey against the library, the Board of Directors, the Morristown Bureau of Police, and other library and municipal officials. The suit alleged that the policy rules were "overbroad" (that is, they failed to specify what actions would be objectionable), "vague," and a violation of Kreimer's First Amendment right of access to information and his Fourteenth Amendment rights of equal protection and due process, as well as his rights under the New Jersey Constitution.

The district court upheld Kreimer's complaint that the policy violated his First and Fourteenth Amendment rights. The library appealed the decision to the Court of Appeals, and the court reversed the decision, validating the library's policy, finding that a library, by its very nature, cannot support all First Amendment activities, such as speech-making and interactive debate. Therefore, a library is a "limited public forum," and the rules of the Morristown Library were appropriate to its limited functions of reading, studying, and using library materials (*Kreimer v. Bureau of Police for Morristown*, 958 F.2d 1242 [3rd Cir. 1992]).

LOITERING OR WANDERING. In 2000 homeless street dwellers and shelter residents of the Skid Row area (the plaintiffs) sought a temporary restraining order (TRO) against the Los Angeles Police Department (the defendants), claiming their First and Fourth Amendment rights were being violated. The plaintiffs alleged they were being stopped without cause and their identification demanded on threat of arrest, that they were being ordered to "move along" although they were not in anyone's way, that their belongings were being confiscated, and that they were being ticketed for loitering. In *Justin v. City of Los Angeles* (No. CV-00-12352 LGB, 2000 U.S. Dist. Lexis 17881 [C.D. Cal. Dec. 5, 2000]), Judge Lourdes Baird denied a TRO that would have prevented the defendants from asking the plaintiffs to "move along." The TRO was granted with reference to the following actions when in the Skid Row area:

- Detention without reasonable suspicion.

- Demand of identification upon threat of arrest.

- Searches without probable cause.

- Removal from sidewalks unless free passage of pedestrians was obstructed.

- Confiscation of personal property that was not abandoned.

- Citation of those who may "annoy or molest" if interference was reasonable and free passage of pedestrians was not impeded.

LIVING IN AN ENCAMPMENT. In 1996 advocates for the homeless sought an injunction against a Tucson resolution barring homeless encampments from city-owned property on Eighth Amendment and Equal Protection grounds. The court, in *Davidson v. City of Tucson* (924 F. Supp.989), held the plaintiffs did not have standing to raise a cruel and unusual punishment claim, as they had not been convicted of a crime and no one had been arrested under the ordinance. The Equal Protection claim failed because the court did not consider homeless people a suspect class and the right to travel did not include the right to ignore trespass laws or remain on property without regard to ownership.

SITTING OR LYING ON THE SIDEWALK. In 1995 homeless persons challenged Cincinnati ordinances prohibiting sitting or lying on sidewalks and solicitation on First and Fourteenth Amendment grounds. In 1998, in *Clark v. Cincinnati* (No. 1-95-448, S.D. Ohio, October 25, 1995), determining that the ordinances likely infringed on the plaintiffs' First Amendment right to freedom of speech, the U.S. District Court issued a preliminary injunction to stop the city from enforcing the ordinances, except for the specific provision of the sidewalk ordinance that prohibited lying down.

LOITERING IN A TRAIN STATION. In 1995 plaintiffs challenged Amtrak's policy of arresting or ejecting persons who appeared to be homeless or loitering in Penn Station in New York City, even though the individuals were not apparently committing crimes. The district court, in *Streetwatch v. National R.R. Passenger Corp.* (875 F. Supp. 1055), issued a preliminary injunction prohibiting Amtrak from continuing the practice, finding that Amtrak's rules of conduct were vague and that their enforcement impinged on plaintiffs' rights to freedom of movement and due process.

PANHANDLING. One of the notable court cases addressing panhandling involved Jennifer Loper, who moved from her parents' suburban New York home to beg on the streets of New York City. From time to time she and her friend William Kaye were ordered by police to move on, in accordance with the city ordinance stating: "A person is guilty of loitering when he: '(1) Loiters, remains or wanders about in a public place for the purpose of begging.'" In 1992 Loper and Kaye sued the city, claiming that their free speech rights had been violated and that the ordinance was unconstitutional. A district court declared the ordinance unconstitutional on First Amendment grounds. On appeal, the police department argued that begging has no expressive element that is protected by the First Amendment. In *Loper v. New York City Police Department* (999 F.2d 699 [2d Cir. 1993]), the U.S. Court of Appeals, Second Circuit declared the city's ban on begging invalid, noting that the regulations applied to sidewalks, which have historically been acknowledged to be a public forum. The Court agreed that the ban deprived beggars of all means to express their message. Even if a panhandler does not speak, "the mere presence of an unkempt and disheveled person holding out his or her hand or a cup to receive a donation itself conveys a message of need for support and assistance."

ZONING THE HOMELESS OUT OF DOWNTOWN. In 1998 Alan Mason, a homeless man, sought an injunction, damages, and relief against the city of Tucson and the city police for "zoning" homeless people. The suit alleged that homeless people were arrested without cause, were charged with misdemeanors, and were then released only if they agreed to stay away from the area where they had been arrested. Mason himself had been restricted from certain downtown areas, including state, local, and federal courts (including the court in which his case was tried); voter registration facilities; a soup kitchen; places of worship; and many social and transportation agencies.

The plaintiff argued that such restrictions violated his constitutional right to travel, deprived him of liberty without due process in violation of the Fifth Amendment, and implicated the Equal Protection clause of the Fourteenth Amendment. In July 1998, the district court, in *Mason v. Tucson* (D. Arizona, 1998) granted a temporary injunction against enforcing the law, saying the zone restrictions were overbroad. Subsequently, the parties entered into settlement negotiations.

HOMELESS COURT

A recent solution to the increasing backlog of court cases involving petty offenses committed by the homeless is the Homeless Court Program, founded in 1996 by Steven R. Binder, Deputy Public Defender for San Diego County. The program is now a model for other jurisdictions. In a typical program, a courtroom is set up in a shelter or in a Health Care for the Homeless office, and defendants charged with criminal misdemeanor warrants are tried in the presence of a judge, a clerk, a public defender and a prosecutor who are familiar with the problems of the homeless. The guiding principle is rehabilitation, not punishment. According to Justin Graf of the American Bar Association, in an online review of Binder's *The Homeless Court Program: Taking the Court to the Streets* (The American Bar Association Commission on Homelessness & Poverty, Washington, D.C., 2002): "The key players involved in the program realize that outstanding criminal warrants often preclude homeless people from accessing vital services such as employment, housing, public benefits, and treatment for mental health and/or substance abuse problems. As such, the court seeks to address the legal problems of the homeless participants as well as linking them with appropriate services and treatment programs."

CHAPTER 7
THE HEALTH OF THE HOMELESS

LIVING IN PUBLIC: INCREASED HEALTH PROBLEMS

Virtually all Americans suffer illness and disease at some time in their lives, but for people experiencing homelessness and poverty, illness all too often means serious health concerns or premature death. Health problems that may not be so apparent at other income levels, like alcoholism, mental illnesses, diabetes, and depression, become visible and more pronounced with homeless people. Other, more serious illnesses (tuberculosis, for example) are almost exclusively associated with poverty. Homeless people suffer from more types of illnesses, for longer periods of time, and with more harmful consequences than housed people.

The Homeless/Morbidity Connection

One way of measuring the health of a population is to measure its morbidity rate—the rate of incidence of a disease or a mental or substance abuse disorder. (Morbidity does not mean a person is about to die from the disease or condition.) The homeless often exhibit two or more conditions simultaneously, a phenomenon known as comorbidity or co-occurring disorders. Researcher Mary Ann Burg, in "Health Problems of Sheltered Homeless Women and Their Dependent Children" (*Health and Social Work*, 1994), explored the relationship between ill health and poverty and categorized the health problems of homeless women and their dependent children living in shelters. Burg's study revealed three general classifications of illnesses related to homelessness:

- Illnesses resulting from homelessness

- Illnesses intensified by the limited health-care access of the homeless

- Illnesses associated with the psychosocial burdens of homelessness

Poor health has also been reported as a cause of homelessness. In a frequently-cited 1987 national survey of homeless patients (James D. Wright and Eleanor Weber, *Homelessness and Health,* McGraw Hill, Washington, DC, 1987), 13 percent of the patients said that poor physical health was a factor in their becoming homeless. Of those responding in the affirmative, half said health was a "major factor" and 15 percent said that it was the "single most important" factor. Wright and Weber also found that up to 40 percent of the homeless suffered from a major mental illness; in the case of the mentally ill and the alcoholic and drug-addicted homeless, the authors asserted that the failure of America's health-care system must bear a major share of the blame for their homelessness.

The Homeless/Mortality Connection

Mortality refers to the proportion of deaths to population. San Francisco, estimated to have one of the largest homeless populations in the country (7,200 in 2002), has been tracking homeless mortality data since 1985. Since 1988 the annual number of homeless deaths has exceeded 100 and reached 169 in the one-year period ending June 30, 2003 (a rate of one death every other day). In an analysis of deaths among San Francisco's homeless (Ricardo Bermúdez et al., *San Francisco Homeless Deaths Identified from Medical Examiner Records: December 1996–November 1997*), the authors noted that it was obvious from this and previous reports that the homeless had a higher mortality rate than the housed population. The homeless die at younger ages; in 1997 the average age of death among the homeless was 43.3 years, compared with 72.6 years for the general population. The leading cause of death was substance abuse (50 percent of all deaths); 31 percent of deaths were caused by illicit drug use and 19 percent by alcohol use.

Doctor James O'Connell, a physician with the Boston Health Care for the Homeless (BHCH) program, concluded in "Death on the Streets" (*Harvard Medical Alumni Bulletin*, Winter 1997) that while the causes of the higher morbidity and mortality rates among Boston's homeless people are complex, there are elements of the homeless life that encourage early death. Some of these are: exposure to extremes of weather and temperature; crowded shelter living, which increases the spread of communicable diseases such as tuberculosis (TB) and pneumonia; violence; the high frequency of medical and psychiatric illnesses; substance abuse; and inadequate nutrition.

A 1998 study of 558 homeless adults in the city of Boston, Massachusetts, conducted by the Inner City Health Program (*Risk Factors for Death in Homeless Adults in Boston*), found that males, whites, and substance abusers were most likely to die while living on the streets. The strongest risk factors for death were AIDS, renal (kidney) disease, recurrent cold-related injuries, liver disease, and arrhythmia (irregular heartbeat). A history of substance abuse involving alcohol or injected drugs also increased the risk of mortality.

A ten-year follow-up study of 750 homeless people who in 1991 had stayed in homeless shelters in Copenhagen, Denmark, found that homeless people were four times more likely to die early than people in the general population (Merete Nordentoft and Nina Wandall-Holm, "10-Year Follow Up Study of Mortality Among Users of Hostels for Homeless People in Copenhagen," *British Medical Journal*, July 12, 2003). Mortality was particularly high for homeless people aged 15 to 34 years, among women, and among people who had stayed for only a short time in a shelter or who stayed more than once during the year.

The Causes

According to the Danish researchers, "Other predictors of early death were adverse childhood experiences, such as death of the father, and misuse of alcohol and sedatives." According to health-care experts, the following socioeconomic conditions contribute to the greater prevalence of illness and early death among the poor and homeless population:

- Poor diet
- Inadequate sleeping locations
- Contagion from overcrowded shelters
- Limited facilities for daily hygiene
- Exposure to the elements
- Exposure to violence
- Social isolation
- Lack of health insurance

The Severity of the Problem

There is a growing belief in the health-care field that homelessness needs to be considered in epidemic terms—

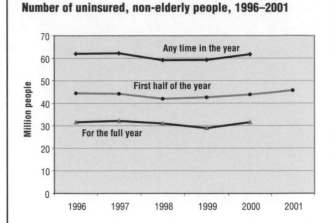

FIGURE 7.1

Number of uninsured, non-elderly people, 1996–2001

SOURCE: Jeffrey A. Rhoades, Ph.D., and Joel W. Cohen, Ph.D., "Figure 2. MEPS 1996-2001, Uninsured Status, Non-elderly," in "The Uninsured in America–1996-2001: Estimates for the Civilian Noninstitutionalized Population Under Age 65," *Statistical Brief #6*, Medical Expenditure Panel Survey [Online] http://www.meps. ahrq.gov/papers/st6/stat06.pdf [accessed September 11, 2003]

that massive increases in homelessness may result in a hastened spread of illness and disease, overwhelming the health-care system. Researcher W. R. Breakey recognized the morbidity rates among the homeless as a major public health concern. In a 1997 article in the *American Journal of Public Health* ("It's Time for the Public Health Community to Declare War on Homelessness"), Breakey proposed that homelessness be responded to with the same urgency as an epidemic of an infectious disease. He urged public health officials to address larger issues—socioeconomic elements such as housing availability and wages—in order to effectively treat afflicted individuals.

The scope of health issues regarding the impoverished and homeless in the United States is related in part to the number of uninsured Americans. In "The Uninsured in America—1996–2001: Estimates for the Civilian Non-institutionalized Population Under Age 65," Jeffrey A. Rhoades, Ph.D., and Joel W. Cohen, Ph.D., reported that in every year from 1996 to 2001 about 60 million people were without insurance at some point. (See Figure 7.1.) Figure 7.2 shows the percentage of people who were without health insurance coverage in 2000, by state. (See Figure 7.2.) New Mexico (23.8 percent) and Texas (21.5 percent) had the highest percentages of uninsured people, while Rhode Island (5.9 percent) had the lowest.

People without insurance are less likely to seek medical care. In "Out of Pocket Medical Spending for Care of Chronic Conditions" (*Health Affairs*, November–December 2001), W. Hwang et al. noted that "among chronically ill persons the uninsured had the highest out-of-pocket spending and were five times less likely to see a medical provider in a given year."

FIGURE 7.2

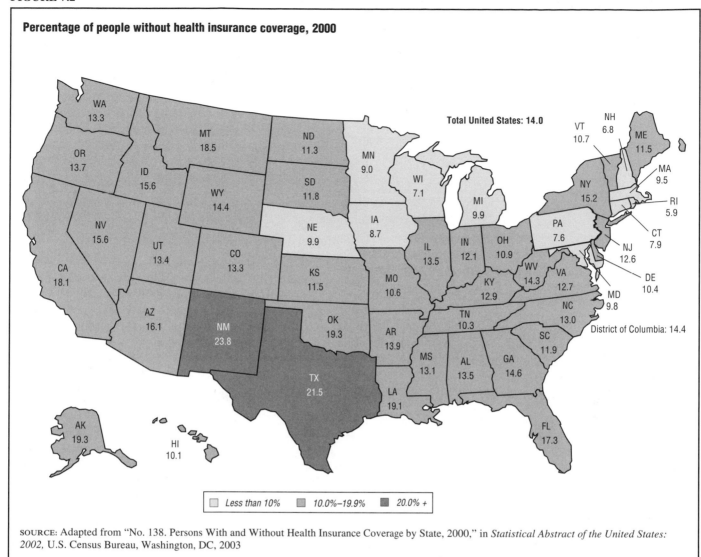

Percentage of people without health insurance coverage, 2000

Total United States: 14.0

WA 13.3
OR 13.7
MT 18.5
ND 11.3
MN 9.0
ID 15.6
WY 14.4
SD 11.8
NE 9.9
IA 8.7
WI 7.1
MI 9.9
NV 15.6
UT 13.4
CO 13.3
KS 11.5
MO 10.6
IL 13.5
IN 12.1
OH 10.9
PA 7.6
NY 15.2
VT 10.7
NH 6.8
ME 11.5
MA 9.5
RI 5.9
CT 7.9
NJ 12.6
DE 10.4
MD 9.8
WV 14.3
VA 12.7
CA 18.1
AZ 16.1
NM 23.8
OK 19.3
AR 13.9
TN 10.3
KY 12.9
NC 13.0
SC 11.9
TX 21.5
LA 19.1
MS 13.1
AL 13.5
GA 14.6
FL 17.3
AK 19.3
HI 10.1

District of Columbia: 14.4

Less than 10% | 10.0%–19.9% | 20.0% +

SOURCE: Adapted from "No. 138. Persons With and Without Health Insurance Coverage by State, 2000," in *Statistical Abstract of the United States: 2002,* U.S. Census Bureau, Washington, DC, 2003

The Health Costs of Street Living

The rates of both chronic and acute health problems are disproportionately high among the homeless population. With the exception of obesity, strokes, and cancer, homeless people are far more likely than the housed to suffer from every category of chronic health problem. Conditions that require regular, uninterrupted treatment, such as TB, HIV/AIDS, diabetes, hypertension, malnutrition, severe dental problems, addictive disorders, and mental disorders, are extremely difficult to treat or control among those without adequate housing.

Street living comes with a set of health conditions that living in a home does not. Human beings without shelter tend to fall prey to parasites, frostbite, leg ulcers, and infections. Homeless people are also at greater risk of physical and psychological trauma resulting from muggings, beatings, and rape. With no safe place to store belongings, proper storage or administration of medications becomes difficult. In addition, some homeless people with mental disorders may use drugs or alcohol to self-medicate, and those with addictive disorders are more susceptible to HIV and other communicable diseases.

Homeless people may also lack the ability to access some of the fundamental rituals of self-care: bed rest, good nutrition, and good personal hygiene. The luxury of "taking it easy for a day or two," for example, is almost impossible for homeless people; they must often keep walking or remain standing all day in order to avoid criminal charges.

Unwell homeless people also remain untreated longer than their sheltered counterparts because obtaining food and shelter takes priority over health care. As a result, relatively minor illnesses go untreated until they develop into major emergencies, requiring expensive acute care treatment and long-term recovery.

The Urban Institute analyzed the results of the 1996 National Survey of Homeless Assistance Providers and

FIGURE 7.3

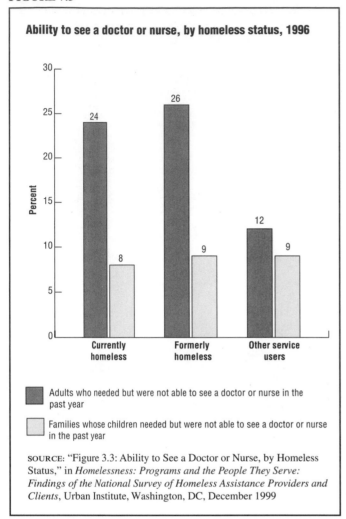

Ability to see a doctor or nurse, by homeless status, 1996

SOURCE: "Figure 3.3: Ability to See a Doctor or Nurse, by Homeless Status," in *Homelessness: Programs and the People They Serve: Findings of the National Survey of Homeless Assistance Providers and Clients*, Urban Institute, Washington, DC, December 1999

FIGURE 7.4

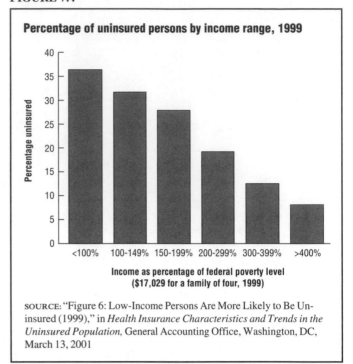

Percentage of uninsured persons by income range, 1999

SOURCE: "Figure 6: Low-Income Persons Are More Likely to Be Uninsured (1999)," in *Health Insurance Characteristics and Trends in the Uninsured Population*, General Accounting Office, Washington, DC, March 13, 2001

Clients, the only survey of its kind (studies of the homeless tend to focus on local populations). The analysis showed that in the year preceding the survey, 25 percent of the clients studied had needed medical attention but were not able to see a doctor or a nurse. The same study also revealed that recently homeless people were even less likely to receive medical help when needed (26 percent). (See Figure 7.3.)

The higher rate of health problems among the newly housed was attributed to: 1) the loss of convenient health care in centers or shelters, 2) the habit of enduring untreated ailments, and/or 3) a lack of health-care benefits (common among people below the poverty level). A 1999 study by the General Accounting Office revealed that 37 percent of those people below the official poverty level (in 1999, $17,029 annual income for a family of four) were likely to be uninsured. (See Figure 7.4.) Of those people earning four times the poverty level (about $68,000) or more, only 8 percent were uninsured.

The results of a study published in February 2000 (L. Gelberg, R.M. Andersen, and B.D. Leake, "The Behavioral Model for Vulnerable Populations: Application to Medical Care Use and Outcomes for Homeless People," *Health Services Research*) on the prevalence of certain disease conditions among homeless adults revealed that 37 percent suffered from functional vision impairment, 36 percent from skin/leg/foot problems, and 31 percent tested positive for TB. The authors of the study indicated that homeless people who had a community clinic or private physician as a regular source of care exhibited better health outcomes. The research study also suggested that clinical treatment of the homeless be accompanied by efforts to help them find permanent housing.

PHYSICAL AILMENTS OF HOMELESS PEOPLE

A March 2000 survey of the homeless in Hartford, Connecticut, performed by The Institute of Outcomes Research for the Hartford Community Health Partnership (E. B. O'Keefe, R. Maljanian, and M. McCormack, *Hartford Homeless Health Survey*), counted 1,365 homeless persons on the evening of December 13, 1999. The vast majority (87 percent) of survey respondents reported a prior diagnosis of at least one of seventeen chronic conditions. The most prevalent of these chronic conditions were drug and alcohol abuse, depression and other mental illnesses, hypertension, chronic bronchitis and emphysema, HIV/AIDS, asthma, and arthritis. Comparing the responses from the homeless survey against the rates for the general Hartford population revealed that depression was almost twice as likely among the homeless (41 percent) than among the general population (23 percent) and the rate of chronic bronchitis and emphysema among homeless survey respondents was 22.7 percent, three times that of Hartford's general population. While these chronic diseases exist throughout the general population, difficulty in providing treatment to the homeless makes them worse, as do hunger and malnutrition.

Gillian Silver of the Johns Hopkins Bloomberg School of Public Health and Rea Pañares summarized the study findings regarding the health problems faced by homeless women, who comprise about one-third (32 percent) of the homeless population. This group was prone to the same physical ailments reported by the general homeless population in Hartford but also reported high rates of gastrointestinal problems, neurological disorders, chronic obstructive pulmonary disease, and peripheral vascular disease. (See Table 7.1.)

Tuberculosis

Several kinds of acute, nonspecific respiratory diseases are common among homeless people. These diseases are spread by living in groups and overcrowded shelters, in stressful situations, and without adequate nutrition. Tuberculosis (TB), a disease at one time almost eliminated from the general American population, has become a major health problem among the homeless. This disease is associated with exposure, poor diet, alcoholism, HIV, injection drug use (IDU), and other illnesses that lower the body's resistance to infection. TB is spread by lengthy personal contact, making it a potential hazard not only to shelter residents but also to the general public.

From 1953 to 1984 the United States experienced a decrease of 73.6 percent in the number of reported TB cases (from 84,304 cases to 22,255 cases). However, in 1984 the number of TB cases began to rise, reaching 25,701 cases in 1990. According to the Centers for Disease Control and Prevention (CDC), rising homelessness and poverty account, in part, for the resurgence of TB. Poor ventilating systems and the inability to quarantine victims allowed it to become prevalent. In a special report from the CDC, 6.3 percent of the homeless population were found to have TB in 1999. (See Table 7.2.) State-by-state breakdowns give some indication of the contagious nature of the disease. In 1999, for example, Montana reported that 35.7 percent of its homeless population tested positive for TB, while Wyoming, Vermont, and Hawaii had no cases of TB among the homeless.

Clinical data from the federally-funded Health Care for the Homeless program (HCH), part of the Bureau of Primary Health Care, found prevalence rates for tuberculosis to be 100 to 300 times higher among the homeless than among the overall population. An additional contributing factor was the emergence of drug-resistant strains of TB. Experts reported that to control the spread of TB, the homeless must receive frequent screenings for TB and the infected must get long-term care and rest. A campaign for increased public awareness, particularly among

TABLE 7.1

Summary of study findings related to health problems faced by homeless women, 2000

Health Issue	Key findings
Chronic disease	▪ The most common chronic physical conditions (excluding substance abuse) are hypertension, gastrointestinal problems, neurological disorders, arthritis and other musculoskeletal disorders, chronic obstructive pulmonary disease, and peripheral vascular disease.
Infectious disease	▪ The most common infectious diseases reported were chest infection, cold, cough, and bronchitis; reporting was the same for those formerly homeless, currently homeless, and other service users. ▪ Homeless patients wth tuberculosis were more likely to present with a more progressed form than non-homeless. ▪ Widespread screening for TB in shelters may miss most homeless persons becuase many do not live in the shelter, and instead present in emergency departments.
STDs/ HIV/AIDS	▪ A mobile women's health unit in Chicago reported that of 104 female homeless clients, 30 percent had abnormal Pap smears – 14 percent with atypia and 10 percent with inflammation; the incidence of chlamydia was 3 percent, gonorrhea 6 percent, and trichomoniasis 26 percent. ▪ HIV infection was found to be 2.35 times more prevalent in homeless, drug-abusing women than homeless, drug-abusing men.
Stress	▪ Homeless mothers reported higher levels of stress, depression, and avoidance and anti-cognitive coping strategies than low-income, housed mothers.
Nutrition	▪ Currently and formerly homeless clients are more likely to report not getting enough to eat (28 and 25 percent reprectively) than among all U.S. households (4 percent) and among poor households (12 percent). ▪ Contrary to their opinions, homeless women and their dependents were consuming less than 50 percent of the 1989 recommended daily allowance for iron, magnesium, zinc, folic acid, and calcium. ▪ Subjects of all ages consumed higher than desirable quantities of fats. ▪ The health risk factors of iron deficiency anemia, obesity, and hypercholesterolemia were prevalant.
Smoking	▪ More than half of both homeless mothers and low-income housed mothers were current smokers, compared with 22.6 percent of female adults 18 years and over.
Violence	▪ Poor women are at higher risk for violence than women overall; poverty increases stress and lowers the ability to cope with the environment and live safely. ▪ In a study of 436 sheltered homeless and poor housed women: 84 percent of these women had been severely assaulted at some point in their lives; 63 percent had been severely assaulted by parental caretakers while growing up; 40 percent had been sexually molested at least once before reaching adulthood; 60 percent had experienced severe physical attacks by a male intimate partner, and 33 percent had been assaulted by their current or most recent partner. ▪ A study of 53 women homeless for at least three months in the past year demonstrated that this group is at a very high risk of battery and rape, with 91 percent exposed to battery and 56 percent exposed to rape.
Substance abuse	▪ Homeless women comprise a subpopulation at high risk for substance abuse; rates of substance use disorder range from 16 percent to 67 percent. There exists an imbalance between treatment need and treatment access. ▪ Some homeless people with mental disorders may use drugs or alcohol to self-medicate.
Mental health/ depression	▪ A case-control study of 100 homeless women with schizophrenia and 100 non-homeless women with schizophrenia found that homeless women had higher rates of a concurrent diagnosis of alcohol abuse, drug abuse, antisocial personality disorder, and also had less adequate family support. ▪ Many homeless women with serious mental illness are not receiving care; this is due to lack of perception of a mental health problem and lack of services designed to meet the needs of homeless women.

SOURCE: Gillian Silver and Rea Pañares, "Table 2. Summary of study findings related to health problems faced by homeless women," in *The Health of Homeless Women: Information for State Mental and Child Health Programs,* Women's and Children's Health Policy Center, Johns Hopkins Bloomberg School of Public Health, Baltimore, MD, 2000

TABLE 7.2

Tuberculosis cases by homeless status, 1999

Reporting area	Total cases	Cases with information on homeless status		Percent of cases in homeless persons[1]
		No.	%	
United States	**17,531**	**16,808**	**95.9**	**6.3**
Alabama	314	312	99.4	3.8
Alaska	61	61	100.0	3.3
Arizona	262	258	98.5	14.0
Arkansas	181	180	75.0	3.9
California	3,606	3,554	98.6	6.6
Colorado	88	88	100.0	12.5
Connecticut	121	119	98.3	9.2
Delaware	34	34	100.0	2.9
District of Columbia	70	70	100.0	14.3
Florida	1,277	1,276	99.9	8.7
Georgia	665	632	95.0	7.0
Hawaii	184	184	100.0	0.0
Idaho	16	15	93.8	6.7
Illinois	825	796	96.5	6.7
Indiana	150	133	88.7	3.0
Iowa	58	48	82.8	6.3
Kansas	69	64	92.8	1.6
Kentucky	209	205	98.1	12.2
Louisiana	357	350	98.0	5.7
Maine	23	23	100.0	8.7
Maryland	294	293	99.7	3.1
Massachusetts	270	269	99.6	4.5
Michigan	351	342	97.4	3.5
Minnesota	201	201	100.0	3.0
Mississippi	215	215	100.0	1.4
Missouri	208	197	94.7	14.2
Montana	14	14	100.0	35.7
Nebraska	18	18	100.0	11.1
Nevada	93	92	98.9	8.7
New Hampshire	19	18	94.7	0.0
New Jersey	571	571	100.0	5.3
New Mexico	64	64	100.0	7.8
New York State[2]	377	372	98.7	1.9
New York City	1,460	987	67.6	—
North Carolina	488	486	99.6	7.0
North Dakota	7	6	85.7	16.7
Ohio	317	313	98.7	7.3
Oklahoma	208	208	100.0	11.1
Oregon	123	121	98.4	10.7
Pennsylvania	454	423	93.2	2.1
Rhode Island	53	52	98.1	0.0
South Carolina	315	314	99.7	3.8
South Dakota	21	21	100.0	14.3
Tennessee	382	376	98.4	7.4
Texas	1,649	1,649	100.0	6.6
Utah	40	40	100.0	17.5
Vermont	3	3	100.0	0.0
Virginia	334	334	100.0	2.7
Washington	258	257	99.6	6.2
West Virginia	41	37	90.2	13.5
Wisconsin	110	110	100.0	4.5
Wyoming	3	3	100.0	0.0
American Samoa[3]	4	4	100.0	0.0
Fed. States of Micronesia[3]	...	...	...	...
Guam[3]	69	69	100.0	0.0
N. Mariana Islands[3]	66	66	100.0	0.0
Puerto Rico[3]	200	200	100.0	3.0
Republic of Palau[3]	11	11	100.0	0.0
U.S. Virgin Islands[3]	...	...	...	...

[1] Homeless within past 12 months. Percentage for U.S. based on 52 reporting areas (50 states, New York City, and the District of Columbia). Percentages shown only for reporting areas with information reported for ≥75% of cases.
[2] Excludes New York City.
[3] Not included in U.S. totals.
    Ellipses indicate data not available.

SOURCE: "Table 24. Tuberculosis Cases by Homeless Status: 59 Reporting Areas, 1999," Centers for Disease Control and Prevention, National Center for HIV, STD, and TB Prevention, Atlanta, GA, 1999.

members of the medical community, was launched in 1990 to identify and screen those at the greatest risk for TB. The number of reported TB cases declined to 15,991 in 2001.

Malnutrition

Homeless people face a daily challenge to fulfill their basic need for food. They often go hungry. This was borne out in an analysis of the findings of the 1996 National Survey of Homeless Assistance Providers and Clients by Martha R. Burt et al. (*Homelessness: Programs and the People They Serve,* Urban Institute, August 1999). Clients of homeless assistance programs were found to have higher levels of food problems than poor people in general; 28 percent reported not getting enough to eat sometimes or often, compared with 12 percent of poor American adults. More than one-third of the homeless clients had been hungry in the past 30 days but did not eat because they had no money for food (39 percent) and 40 percent reported going at least one whole day without eating. (See Figure 7.5.) Undernourishment and vitamin deficiency can cause or aggravate other physical conditions.

The diet of the homeless is generally not balanced or of good quality, even among those who live in shelters or cheap motels. Homeless people often rely on ready-cooked meals, fast-food restaurants, garbage cans, and the sometimes infrequent meal schedules of free food sources, such as shelters, soup kitchens, and drop-in centers. Many soup kitchens serve only one meal a day, and many shelters that serve meals—and not all of them do—serve only two meals a day.

BARRIERS TO ADEQUATE NUTRITION. People who live below the poverty level, including the homeless, are eligible for food stamps, but many people are not aware that they are eligible. In her speech before the New York City Coalition Against Hunger on June 16, 2003, public advocate Betsy Gotbaum described an investigation into the reasons why New Yorkers' participation in the food stamp program was declining even though the city had endured high unemployment as a result of the national recession that began in March 2001, combined with the further blow to the city's economy caused by the terrorist attacks of September 11, 2001. The investigation revealed that welfare participants who had left the welfare rolls following the 1996 welfare reform legislation were not aware that they could still receive food stamps. Those who were aware of their entitlement were required to fill out a 17-page form to receive benefits. This is the type of barrier that prevents the poor and homeless from accessing or effectively using federal assistance programs.

In 2002 the U.S. Conference of Mayors reported that every one of the 25 cities they surveyed reported an increase in requests for emergency food assistance over the course of the year, but 16 percent of the requests had gone unmet. Fewer than half (48 percent) of the cities

FIGURE 7.5

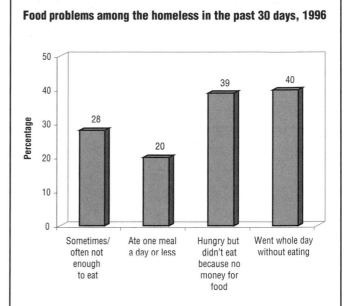

Food problems among the homeless in the past 30 days, 1996

SOURCE: "Figure 2.9: Frequency of Food Problems in the Past 30 Days Among Homeless Clients," in *Homelessness: Programs and the People They Serve: Findings of the National Survey of Homeless Assistance Providers and Clients,* Urban Institute, Washington, DC, December 1999

reported that their facilities were able to provide an adequate amount of food.

Alcoholism, drug use, mental illness (especially severe depression), and physical illness contribute to nutritional deficiencies or lack of appetite. Some soup kitchens and shelters exclude persons high on drugs or alcohol from partaking of meals at their facilities. Intoxicated persons may not be interested in food and can lose a substantial amount of weight as a result. Some advocates for the homeless suggest providing vitamin and mineral supplements to homeless substance abusers.

Skin and Blood Vessel Disorders

Frequent exposure to severe weather, insect bites, and other infestations make skin lesions fairly common among the homeless. Being forced to sit or stand for extended periods results in many homeless people being plagued with edema (swelling of the feet and legs), varicose veins, and skin ulcerations. This population is more prone to conditions that can lead to chronic phlebitis (inflammation of the veins). A homeless person with circulatory problems who sleeps sitting up in a doorway or a bus station can develop open lacerations that may become infected or maggot-infested if left untreated.

Regular baths and showers are luxuries to most homeless people, so many suffer from various forms of dermatitis (inflammation of the skin), often due to infestations of lice or scabies (a contagious skin disease caused by a parasitic mite that burrows under the skin to deposit eggs, causing intense itching). The lack of bathing increases the opportunity for infection to develop in cuts and other lacerations.

AIDS

The Centers for Disease Control and Prevention (CDC) reported in 2002 that between 150,000 and 950,000 Americans are living with HIV, the virus that causes AIDS, and nearly 385,000 of those had full-blown AIDS. AIDS diagnoses increased in 2002 for the first time in 10 years (42,136 new cases were diagnosed). In November 2002 the Food and Drug Administration approved a rapid test for HIV infection that can provide results in 20 minutes. U.S. Health and Human Services Secretary Tommy G. Thompson explained the significance of the test: "Each year, 8,000 HIV-infected people who come to public clinics for HIV testing do not return a week later to receive their test results. . . . With this new test, in less than a half an hour they can learn preliminary information about their HIV status, allowing them to get the care they need to slow the progression of their disease and to take precautionary measures to help prevent the spread of this deadly virus."

The CDC estimates that up to one-fourth of those infected with HIV are not aware of their condition. The CDC is working with health officials to make the rapid test widely available, particularly in places where likely victims reside, such as homeless shelters, drug treatment centers, and jails.

A study of AIDS patients in San Francisco found that poor people die sooner from AIDS ("Study: Disparity Between Rich and Poor Mortality: Poor, Disadvantaged People Develop AIDS Faster," *AIDS Alert,* August 2003). Within five years of diagnosis, fewer than 70 percent of people living in the city's poorest neighborhoods were still alive, compared with more than 85 percent of people who lived in the richest neighborhoods. Poor people with HIV usually have a number of co-occurring disorders, such as drug dependence, mental illness, and unstable housing arrangements. The lack of affordable and appropriate housing can be an acute crisis for these individuals, who need a safe shelter that provides protection and comfort, as well as a base from which to receive services, care, and support.

The University of California at San Francisco, in *HIV Prevention: Looking Back, Looking Ahead* (1995), reported that almost half the homeless are estimated to have two or more of the risk factors associated with HIV—unprotected sex with multiple partners, IDU (intravenous drug use), sex with an IDU partner, or the exchange of unprotected sex for money or drugs. One-fourth report three or more risk factors. Having multiple sex partners is a risk for HIV, but it is extremely difficult for homeless people to form safe or stable intimate relationships due to drug use, mental illness, violence, or transient living conditions. Many homeless women are victims of rape or battery, and many women and children engage in "survival sex" or the exchange of sex for money, drugs, food, or housing.

THE MENTAL HEALTH OF HOMELESS PEOPLE

Before the 1960s people with chronic mental illness were often committed involuntarily to state psychiatric hospitals or "asylums." The development of medications that could control the symptoms of mental illness coincided with a growing belief that involuntary hospitalization was warranted only when a mentally ill person could be deemed a threat to him or herself or to others. Gradually, large numbers of mentally ill people were discharged from hospitals and other treatment facilities, often into homelessness. Often, too, the community-based treatment centers that were supposed to take the place of state hospitals were either inadequate or nonexistent. Many homeless people do not realize how ill they are and how dependent they are on regular treatment. Others no longer believe the system can or will help them. This seems to have been borne out by a 1999 survey of 301 homeless adults in Buffalo, New York (O. Acosta and P.A. Toro, "Let's Ask the Homeless People Themselves: A Needs Assessment Based on a Probability Sample of Adults," *American Journal of Community Psychology,* vol. 28, 2000). When asked what were their greatest needs, the respondents listed affordable housing, safety, education, transportation, medical treatment, and job training/placement. Needs for formal mental health and substance abuse services were rated as unimportant by comparison, easy to obtain, and not very satisfactory to those who had used them.

In a 1998 study of 132 homeless adults (E. M. Reichenbach et al., "The Community Health Nursing Implications of the Self-Reported Health Status of a Local Homeless Population," *Public Health Nurse*, December 1998), researchers explored the personal characteristics and the health and health-related concerns of homeless health clinic clients. The study examined the significant differences in health and well-being between homeless shelter residents and nonshelter residents. The homeless population studied featured a majority of males, average age in the mid-thirties, a high rate of unemployment, and a low rate of health insurance. One-third of respondents reported their own health status as fair or poor. Joint problems and cardiovascular disease were the two most common physical ailments mentioned, while depression was the most common self-identified mental health problem. The most common fear mentioned by study participants was loneliness, but homeless people staying in shelters reported this fear much less often than those who did not stay in shelters.

Table 7.1 describes a study of 100 homeless women with schizophrenia and 100 non-homeless women with schizophrenia. (See Table 7.1.) The study, summarized by Silver and Pañares, found that homeless schizophrenic women had higher rates of co-occurring disorders, including alcohol and/or drug abuse and antisocial personality disorder; the homeless women were less likely to have adequate family support.

Silver and Pañares reported that families with children comprise about 40 percent of the total homeless population, and the vast majority (about 90 percent) are female-headed. The authors reported on a study of 436 sheltered homeless and low-income housed mothers. The study found that 84 percent of all of these women had a history of having been severely assaulted at some point in their lives. Research has shown that mothers with a history of abuse are more likely to have children with mental health problems.

Perceptions of and about Mental Illness and the Homeless

Homeless people may be looked upon as mentally ill when their "abnormal" actions may actually be behavior caused by social and economic problems. For example, some homeless women act strangely and neglect personal hygiene as a way to protect themselves from attack. A 1988 report on homeless women in San Francisco (C. J. Cooper, "Brutal Lives of Homeless S.F. Women," *San Francisco Examiner*, December 18, 1988) revealed a high rate of rape and sexual assault—some of the women had been raped as many as 17 times. The report stated that to protect themselves from attack, homeless women would wear 10 pairs of panty hose at once and bundle up in layers of clothing.

Prevalence and Treatment

There is some debate over the rate of mental disorders among homeless populations, but there is general agreement that it is greater among the homeless than the general population. The 2000 U.S. Conference of Mayors study reported that an average of 22 percent of the homeless in the 25 surveyed cities were considered severely mentally ill. This was a 3 percent increase over 1999 (19 percent), but the second lowest reported percentage since 1985. The National Resource Center on Homelessness and Mental Illness reported that a disproportionate percentage of the homeless population suffers from serious mental illnesses of the most "personally disruptive" kind, "including severe, chronic depression; bipolar disorder; schizophrenia; schizoaffective disorders; and severe personality disorders." An estimated 20 to 25 percent of the homeless population is afflicted, compared with 4 percent of the general population.

Mentally ill homeless people present special problems for health-care workers. They may not be as cooperative and motivated as other patients. Because of their limited resources, they may have difficulty getting transportation to treatment centers. They frequently forget to show up for appointments or take medications. They are often unkempt. The addition of drug abuse can make them unruly or unresponsive. Among people with severe mental disorders, those at greatest risk of homelessness are both the most severely ill and the most difficult to help.

SUBSTANCE ABUSE

The abuse of alcohol and other drugs has long been recognized as a major factor contributing to the problems of the homeless. Being intoxicated or high in public is considered socially unacceptable. Housed substance abusers have the luxury of staying out of public scrutiny when in such a condition. But homeless people may have no place else to be except outside; many homeless shelters refuse to provide shelter to intoxicated persons. Consequently, homeless substance abusers are often more visible than those in the general population, which may lead to inflated statistics. According to the National Coalition for the Homeless, though, in *No Open Door: Breaking the Lock on Addiction Recovery for Homeless People* (December 1998), the number of addictive disorders per capita within the homeless population is nearly twice that of the general population, and even higher in certain localities.

Children, either in families or on their own, are the fastest-growing segment of the homeless population. In "Substance Use Among Runaway and Homeless Youth in Three National Samples" (*American Journal of Public Health*, 1997), researchers J. M. Greene, S. T. Ennett, and C. L. Ringwalt found that 81 percent of street youth (children under 18 who have been on their own for an extended period of time) and 67 percent of homeless youth in shelters were using alcohol. In addition, 75 percent of street youth and 52 percent of sheltered youth were using marijuana, and 26 percent of street youth and 8 percent of sheltered youth were using crack cocaine. Among housed youth, 64 percent used alcohol, 25 percent used marijuana, and 2 percent used crack cocaine.

The U.S. Conference of Mayors found that in 2002, 32 percent of the homeless in surveyed cities were substance abusers, down from a high of 48 percent in 1993.

Dual Diagnosis and Substance Abuse

The National Institute of Mental Health (NIMH) and the National Institute on Alcohol Abuse and Alcoholism (NIAAA) report that mental illness and substance abuse frequently occur together. Clinicians call this co-occurring disorders, or dual diagnosis. Experts report that in the absence of appropriate treatment, persons with mental

FIGURE 7.6

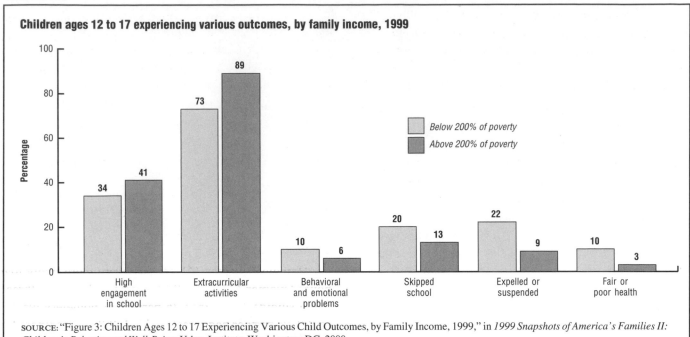

Children ages 12 to 17 experiencing various outcomes, by family income, 1999

SOURCE: "Figure 3: Children Ages 12 to 17 Experiencing Various Child Outcomes, by Family Income, 1999," in *1999 Snapshots of America's Families II: Children's Behavior and Well-Being,* Urban Institute, Washington, DC, 2000

illness often resort to "self-medication," using alcohol or drugs to silence the voices or calm the fears that torment them. Homeless people with dual diagnoses are frequently excluded from mental health programs because of treatment problems created by their substance abuse and are excluded from substance abuse programs due to problems in treating their mental illness. Experts report that the lack of an integrated system of care plays a major role in their recurrent homelessness. They stress that transitional or assisted housing initiatives for homeless substance abusers must realistically address the issue of abstinence and design measures for handling relapses that do not place people back on the streets.

Welfare Reform and Substance Abusers

Some people fear that welfare policy changes have increased homelessness among impoverished people with addiction disorders. In 1996 Congress passed the Personal Responsibility and Work Opportunity Reconciliation Act (PL 104-193), which, among other things, denies Social Security Income (SSI), Social Security Disability Insurance (SSDI) benefits, and Medicaid to people whose addictions are a "contributing factor" in their disability. More than 200,000 people were affected by the cutoff. In "Welfare Reform and Housing: Assessing the Impact to Substance Abuse," (T.L. Anderson et al., *Journal of Drug Issues,* Winter 2002), the authors reported on their study of the effects of terminating the addiction disability "at a time of diminishing social services and a housing market explosion." Former recipients reported increased homelessness and were found to be at risk of drug and alcohol use, criminal participation, and criminal victimization.

SPECIAL POPULATION CONCERNS

Children

While a quarter of all homeless people may suffer from mental illness, and many more have a past or current drug or alcohol addiction, these common stereotypes of the homeless do not fit a significant segment of the homeless population. Children under 18 years of age, for example, make up from 8 to 12 percent of the homeless.

One research team (E. R. Danseco and E. W. Holden, "Are There Different Types of Homeless Families? A Typology of Homeless Families Based on Cluster Analysis," *Family Relations*, 1998) sought to identify different types of homeless families and to examine children from these families. The researchers studied 180 families, with a total of 348 children, that participated in a comprehensive health-care program for children of homeless families. The results showed that homeless children consistently exhibited greater behavior problems and showed a trend of poorer cognitive, academic, and adaptive behaviors than children in the general population.

Similar results were found in a 1999 Urban Institute study. Figure 7.6 shows that poor children are less involved in school than their more well-off peers—41 percent of children above 200 percent of the poverty level have a high engagement in school, versus 34 percent of children below 200 percent of the poverty level. Lower-income children had 4 percent more behavioral and emotional problems, skipped school 7 percent more often, were expelled or suspended more than twice as often, and reported fair or poor health more than three times as frequently as children above 200 percent of the poverty level.

Homeless children experience delays in immunizations, which leaves them vulnerable to preventable diseases. Failure to treat certain childhood conditions early (ear infections, for example) can lead to a lifetime of health problems.

Unaccompanied Youth

Unaccompanied youth is the term used to describe children under the age of 18 who are either runaways (away without permission), thrownaways (told or forced to leave or abandoned), or street youth (long-term runaways or thrownaways). The National Runaway Switchboard estimates that between 1.3 and 2.8 million runaway and homeless youth live on America's streets and that one out of every seven children will run away before the age of 18. Many of these children are escaping physical and sexual abuse, strained family relationships, addiction of a family member, and/or parental neglect. These children might be expected to exhibit a variety of behavioral and/or health disorders.

Access to health care at traditional health-care centers is complicated for this segment of the homeless population by parental permission requirements, lack of insurance, and a reluctance to trust health-care professionals.

Veterans

The U.S. Department of Veterans Affairs (VA) estimates that between 250,000 and 275,000 veterans are homeless on any given night. Twice as many may be homeless in a given year. A one-day count in September 1997 revealed that approximately one-fourth of the patients in VA hospitals were homeless. In 2000 the U.S. Conference of Mayors reported that veterans made up 15 percent of the homeless in the surveyed cities, a decrease of 7 percent from two years before.

To some, the homelessness of veterans is hard to understand. Since World War II, U.S. veterans have been offered a broad range of special benefits, including educational assistance, home loan guarantees, pension and disability payments, and free health care. In fact, veterans consistently have higher median incomes, lower rates of poverty and unemployment, and better education than U.S. males in similar age groups. Veterans, those observers claim, should be less vulnerable to homelessness than other Americans.

The belief that veterans become homeless because of combat-related stress has received much attention of late. Health-care professionals believe that there may be a link between the persistence of Post Traumatic Stress Disorder (PTSD) in veterans and the stresses of street living, though research on this topic is as yet inconclusive.

Victims of Violence

VIOLENCE TOWARD HOMELESS WOMEN. Angela Browne, Ph.D., and Shari Bassuk, in a study funded by the National Institute of Mental Health and the Maternal and Child Health Bureau, found that lifetime prevalence rates of physical and sexual assault among homeless women were particularly high. The study, "Intimate Violence in the Lives of Homeless and Poor Housed Women: Prevalence and Patterns in an Ethnically Diverse Sample" (*American Journal of Orthopsychiatry*, April 1999), which surveyed both homeless and very poor housed women, found that although violence by intimate male partners was high in both groups, homeless women experienced violence at a somewhat higher rate (63.3 percent) than poor housed women (58 percent).

Homeless women (41 percent) were more likely than housed women (33 percent) to report a male partner threatening suicide. More than 36 percent of homeless women said their partner had threatened to kill them, compared to 31 percent of poor housed women. Almost 27 percent of homeless women and 19.5 percent of poor housed women needed or received medical treatment because of physical violence. Table 7.1 summarizes other studies related to violence and homeless women.

HATE CRIMES. According to the National Coalition for the Homeless (NCH), homeless advocates are demanding that crimes against the homeless be defined as hate crimes, which may result in harsher penalties in federal courts. Determining how many of these crimes occur is difficult. Some factors that have an effect on the accuracy of the count are:

- The bodies of the victims are not always discovered.

- Bodies may be badly decomposed, preventing accurate identification of the cause of death.

- Local authorities may rule causes of death other than violence.

- Survivors do not always report crimes, and murdered victims cannot tell their own stories.

In April 2003 the NCH released the results of a four-year study of hate crimes and violence committed against homeless people (*Hate, Violence, and Death on Main Street, USA: A Report on Hate Crimes and Violence Against People Experiencing Homelessness from 1999–2002*, Washington, D.C.). The NCH identified 123 hate crime deaths and 89 nonlethal attacks on homeless people over the four-year period. The crimes occurred in 98 cities in 34 states and in Puerto Rico. According to the NCH, the five most dangerous cities for people experiencing homelessness are: Denver, Las Vegas, Rapid City (South Dakota), Toledo, and New York.

The NCH recommended the following actions to address the problem of violence against homeless individuals:

- "A public statement by the U.S. Department of Justice acknowledging that hate crimes and/or violence against people experiencing homelessness is a serious national trend."

- "A database to be maintained by the U.S. Department of Justice, in cooperation with the National Coalition for the Homeless, to track hate crimes and/or violence against people who become homeless."

- "Inclusion of housing status in the pending federal hate crimes legislation."

- "Sensitivity/Awareness training at police academies and departments nationwide for trainees and police officers on how to deal effectively and humanely with people who become homeless in their communities."

- "A General Accounting Office (GAO) investigation into the nature and scope of hate crimes and/or violent acts and crimes that occur against people experiencing homelessness. This proposed study will address the following: causes of hate crimes/violence; circumstances that contribute to or were responsible for the perpetrators' behavior, beliefs held by the perpetrators of these crimes and how their beliefs have changed since conviction, thoughts and advice from the perpetrators to others who are considering hate crimes/violence against the homeless population; and community education, prevention and law enforcement strategies."

PROBLEMS IN TREATING THE HOMELESS

To understand why health care may not be readily available to the homeless population, one must look at American health care in general. In "U.S. Health-Care System Faces Cost and Insurance Crises: Rising Costs, Growing Numbers of Uninsured and Quality Gaps Trouble World's Most Expensive Health-Care System" (*The Lancet*, August 2, 2003), Michael McCarthy described a system "lurching towards crisis." Costs continue to rise, as do the numbers of people who do not have insurance. Meanwhile, the country entered a recession in 2001 and there seemed to be little political will to reform the health-care system.

McCarthy noted that while most hospitals by law must provide care for the indigent, in reality an uninsured patient is less likely to receive any care at all and, if hospitalized, is less likely to receive the same quality of care as an insured patient. He cited a 2002 study by the U.S. National Academy of Sciences Institute of Medicine (*Care Without Coverage: Too Little, Too Late*, National Academies Press). That study found that "uninsured patients who are hospitalized for a range of conditions are more likely to die in the hospital, to receive fewer services when admitted, and to experience substandard care and resultant injury than are insured patients."

Medicaid

Medicaid is the federal health insurance program for low-income families with children, among others. In "'I Abhor the Status Quo': HHS Secretary Tommy G. Thompson's Plan to Revamp the Healthcare Industry" (Michael T. McCue, *Managed Healthcare Executive*, March 2003), Tommy Thompson, Secretary of Health and Human Services, described Medicaid as an outdated system that does not adequately serve the mentally or chronically ill, people with substance abuse problems, or childless adults (who make up a significant portion of the homeless population).

Some medical providers turn Medicaid patients away. A 2000 study (*Oral Health: Factors Contributing to Low Use of Dental Services by Low-Income Populations*, U.S. General Accounting Office, Washington, D.C., 2001) found that dentists were refusing to treat Medicaid patients, citing low payment rates, red tape, and frequently missed appointments. A 2002 survey of physicians conducted by the Medicare Payment Advisory Commission found that more than 30 percent of physicians surveyed refused to accept any new Medicaid patients.

A Fragile Safety Net

Many homeless people depend on a network of federally funded community and migrant health centers and programs funded by local public health departments, hospitals, and other community-based groups. The Bureau of Primary Health Care reported in 2003 that public benefits for those who are unable to work have decreased significantly since the 1980s. The downward trend is expected to continue as welfare programs are shifted from the federal level to the states, which face severe budget crises.

Shortages of Medical Personnel

High malpractice insurance rates have caused some doctors to discontinue the practice of medicine. Newspapers report that physicians who volunteer their services at free clinics have been turned away because they lack malpractice insurance. Analysts predict a critical shortage of nurses and other healthcare workers.

HEALTH CARE FOR THE HOMELESS

In 1987 Congress passed the Stewart B. McKinney Homeless Assistance Act (PL 100-77) to provide services to the homeless, including job training, emergency shelter, education, and health care. Title VI of the Act funds Health Care for the Homeless (HCH) programs. HCH has become the national umbrella under which most homeless health-care initiatives operate. In 1994 there were 119 HCH

TABLE 7.3

Profile of clients served by Health Care for the Homeless programs, 2001

Characteristic	Percent
Male	60.0
Female	40.0
Age 0-14	13.0
Age 15-19	5.0
Age 20-44	57.0
Age 45-64	23.0
Age 65+	2.0
African American	40.0
Hispanic	17.5
Asian/Pacific Islander	2.0
Native American/Alaskan Native	2.0
Lived in shelter	40.0
Lived on the street	12.0
No medical insurance	73.0
Medicaid-eligible	20.0
Medicare-eligible	2.0
Private insurance	1.0
Other public insurance	4.0
At 100 percent or below poverty level	90.0

SOURCE: Adapted from data provided by the U.S. Department of Health and Human Services, Health Resources and Services Administration, Bureau of Primary Health Care, Bethesda, MD [Online] http://bphc.hrsa. gov/hchirc/about/prog_successes.asp [accessed September 17, 2003]

programs in the United States; by 2001, 154 programs provided health care to about a half million people each year. In the year 2000 the government appropriated $88 million for HCH programs, up $8 million from 1999 and almost double the $46 million appropriation of 1987, the first year of the program. Approximately $122 million was appropriated for 2003 and President George W. Bush requested $131 million for the program for 2004. Nonprofit private organizations and public entities, including state and local government agencies, may apply for grants. The grants may be used to continue to provide services for up to one year to individuals who have obtained permanent housing if services were provided to them when they were homeless.

The goal of the HCH program is to improve health status for homeless individuals and families by improving access to primary health care and substance abuse services. HCH provides outreach, counseling to clients explaining available services, case management, and linkages to services such as mental health treatment, housing, benefits, and other critical supports. Access to around-the-clock emergency services is available, as well as help in establishing eligibility for assistance and obtaining services under entitlement programs.

Table 7.3 shows characteristics of people treated in HCH centers in 2001. The majority of clients (60 percent) were male; 40 percent were female, up 5.3 percent over the preceding year. Almost two-thirds (62 percent) of homeless clients were minorities: African Americans made up 40 percent; Hispanics, 17.5 percent; Asians/Pacific Islanders, 2 percent; and Native Americans/Alaskan natives, 2 percent.

Clients between the ages of 20 and 44 represented the largest portion of people served by the HCH programs (57 percent), followed by individuals between the ages of 45 and 64 (23 percent), children up to age 14 (13 percent), and teenagers between the ages of 15 and 19 (5 percent). Homeless persons over 65 comprised 2 percent of clients served.

Of clients seen in HCH centers, 40 percent lived in shelters at some point during treatment, while 12 percent lived on the street. The remainder lived in transitional housing, with family or acquaintances, or in some other type of living arrangement. The majority (73 percent) of HCH users had no medical care coverage. Of those who had some type of insurance, one-fifth (20 percent) were eligible for Medicaid (although they may not have been enrolled), 2 percent were eligible for Medicare, 1 percent had private insurance, and 4 percent had some other type of insurance.

IMPORTANT NAMES AND ADDRESSES

America's Second Harvest
35 E. Wacker Dr., #2000
Chicago, IL 60601
(312) 263-2303
(800) 771-2303
URL: www.secondharveSt.org

Association of Rescue Gospel Missions
1045 Swift Street
Kansas City, MO 64116-4127
(816) 471-8020
FAX: (816) 471-3718
URL: www.agrm.org/

Center on Budget and Policy Priorities
820 1st Street, NE, #510
Washington, DC 20002
(202) 408-1080
FAX: (202) 408-1056
E-mail: bazie@cbpp.org
URL: www.cbpp.org

Children's Defense Fund
25 E Street, NW
Washington, DC 20001
(202) 628-8787
E-mail: cdfinfo@childrensdefense.org
URL: www.childrensdefense.org

Fannie Mae Foundation
4000 Wisconsin Ave., NW
North Tower, Suite One
Washington, DC 20016-2804
(202) 274-8000
FAX: (202) 274-8100
URL: www.fanniemaefoundation.org

Food Research and Action Center
1875 Connecticut Ave., NW, #540
Washington, DC 20009
(202) 986-2200
FAX: (202) 986-2525
URL: www.frac.org

Habitat for Humanity International
121 Habitat Street
Americus, GA 31709-3498
(229) 924-6935
E-mail: publicinfo@hfhi.org
URL: www.habitat.org

Health Care for the Homeless Information Resource Center
Bureau of Primary Health Care
U.S. Department of Health and Human Services
East West Towers
4350 East West Highway
Bethesda, MD 20814
URL: http://bphc.hrsa.gov/hchirc/

Homes for the Homeless
The Institute for Children and Poverty
36 Cooper Square, 6th Floor
New York, NY 10003
(212) 529-5252
FAX: (212) 529-7698
E-mail: info@homesforthehomeless.com
URL: www.HomesfortheHomeless.com

Housing Assistance Council
1025 Vermont Avenue, NW #606
Washington, DC 20005
(202) 842-8600
FAX: (202) 347-3441
E-mail: hac@ruralhome.org
URL: www.ruralhome.org

Institute for Research on Poverty
University of Wisconsin-Madison
1180 Observatory Dr.
3412 Social Science Building
Madison, WI 53706-1393
(608) 262-6358
FAX: (608) 265-3119
URL: www.ssc.wisc.edu/irp/

Interagency Council on Homelessness
451 Seventh Street SW, Ste. 2100
Washington, DC 20410
(202) 708-4663
FAX: (202) 708-1216
URL: www.ich.gov/

National Alliance of HUD Tenants
42 Seaverns Avenue
Boston, MA 02136
(617) 267-9564
FAX: (617) 267-4769
E-mail: naht@erols.com
URL: www.saveourhomes.org/

National Alliance to End Homelessness
1518 K Street NW, #206
Washington, DC 20005
(202) 638-1526
E-mail: naeh@naeh.org
URL: www.endhomelessness.org

National Center for Homeless Education
P.O. Box 5367
Greensboro, NC 27435
(800) 308-2145
(800) 755-3277
E-mail: homeless@serve.org
URL: www.serve.org/nche

National Coalition for Homeless Veterans
333 1/2 Pennsylvania Ave., SE
Washington, DC 20003 1148
(202) 546-1969
(800) VET-HELP
FAX: (202) 546-2063
E-mail: nchv@nchv.org
URL: www.nchv.org

National Coalition for the Homeless
1012 Fourteenth Street, NW, #600
Washington, DC 20005-3471
(202) 737-6444
FAX: (202) 737-6445

E-mail: info@nationalhomeless.org
URL: www.nationalhomeless.org/

National Health Care for the Homeless Council
P.O. Box 60427
Nashville, TN 37206-0427
(615) 226-2292
FAX: (615) 226-1656
E-mail: council@nhchc.org
URL: www.nhchc.org

National Housing Conference
1801 K Street, N.W., Suite M-100
Washington, DC 20006-1301
(202) 466-2121
FAX: (202) 466-2122
E-mail: nhc@nhc.org
URL: www.nhc.org

National Housing Law Project
614 Grand Avenue, Ste. 320
Oakland, CA 94610
(510) 251-9400
FAX: (510) 451-2300
E-mail: nhlp@nhlp.org
URL: www.nhlp.org

National Law Center on Homelessness and Poverty
1411 K Street NW, Suite 1400
Washington, DC 20005
(202) 638-2535
FAX: (202) 628-2737
E-mail: nlchp@nlchp.org
URL: www.nlchp.org

National Low Income Housing Coalition
1012 14th Street NW, #610
Washington, DC 20005
(202) 662-1530
FAX: (202) 393-1973
E-mail: info@nlihc.org
URL: www.nlihc.org

National Resource Center on Homelessness and Mental Illness
Policy Research Associates
345 Delaware Avenue
Delmar, NY 12054
FAX: (518) 439-7612
(800) 444-7415
E-mail: nrc@prainc.com
URL: www.nrchmi.com/

National Rural Housing Coalition
1250 Eye Street, NW, Suite 902
Washington, DC 20005
(202) 393-5229
FAX: (202) 393-3034
E-mail: nrhc@nrhcweb.org
URL: www.nrhcweb.org/

National Student Campaign Against Hunger and Homelessness (NSCAHH)
233 N. Pleasant Ave.
Amherst, MA 01002
(413) 253-6417
FAX: (413) 256-6435
(800) NO-HUNGR
E-mail: info@studentsagainsthunger.org
URL: www.pirg.org/nscahh

Urban Institute
2100 M Street, NW

Washington, DC 20037
(202) 833-7200
E-mail: paffairs@ui.urban.org
URL: www.urban.org

U.S. Conference of Mayors
Task Force on Hunger and Homelessness
1620 I Street NW, #400
Washington, DC 20006
(202) 293-7330
FAX: (202) 293-2352
E-mail: info@usmayors.org
URL: www.usmayors.org/uscm

U.S. Department of Education
Education for Homeless Children
400 Maryland Avenue, SW
Washington, DC 20202
(800) USA-LEARN
FAX: (202) 401-0689
E-mail: customerservice@inet.ed.gov
URL: www.ed.gov/programs/homeless/
resources.html?exp=0

U.S. Department of Housing and Urban Development
451 7th Street SW
Washington, DC 20410
(202) 708-1112
URL: www.hud.gov

U.S. General Accounting Office
441 G Street, NW
Washington, DC 20548
(202) 512-4800
E-mail: webmaster@gao.gov
URL: www.gao.gov

RESOURCES

Many different organizations study the homeless and the poor. Notable among them for their many large studies on homelessness is The Urban Institute. This organization's ongoing studies of the homeless are among the largest and most comprehensive in the United States. Their publications were a major source of information for this volume, especially: *The 1996 National Survey of Homeless Assistance Providers and Clients: A Comparison of Faith-Based and Secular Non-Profit Programs* (2002), *America's Homeless II: Populations and Services* (2000), *Homelessness: Programs and the People They Serve. National Survey of Homeless Assistance Providers and Clients* (December 1999), and *On the Bottom Rung, A Profile of Americans in Low-Income Working Families* (October 2000). These statistics were very useful.

Three other excellent sources of information on the national homeless population are the National League of Cities, the U.S. Conference of Mayors, and the Association of Gospel Rescue Missions. The publication *The State of America's Cities: Seventeenth Annual Opinion Survey of Municipal Elected Officials* (National League of Cities, 2001) contains much valuable data on the scope of urban homelessness and how cities and regions try to deal with it. *A Status Report on Hunger and Homelessness in America's Cities* (U.S. Conference of Mayors, 2002) and *1999 Snap Shot Survey of the Homeless* (Association of Gospel Rescue Missions, November 1999) also provide a great deal of information on the homeless population.

The many organizations that advocate for the homeless and their issues are also crucial sources for this book. The National Coalition for the Homeless is certainly one of the most important of these organizations. Their publications *Homelessness in America: Unabated and Increasing—A Ten-Year Perspective* (1997), *Illegal to Be Homeless: The Criminalization of Homelessness in the United States,* (2003), and *Welfare to What? Part II: Laying the Groundwork for the 2002 Congressional TANF Reauthorization Debate* (2001; in conjunction with the Los Angeles Coalition to End Hunger & Homelessness and the National Welfare Monitoring and Advocacy Partnership) are particularly recommended. The National Low Income Housing Coalition is another advocacy organization with much useful information on homelessness, including *Out of Reach, The Growing Gap Between Housing Costs and Income of Poor People in the United States* (September 2000) and *Rental Housing for America's Poor Families: Farther Out of Reach Than Ever, 2002* (2002).

Applied Survey Research, Economic Policy Institute, Joint Center for Housing Studies of Harvard University, Health Care for the Homeless, National Coalition for Homeless Veterans, Millennial Housing Commission, National Multi Housing Council, and the National Law Center on Homelessness & Poverty, all provide extensive coverage of important aspects of the housing and homelessness issues.

No list of major sources of information on the homeless and poor would be complete without mentioning the federal government. While the government has done relatively few studies on the homeless since the 1980s, it remains the premier source of facts on many issues closely related to homelessness, including poverty, employment, welfare, and housing. There are far too many worthwhile publications to list here, but some particularly excellent sources of information that the Gale Group relied on in producing this book are: *Emergency and Transitional Shelter Population: 2000* (U.S. Census Bureau, October 2001); *Employment and Earnings* (Bureau of Labor Statistics, January 2001); *Homelessness: Coordination and Evaluation of Programs Are Essential* (General Accounting Office, 1999); *A Profile of the Working Poor, 1999* (Bureau of Labor Statistics, February 2001); *Rental Housing Assistance—The Worsening Crisis* (Office of Policy Development and

Research, U.S. Department of Housing and Urban Development, March 2000); and *Rural Homelessness: Focusing on the Needs of the Rural Homeless* (Department of Agriculture, 1996). In addition to these specific publications, the Gale Group recommends that anyone who is interested in homelessness and related issues make use of the latest government reports from the Bureau of the Census, the Department of Health and Human Services, the Centers for Disease Control and Prevention, and the Department of Housing and Urban Development.

INDEX

Homeless in America: How Could It Happen Here?